Supply Chain Management in Practice

This book provides a foundational understanding of Supply Chain Management (SCM), covering the strategic end-to-end process of procurement, production, and distribution of goods. Organised around proven frameworks and operational models, this book emphasises how effective SCM contributes to business efficiency, competitiveness, profitability, and customer satisfaction.

Unlike typical introductory textbooks that may overemphasise theoretical frameworks, this book presents essential concepts and models, such as the SCOR Model and key risk management strategies, in a digestible manner. It supplements these with clear opportunities to apply knowledge to modern challenges, demonstrating how strategic thinking can be constructively implemented to achieve global success. The textbook is structured to guide readers from foundational knowledge to advanced application, covering topics from the Definition and Importance of Supply Chain Management to Key Frameworks, Models, and Theories in SCM, and the critical role of Digital Innovations, Operations, and Sustainability. Students will gain the ability to explain core SCM concepts and develop analytical skills through diverse, contemporary cases. Template KPIs, warehouse and supply chain performance formulas, and a list of common acronyms are also included as an appendix.

This textbook is ideal for undergraduate courses in supply chain management. Its focus on applications will also make it attractive to students taking vocational training at technical institutes.

Drew Dale is an experienced practitioner and educator in Supply Chain Management, specialising in operations, risk management, and the strategic integration of digital innovations and sustainable practices. He holds an MBA (UniSC) and is a Fellow of the Institute of Managers and Leaders.

Supply Chain Management in Practice

Integrating Digital Innovations, Operations, and Sustainability for Global Success

Drew Dale

Routledge
Taylor & Francis Group
LONDON AND NEW YORK

Designed cover image: Getty Images

First published 2026
by Routledge
4 Park Square, Milton Park, Abingdon, Oxon OX14 4RN

and by Routledge
605 Third Avenue, New York, NY 10158

Routledge is an imprint of the Taylor & Francis Group, an informa business

For Product Safety Concerns and Information please contact our EU representative GPSR@taylorandfrancis.com. Taylor & Francis Verlag GmbH, Kaufingerstraße 24, 80331 München, Germany.

British Library Cataloguing-in-Publication Data
A catalogue record for this book is available from the British Library

ISBN: 978-1-041-24180-5 (hbk)
ISBN: 978-1-041-24179-9 (pbk)
ISBN: 978-1-003-74056-8 (ebk)

DOI: 10.4324/9781003740568

Typeset in Galliard
by SPi Technologies India Pvt Ltd (Straive)

Access the Support Material: www.routledge.com/9781041241799

Contents

Figures

Tables

Preface

Supply Chain Management in Practice: The Motivation

The Strategic Imperative of Modern Supply Chain Management

The discipline of Supply Chain Management (SCM) has undergone a fundamental transformation, transitioning from a reactive logistical function focused solely on cost minimisation to a proactive, strategic core competency essential for competitive advantage, long-term resilience, and global relevance (Chapter 1). SCM is defined today as the integrated planning, execution, and control of all activities involved in sourcing, procurement, conversion, and logistics management, augmented by coordination and collaboration to create net value and sustainable competitive advantage (Chapter 1). This comprehensive scope demands that contemporary SCM professionals possess a robust, interdisciplinary skillset to navigate economic volatility, geopolitical complexity, and technological disruption.

The foundational shift in SCM lies in recognising that the supply chain is the operational mechanism for delivering organisational strategy. It is the crucial domain where efficiency encounters scale, where risk is proactively managed, and where digital capabilities are converted into measurable commercial outcomes. Therefore, mastering SCM is synonymous with mastering modern business strategy.

The Economic Significance of Global Supply Chains

The sheer scale and aggressive expansion of the SCM sector underscore its indisputable status as a high-growth, economically critical industry, validating the investment in specialised, advanced instruction.

The global SCM market size was valued at approximately USD 31.77 billion in 2024 and is forecast to exceed USD 35 billion by 2025. This sector is projected to maintain a Compound Annual Growth Rate (CAGR) of between 10.92% and 11.7% through 2034, confirming SCM's status as a top-tier domain in global commerce. This rapid acceleration in market valuation confirms that SCM is no longer viewed as a passive, back-office cost function, but rather as an active driver of investment and value capture across international boundaries. The market-leading position of North America before the 2025 tariff wars further highlights the immense professional demand for strategic SCM expertise capable of orchestrating complex, multi-jurisdictional networks (Chapter 4) (Fortune Business Insights, 2024; Precedence Research, 2025).

The Paradigm Shift: From Cost Centre to Strategic Enabler

The pursuit of competitive advantage relies heavily on the strategic maturity of an organisation's supply chain (Chapter 3). The modern SCM mandate operates across a multi-dimensional framework, moving beyond simply reducing expenses to actively shaping market position.

1 Efficiency and Cost Leadership: This mandate is achieved through the rigorous application of Lean SCM principles and Total Cost of Ownership (TCO) models (Chapters 3 and 7). This approach, exemplified historically by organisations like Toyota in implementing its Just-In-Time (JIT) system, demands relentless elimination of waste, optimisation of process flow, and meticulous control of inventory across all tiers of the network.
2 Responsiveness and Differentiation: Superior market positioning is secured via Agile SCM methodologies and customised distribution networks (Chapters 3 and 7). This capability enables companies like Zara and Apple to rapidly adapt to shifts in consumer preferences, shorten time-to-market, and deliver a superior, differentiated customer experience that commands premium pricing (Chapters 2 and 3).
3 Sustainability and Social Value (ESG): SCM is the operational heart of Environmental, Social, and Governance (ESG) commitments, moving sustainability "From Compliance to Strategy". Modern procurement, production, and logistics must integrate ethical sourcing, circular economy principles, and waste minimisation to build social value, meet regulatory requirements, and enhance brand resilience (Chapters 3 and 7) (Liferay, n.d.).

The Dual Challenge: Digital Acceleration and Systemic Risk

The need for highly capable SCM professionals is intensified by the twin forces that define the current operating environment: pervasive digital acceleration and critical exposure to systemic global risk.

Digital Acceleration and the Orchestration Imperative: Top industry trends for 2025 identify the dominance of Artificial Intelligence (AI), Big Data and Advanced Analytics, and Automation as central enablers of SCM advancement. AI-enabled forecasting, for instance, enables predictive decision-making that significantly reduces forecast error and minimises inventory distortion across complex, multi-echelon networks (Chapter 5) (Association for Supply Chain Management (ASCM), 2025; Liferay, n.d.). The rapid advancement of these technologies means the digital manager is constantly challenged to align new tools with business outcomes.

The formal impact analysis of these trends reveals a profound effect on the fundamental SCOR "Orchestrate" process. This indicates that digital technologies are not merely improving isolated functions but are fundamentally changing the governance and coordination required to align global supply networks. This mandates that the successful SCM manager must operate as the *conductor* of digital transformation, ensuring seamless data flow and strategic coherence across the entire system (Chapters 2 and 10) (Association for Supply Chain Management (ASCM), 2025).

Systemic Risk and the Resilience Imperative: The strategic priority has decisively shifted from pure efficiency to risk-centric planning. Global Trade Dynamics, Geopolitical Policies, and Cybersecurity rank among the highest criticality threats facing SCM in 2025 and beyond (Liferay, n.d.; Association for Supply Chain Management (ASCM), 2025).

Table 0.1 Global Supply Chain Market and Critical Trends (2025)

Metric/Trend	*Economic Context (2024–2034)*	*Strategic Implication for SCM*	*Relevant Chapter(s)*
Market Size (2024)	USD 31.77 billion	High commercial valuation and professional opportunity.	Chapter 1
Projected CAGR (2025–2034)	–	Requirement for rapid capability scaling and technology adoption.	Chapters 1 and 10
Top Critical Trends (2025)	AI, Geopolitical Dynamics, Cybersecurity, Agility/Resilience	SCM priority shift from pure efficiency to risk mitigation and strategic adaptation.	Chapters 4, 10, 11
Strategic Focus	ESG, Strategic Sourcing, Visibility/ Traceability	Embedding social responsibility and data transparency into core operations.	Chapters 3 and 7

The systemic risks observed in recent history illustrate the interdependencies of the global economy. Global concentration of manufacturing often leads to single points of failure, as demonstrated by the widespread disruption following the 2021 Suez Canal blockage. Simultaneously, increased digital connectivity for optimisation increases exposure to sophisticated cyber threats, such as the operational paralysis inflicted upon Maersk during the NotPetya attack. This complex relationship requires the modern SCM professional to prioritise risk management (Chapter 11) and to use advanced tools (AI, Digital Twins) to model and counter complex, cascading threats across global networks (Chapter 4).

Table 0.1 provides a synthesis of the economic context and strategic imperatives that necessitate the advanced training offered by this book.

The Objectives of the Book

Addressing the Pedagogical Gap in SCM Education

Traditional SCM education often fails to adequately prepare professionals for the rigorous, integrated demands of the modern global economy (Chapter 1). Curricula frequently focus on siloed functional areas or abstract theories, failing to link operational decisions to strategic business outcomes. This textbook is explicitly designed to bridge the chasm between foundational academic theory and the urgent need for practical, data-driven, and strategic application in the industrial environment (Chapter 1). The volume aims to replace fragmented, siloed instruction with a holistic, end-to-end perspective that views the supply chain as a dynamic, interconnected system (Chapter 1).

Defining the Target Audience and Learner Profile

This book is intended for a sophisticated audience requiring advanced, applied SCM training (Chapter 1). The material is deliberately pitched to empower learners transitioning into leadership roles.

1 Graduate Students (Masters and Advanced Undergraduate): This cohort requires a robust, integrated curriculum that covers the full range of SCM theory, analytical models (SCOR, Lean/Agile), and contemporary challenges (Risk, IT) (Chapter 1).
2 SCM Professionals and Practitioners: This includes experienced functional managers (e.g., Logistics Managers, Procurement Specialists) transitioning into strategic management or executive positions that demand cross-functional mastery and the ability to link departmental actions to corporate strategy (Chapter 1).

The core objective of the book is to produce managerial talent capable of informed, strategic decision-making and problem-solving in the face of market volatility and systemic threats.

Core Learning Outcomes: Analytical and Applied Competencies

The curriculum is rigorously structured to ensure measurable competence, focusing on higher-order analytical and applied skills, as evidenced in the learning outcomes for every chapter. Upon completion, the reader will acquire the ability to:

- Strategic Alignment and Framework Selection: Explain and apply the strategic role of SCM, learning to select and apply appropriate organisational frameworks (e.g., contrasting Lean vs Agile) based on unique product characteristics and shifting market needs (Chapter 2).
- Quantitative Operational Mastery: Apply analytical and quantitative techniques to core functions. This includes the ability to calculate critical inventory metrics, such as safety stock and Economic Order Quantity (EOQ) (Chapter 6). Furthermore, proficiency will be developed in applying sophisticated cost models, such as TCO, in strategic sourcing decisions (Chapter 7), and in utilising established quality management tools, such as DMAIC and Statistical Process Control (SPC), to analyse and resolve operational defects (Chapter 8).
- Digital Enabler Evaluation: Assess and justify the strategic adoption of advanced technologies (Chapter 10). This involves understanding the role of Enterprise Resource Planning (ERP) systems as the transactional core; evaluating the progression of Supply Chain Analytics (SCA) to prescriptive capability; and determining the optimal use of AI, IoT, and Blockchain (for provenance and trust). The focus is on leveraging these tools to enhance visibility, traceability, and automated decision-making (Chapter 10).
- Resilience Design and Risk Quantification: Identify, assess, and prioritise supply chain risks (including demand, geopolitical, and cyber threats) and develop actionable mitigation strategies. This requires designing resilient systems through portfolio sourcing, implementing targeted buffering, and creating comprehensive business continuity plans (Chapter 11).
- Practical Synthesis and Recommendation: A key objective is to foster managerial judgement by enabling the reader to evaluate and critique complex, real-world SCM examples and use theoretical knowledge to "recommend one improvement to enhance resilience or value" in a given scenario (Chapter 1).

The Pedagogical Approaches of the Book

The learning architecture is founded on an applied, experiential, and practical methodology, ensuring clear, constructive alignment between teaching activities, learning outcomes, and measurable assessment (Chapter 1). This design moves training beyond mere comprehension to demonstrable professional capability (Chapter 1).

Foundations in Outcome-Based Education and Applied Learning

This textbook moves beyond passive knowledge acquisition to emphasise active, quantitative problem-solving. The majority of the learning outcomes require demonstrative skills, such as applying frameworks, calculating key metrics, modelling operational scenarios, and proposing evidence-based strategic recommendations. This approach is specifically designed to simulate the fast-paced, high-stakes decision-making environment faced by global SCM leaders.

The Primacy of Real-World Case Studies for Contextual Learning

Theoretical concepts are immediately grounded in operational reality through comprehensive case analysis. Chapter 12 is dedicated to synthesising learning through high-profile, cross-industry examples.

- Models of Excellence and Efficiency: The book examines Toyota's mastery of JIT and lean systems; Amazon's integration of robotics and analytics for hyper-efficient fulfilment; and Apple's rigorous management of complex, high-quality global sourcing (Chapter 12).
- Vulnerability and Strategic Misstep: Critical lessons are drawn from historical failures to adapt (Nokia) and the severe consequences of ethical lapses in multi-tier networks (the Rana Plaza factory collapse) (Chapter 12).

The online Case Studies and Teaching Aids resource document provides structured teaching aids that connect these cases directly back to modular topics (Chapter 12). For example, the materials offer instruction on using the Suez Canal blockage to teach network vulnerability or employing the details of the Maersk cyberattack to teach cyber resilience (Chapter 12). This ensures that conceptual understanding is immediately contextualised within recent global history.

Experiential and Quantitative Learning through Simulation and Design

A cornerstone of this book's pedagogy is the use of high-fidelity quantitative simulation exercises in the Appendices (Appendix D). These modules intentionally move learning from qualitative discussion towards experiential mastery, forcing students to quantify trade-offs and justify solutions based on measurable performance metrics.

- End-to-End Digital Twin Simulation (Appendix D): This is a critical exercise in systems analysis, requiring students to build a simplified model that simulates stochastic demand and transport lead-time variability. The exercise enables students to visualise and quantitatively measure the non-linear, cascading effects of disruption (such as the Bullwhip Effect) and to test the effectiveness of different inventory or sourcing buffers under various service-level targets. This vital practical application translates abstract risk theory into measurable financial and operational consequences.
- Network Redesign Project (Appendix D): Students must apply strategic models to real-world constraints, designing networks that balance cost efficiency with geopolitical resilience, a top priority for SCM executives in 2025 (Association for Supply Chain Management (ASCM), 2025).

- Procurement Negotiation Simulation (Appendix D): A role-play exercise designed to integrate negotiation strategy, contract risk allocation, and the practical inclusion of ethical and sustainability clauses into binding agreements (linking directly to the Unilever relational sourcing model discussed in Chapter 7) (Appendix D).
- Supplier Scorecard and Smallholder Yield Simulation (Appendix D): This quantitative worksheet requires the hands-on application of metrics, balancing commercial KPIs (Price, On-Time Delivery) with social impact scores (Traceability, Social Value) (Appendix D).

Assessment and Rigor: Bridging Theory to Measurable Performance

Rigour is maintained through detailed rubrics (Appendix D) that provide specific guidance for assessing student performance, model correctness, strategic justification, and the feasibility of implementation plans. Furthermore, every core chapter (Chapters 1–11) (Appendix C) includes a dedicated Q&A Section, ensuring continuous knowledge consolidation and immediate feedback on applied problem-solving skills throughout the learning journey.

Overview of the Book

The book, *Supply Chain Management in Practice: Integrating Digital Innovations, Operations, and Sustainability for Global Success*, is structured into 12 chapters across four progressive modules, guiding the reader from core definitional principles and strategic frameworks to deep functional expertise, culminating in a synthesis of digital technologies and resilient risk management (Chapter 1).

Module I: Foundations and Competitive Strategy (Chapters 1–3)

This introductory module establishes the context, necessity, and fundamental analytical frameworks required for strategic SCM.

- Chapter 1: Definition and Importance of Supply Chain Management: Defines SCM, traces its evolution (from early logistics to modern digital integration), outlines its strategic role in value creation, and introduces the impact of key technological and sustainability trends.
- Chapter 2: Key Frameworks, Models, and Theories in SCM: Provides a comprehensive and comparative analysis of essential models: the SCOR Model (Plan, Source, Make, Deliver, Return), the strategic trade-offs between Lean (waste elimination, JIT) and Agile (flexibility, responsiveness), the systemic focus of the Theory of Constraints, and the destructive effects of the Bullwhip Effect.
- Chapter 3: Supply Chain Management as a Competitive Advantage: Analyses how organisations achieve Cost Leadership and Differentiation through SCM, emphasising the essential concept of Strategic Alignment and the catalytic role of Technology and the Triple Bottom Line (ESG) in modern competition.

Module II: Core Operational Disciplines (Chapters 4–9)

This module delivers the deep functional expertise required to manage the operational core of the supply chain.

- Chapter 4: Global Supply Chains: Addresses the unique complexity and risks of international operations, detailing the Structural and Operational Challenges posed by global disruptions, regulatory fragmentation, and cultural variance. This provides essential context for managing global trade dynamics.
- Chapter 5: Demand Forecasting and Planning: Explores the methodologies of forecasting (Qualitative vs Quantitative), details the challenges in accuracy (e.g., forecast error), and examines the necessity of integrated Demand Planning to align commercial objectives with operational capacity.
- Chapter 6: Inventory Management: Covers the foundational concepts: the purpose of inventory, calculating EOQ, the implementation demands of JIT, and the calculation and strategic management of Safety Stock to manage the critical cost/service trade-off.
- Chapter 7: Procurement and Supplier Management: Details the complete procurement lifecycle, emphasising TCO over mere purchase price, the mechanics of strategic sourcing, and the post-contractual value derived from Supplier Relationship Management. Includes practical strategies for managing supplier risk and embedding ESG criteria.
- Chapter 8: Production and Operations Management: Focuses on converting inputs to finished goods efficiently through production planning (MPS, S&OP/IBP), the transformative principles of Lean Manufacturing (including the identification and elimination of the eight wastes), and rigorous Quality Management (TQM, Six Sigma, SPC).
- Chapter 9: Logistics and Distribution: Explores the physical movement and storage of goods, covering Transportation Management (mode selection, multimodal solutions), Warehouse Management (automation, layout, KPIs), and Distribution Network Design (centralised vs decentralised topologies).

Module III: Digital Enablers and Resilience (Chapters 10–11)

This module synthesises the technological capabilities and robust risk management frameworks essential for operating in the modern environment.

- Chapter 10: Introduction to Information Technology in SCM: Examines the digital architecture underpinning SCM, detailing ERP systems as the transactional core, the progression of SCA to prescriptive capability, and the game-changing applications of Emerging Technologies such as IoT, AI/ML, Blockchain (for provenance/trust), and Digital Twins (for simulation and scenario testing).
- Chapter 11: Risk Management in Supply Chains: Provides a structured approach to resilience, covering risk typology (geopolitical, cyber, demand, supply), quantitative and qualitative assessment, mitigation strategies (e.g., diversification, buffers, control towers), and the creation of comprehensive response and recovery plans.

Module IV: Applied Synthesis and Teaching Aids

These concluding sections transform learned theory into practical judgement and professional capacity.

- Chapter 12: Case Studies: Presents foundational cross-industry case materials for critical analysis and comparative learning, covering strategy, technology, operational efficiency, and ethical failure.
- Online Case Studies and Teaching Aids: Provides a resource for instructors and advanced learners, linking core concepts to real-world incidents (e.g., NotPetya, Suez Canal) and guiding students through highly applicable projects such as the Digital Twin Simulation and Procurement Negotiation Role Play. This strongly emphasises the book's commitment to generating actionable insights and professional capability.

References

Association for Supply Chain Management (ASCM). (2025). "Top 10 supply chain trends report 2025: AI, geopolitical dynamics, and cybersecurity." www.ascm.org/globalassets/ascm_website_assets/docs/top-10-trends-report-2025.pdf

Fortune Business Insights. (2024). "Supply chain management market size, share & COVID-19 impact analysis." www.fortunebusinessinsights.com/supply-chain-management-market-102977

Liferay. (n.d.). "5 Supply chain trends every business should watch in 2025: ESG: From compliance to strategy." www.liferay.com/blog/category/5-supply-chain-trends-every-business-should-watch-in-2025

Precedence Research. (2025). "Supply chain management market size and forecast 2025 to 2034." www.precedenceresearch.com/supply-chain-management-market

Acronyms

3PL	Third-Party Logistics
4PL	Fourth-Party Logistics
ABC	Stock Categories
ACV	Annual Contract Value
AD	Authorised Distributor
ASAP	As soon As possible
ASL	Approved Supplier List
ATO	Assemble to Order
ATP	Available to Promise
BOL	Bill of Lading
BOM	Bill of Materials
CAGR	Compound Annual Growth Rate
CAN	Cargo Arrival Notice
Capex	Capital Expenses
Category A	items are high-value, i.e. the top 20% that generate 70–80% of the value.
Category B	items are the next 30% contributing 15–25%.
Category C	are the low-value items, i.e. the remaining 50%.
CFS	Container Freight Station
CI	Continuous improvement
CIF	Cost, Insurance, and Freight
CNC	Computer Numerical Control
COGS	Cost of Goods Sold
COO	Country of Origin
CPFR	Collaborative Planning, Forecasting, and Replenishment
CTO	Configure to Order
DC	Distribution Centre
DN	Delivery Note
DOI	Days of Inventory
DRP	Distribution Resource Planning
DTV	Design to Value
EDA	Expected Date of Arrival
EDD	Expected Delivery date
EDI	Electronic Data Interchange
EOD	End of Day
EOQ	Economic Order Quantity
ERP	Enterprise Resource Planning

ETA	Expected Time of Arrival
ETD	Estimated Time of Delivery
EX-W	Ex-Work
FIFO	First In, First Out
FMS	Flexible manufacturing system
FOB	Free On Board
FOC	Free of Charge
FTE	Full-Time Equivalent
FTL	Full Truckload
GOP	Global Order promise
GPS	Global Positioning System
GRN	Goods receipt Note
HSS	High Sea Sale
IBP	Integrated Business Planning
INCOTERMS	International Commercial Terms
IR	Invoice receipt
KPI	Key Performance Indicator
LIFO	Last In, First Out
LPO	Local Purchase Order
LTL	Less Than Truckload
MIR	Material Issue Receipt
MIS	Management Information System
MOM	Minutes of meeting
MOQ	Minimum Order Quantity
MPS	Master Production Schedule
MRO	Maintenance, Repair, and Operations
MRP	Material Requirements Planning
OEM	Original Equipment manufacturers
OPEX	Operation Expenses
OTD	On Time Delivery
OTIF	On Time In Full
PCC	Periodic Cycle Count
PFI	Pro Forma Invoice
PO	Purchase Order
POD	Proof of delivery
POS	Point of Sale
POU	Point of Use
RFID	Radio-Frequency Identification
RFP	Request for Proposal
RFQ	Request for Quotation
ROI	Return on Investment
ROL	Re-order level
S&OP	Sales and Operations Planning
S/O	Service Order
SCM	Supply Chain Management
SCO	Supply Chain Optimisation
SCOR	Supply Chain Operations Reference
SKU	Stock Keeping Unit

SLA	Service Level Agreement
SO	Sales Order/Service Order
SO	Stock Out
SOB	Share of business
SoB	Share of business EEOQ
SOH	Stock on Hand
SPOC	Single point of contact
SS	Safety Stock
TCO	Total Cost of Ownership
TCV	Total Contract Value
TMS	Transportation Management System
VMI	Vendor-Managed Inventory
VSM	Value Stream Mapping
WIP	Work in Progress
WMS	Warehouse Management System
WO	Work Order

1 Definition and Importance of Supply Chain Management

Learning Outcomes

By the end of this chapter, learners will be able to:

- Define key supply chain concepts and summarise the historical evolution of Supply Chain Management (SCM).
- Explain the strategic role of SCM in business value creation and risk management.
- Identify the ten key components of modern supply chains and their interdependencies.
- Analyse how technology and sustainability trends are reshaping SCM strategy.
- Evaluate a real-world SCM example and recommend one improvement to enhance resilience or value.

In the contemporary globalised economy, SCM is defined as the integrated planning, execution, and control of all activities involved in sourcing, procurement, conversion, and logistics management, supplemented by coordination and collaboration with channel partners to create net value and competitive advantage. Its primary objective is to create a seamless, cost-effective process that optimises operations, maximises efficiency, and enhances customer satisfaction (ASCM: Association of Supply Chain Management, 2024).

The significance of SCM in today's marketplace is evident. Aligning production with demand provides businesses with a structure that supports adaptability and efficiency. Effective SCM enables companies to remain competitive, meet fluctuating demands, and control costs. As such, SCM influences a business's success across several dimensions, including profitability, customer satisfaction, and reputation (Chopra & Meindl, 2024). SCM's significance extends beyond operational efficiency: it underpins organisational resilience, cost leadership, and customer satisfaction in contexts ranging from the automotive plants of Japan to the e-commerce corridors of Southeast Asia.

DOI: 10.4324/9781003740568-1

1.1 The History of SCM

The term "supply chain management" was first coined by British logistics expert Keith Oliver of Booz Allen Hamilton. In a 4 June 1982 interview with Arnold Kransdorff for the *Financial Times*, Oliver introduced the phrase to describe a new way of looking at the flow of goods and information across multiple functions and organisations (see Figure 1.1) (Ashcroft, 2022).

1.1.1 Original Meaning and Scope

Oliver's original definition of SCM emphasised the end-to-end integration of activities required to move a product from raw material suppliers through manufacturing and distribution to the end customer. Specifically, he described SCM as:

> The process of planning, implementing, and controlling the operations of the supply chain with the purpose of satisfying customer requirements as efficiently as possible. Supply chain management spans all movement and storage of raw materials, work-in-process inventory, and finished goods from point-of-origin to point-of-consumption.

Under this scope, SCM originally included:

1 Strategic sourcing and supplier involvement in product development
2 Inventory management across raw materials, in-process stock, and finished goods
3 Logistics planning (transportation, warehousing, order fulfilment)
4 Cross-functional coordination among manufacturing, marketing, sales, and finance
5 Demand forecasting and production planning

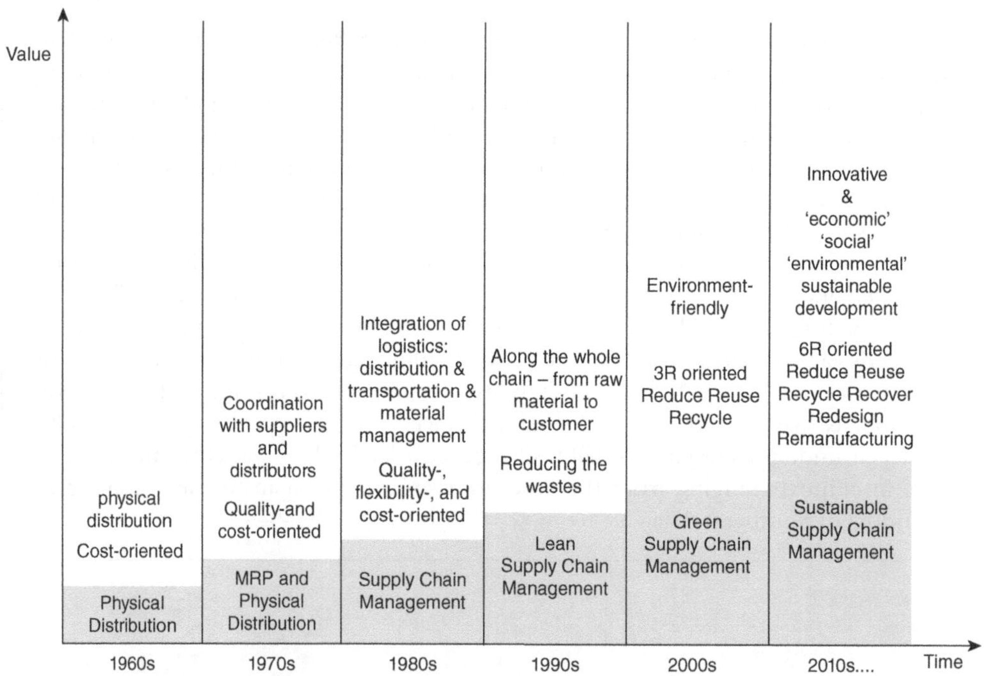

Figure 1.1 The History of SCM.

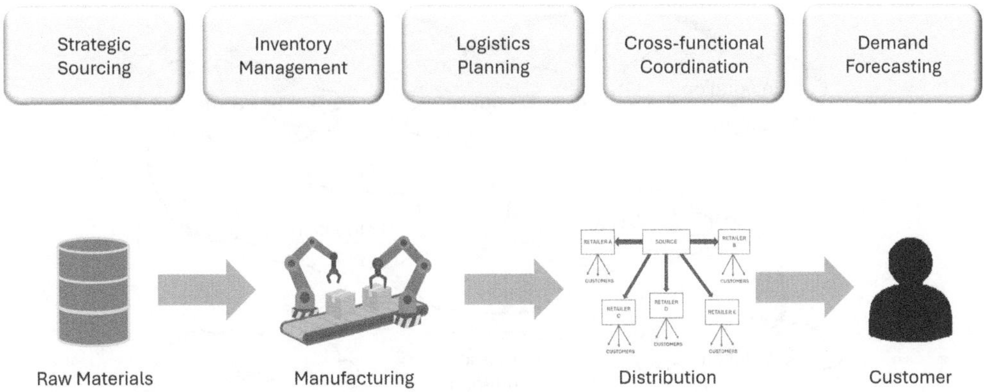

Figure 1.2 Elements of Supply Chain Management.

By framing these disparate activities as parts of a single "chain" (see Figure 1.2), Oliver shifted the focus from isolated functional excellence (e.g., logistics alone) to the holistic management of flows, laying the cornerstone for virtually all later definitions and best practices in the field.

Modern SCM builds on Oliver's definition by introducing Lean SCM in the 1990s, Green SCM in the 2000s, and Sustainable SCM in the 2010s. While the development of these additional principles allows an organisation to remain relevant and meet an increasing demand for decarbonising the supply chain, they do impose additional layers of planning and cost overheads. What makes Modern SCM noteworthy in the contemporary business world is the introduction of Artificial Intelligence (AI), robotics and automation, the Internet of Things (IoT), and Blockchain. These subjects will be explored in detail later in the text.

Case Study – Toyota's Global JIT Network

Toyota's Just-In-Time (JIT) system, originally pioneered in Japan, exemplifies cross-border supplier integration. By coordinating component deliveries from over 300 tier-1 suppliers across Asia and North America, Toyota maintains optimal inventory levels while achieving a sub-two-day supply replenishment cycle in its Texas and Mexico facilities, reducing holding costs by 15% annually (Liker, 2020).

1.2 Key Components of SCM

A supply chain comprises interconnected activities and flows essential to delivering products or services. Understanding these core components (see Figure 1.3) is fundamental to grasping how SCM operates.

An effective system should be agile and functional which leads to strategic decision-making and cost reduction in operations. Moreover, supply chain management tends to work with maximum efficiency and scale up to the capabilities that provide credibility in the operations.

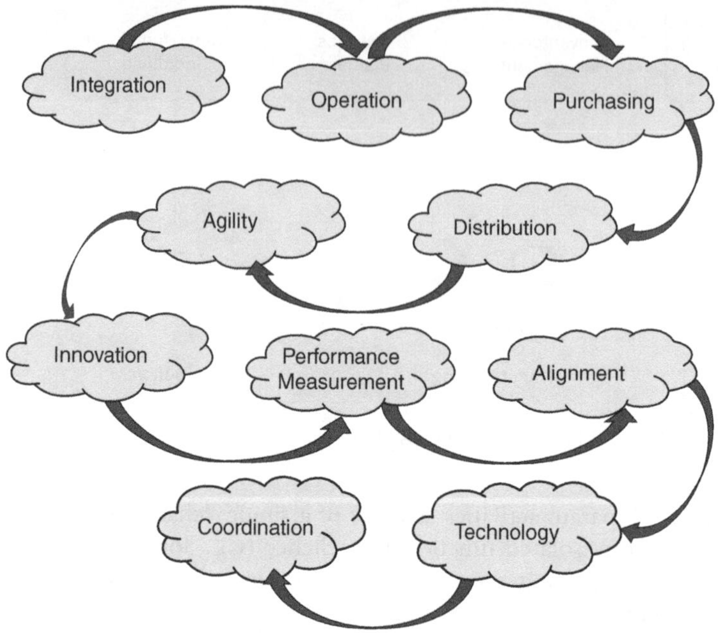

Figure 1.3 The Ten Key Elements of SCM.

The ten key elements of SCM are:

1 **Integration:** Before launching a business, clarity is everything – on purpose, methodology, and execution. Strategic planning isn't a formality; it's foundational. In today's data-driven environment, integrating supply chain processes is non-negotiable. It's how we reduce errors, eliminate waste, and build a responsive operation. That means clearly defining responsibilities across suppliers, third-party logistics (3PL) providers, and co-manufacturers. Integration isn't just good practice; it's what gives leaders the transparency and control to plan, act, and adapt with confidence.
2 **Operations:** Operations sit at the heart of supply chain performance. They're not just about getting product from A to B; they're the engine room of efficiency, insight, and consistency. When done right, operations deliver real-time visibility across functions, allowing us to refine our processes day by day. This leads to smarter decisions, leaner workflows, and improved margins. From warehousing to distribution, every touchpoint should be optimised to anticipate demand and enhance customer satisfaction.
3 **Purchasing:** Effective purchasing is about more than price. It's about ensuring you've got the right materials, the right people, and the right partners in place, at the right time. It's a strategic lever in SCM that impacts everything downstream. Whether you're sourcing raw materials or specialist skills, procurement decisions shape quality, cost, and speed. Combine that with intelligent demand forecasting, and you unlock purchasing's real potential: reducing waste, improving profitability, and future-proofing your supply network.
4 **Distribution:** Once the product is ready, distribution becomes the frontline of customer experience. It's about precision: getting the right product to the right person, in the right place, at the right time. From transport logistics to returns management,

distribution plays a pivotal role in brand perception and profitability. Excellence in distribution isn't accidental; it's the result of good data, reliable partners, and clear service expectations. If your logistics can't keep up, neither can your business.

5 **Agility:** In today's unpredictable market, agility isn't a luxury; it's survival. A supply chain must be built to flex, whether it's due to geopolitical disruptions, supply shocks, or shifting customer preferences. Agile operations give businesses a competitive edge by enabling them to pivot, respond, and recover more quickly than their competitors. Long-term resilience is no longer just about having Plan B; it's about designing supply networks that can self-correct and adapt in real time. The future belongs to the nimble.

6 **Innovation:** Innovation drives progress, and in the supply chain space, it's often the difference between stagnation and growth. Whether it's using AI to predict demand or applying blockchain to trace product origins, innovation enables smarter, faster, and more transparent decision-making. But technology alone won't fix broken systems. It must be paired with effective leadership and clear processes. When those align, innovation becomes a game-changer, driving down costs, improving flow, and solving legacy problems once thought too complex to tackle.

7 **Performance Measurement:** You can't improve what you don't measure. Key Performance Indicators (KPIs), metrics, and dashboards – these aren't just numbers; they're insights. Performance tracking tells us where we're efficient, where we're bleeding time and money, and where we need to recalibrate. The best supply chains are those that continually evaluate their operations and are willing to act on the data's findings. Measurement isn't about ticking boxes; it's about sharpening the edge.

8 **Alignment:** The supply chain doesn't exist in a silo; it must be strategically aligned with your broader business goals. If your supply chain isn't supporting your market position, customer promises, or growth plans, it's holding you back. Alignment requires cross-functional visibility, regular communication, and leadership buy-in. Today, tools such as AI and supply chain analytics (SCA) provide us with deeper insights than ever before. But without a clear strategic framework, even the best tools fall flat.

9 **Technology:** Emerging technologies are rewriting the rules of SCM. AI, IoT, blockchain, and robotics are no longer future-state; they're here, and they're raising the bar. These tools unlock automation, real-time planning, and predictive insight at a scale we've never seen before. The challenge is knowing which tech to adopt and when. It's not about chasing trends; it's about choosing innovations that deliver measurable value and fit your operating model.

10 **Coordination:** Coordination is the glue that holds the supply chain together. From the initial concept through to final delivery, it ensures that every handoff, every process, and every decision is aligned and executed seamlessly. Strong coordination enhances transparency, builds stakeholder trust, and strengthens your market reputation. Without it, even the best strategy can unravel in the execution phase. Coordination is more than a management function; it's a mindset of shared accountability.

At a macro level, creating a viable supply chain involves the interdependence of several components (see Figure 1.4). These interdependent components are:

1 **Organisational Structure:** Backup suppliers, backup subcontractors, facility fortification (including cyber), and workforce resilience.

2 **Informational Structure:** Digital twins, data analytics, visibility, supplier portals, blockchain.

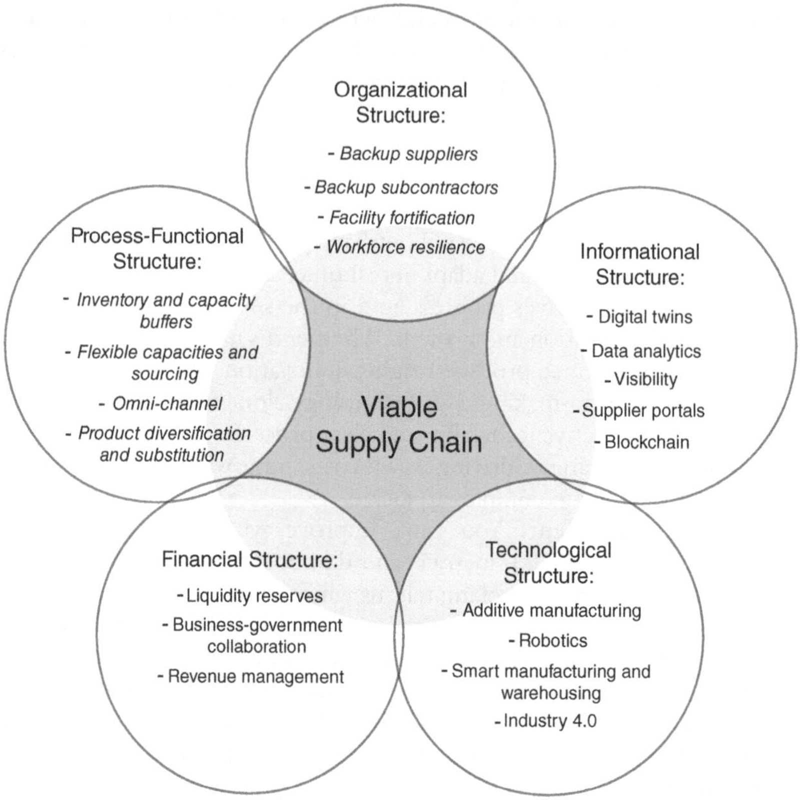

Figure 1.4 Component Interdependencies.

3 **Technological Structure:** Additive manufacturing, robotics, smart manufacturing and warehousing, Industry 4.0.
4 **Financial Structure:** Liquidity reserves, business-government collaboration, revenue management.
5 **Process-Functional Structure:** Inventory and capacity buffers, flexible capacities and sourcing, omni-channel, product diversification, and substitution.

In addition to the Ten Key Elements of SCM discussed above, a modern supply chain comprises five core, interwoven components: procurement and supplier management; production and operations; logistics and distribution; inventory management; and demand forecasting and planning (Wisner, 2022). Each must be optimally configured to balance cost, quality, delivery, and sustainability across international networks.

1 **Procurement and Supplier Management:** Strategic sourcing frameworks emphasise total cost of ownership (TCO), supplier relationship maturity, and risk mitigation (Monczka et al., 2016).

   Case Study: Unilever's Sustainable Agriculture Programme sources from smallholder farmers in India, Brazil, and Nigeria, embedding traceability and social impact metrics into contracts to reduce raw material price volatility by 10% and improve community incomes (Unilever, 2023).

2 **Production and Operations:** Application of Lean Six Sigma drives continuous improvement (CI) and process stability (Womack & Jones, 1996).

   Case Study: Siemens' Amberg Electronics Plant in Germany utilises over 1,200 IoT sensors for real-time defect detection, achieving a 99.9% quality rate and a 20% increase in throughput (Siemens, 2024).

3 **Logistics and Distribution:** Network design models integrate multimodal routing and hub-and-spoke architectures (Christopher, 2016).

   Case Study: DHL's Pan-African eCommerce Express leverages strategic hubs in Nairobi and Johannesburg to cut transit times by 18%, facilitating small and medium-sized enterprises' (SMEs) access to regional markets (DHL, 2023).

4 **Inventory Management:** JIT, EOQ, and Safety-Stock (SS) models align with dynamic demand signals (Chopra & Meindl, 2024).

   Case Study: Zara's fast-fashion model uses real-time point of sale (POS) data from its European, Asian, and American stores to replenish stock bi-weekly, reducing markdowns by 50% (Blanchard, 2022).

5 **Demand Forecasting and Planning:** Advancements in technology have enabled machine learning (ML) and collaborative planning to enhance forecast accuracy (Wang, et al., 2016).

   Case Study: Nestlé's AI-driven forecasting platform in Latin America decreased forecast error by 15% across 14 categories during seasonal peaks (Nestlé, 2024; Quadratyx AI Solutions, 2024).

1.3 Evolution of SCM

SCM has undergone significant evolution from the local, cost-focused logistics of the pre-1980s era, driven by technological advancements, shifting consumer expectations, and changes in the business landscape. Initially focused on internal production and procurement, SCM has expanded into a comprehensive system that integrates external suppliers and customers, encompassing end-to-end processes (Hugos, 2018).

1.3.1 Early Development

In its early stages, SCM primarily focused on production and warehousing. Basic inventory and transport strategies were employed to manage demand and supply. SCM was largely reactive, with organisations responding to demand rather than predicting it.

1.3.2 The Influence of Technology

In the 1990s and 2000s, the advent of digital technologies, including the internet and automation, transformed SCM. Information technology (IT) enabled more accurate forecasting, real-time tracking, and seamless communication across the supply chain. Technologies such as Enterprise Resource Planning (ERP) and Warehouse Management Systems (WMS) allowed for greater control over complex operations and processes.

1.3.3 Globalisation and Outsourcing

During the 2010s and beyond, the rise of global trade has had a profound impact on SCM. Companies began sourcing materials and labour from different countries to reduce costs, increase efficiency, and access larger markets. Global SCM introduced new challenges, including increased lead times, currency fluctuations, and cultural differences. Industry 4.0 technologies (IoT, blockchain, and digital twins) and circular economy pilots are leading in Scandinavia and the Gulf Cooperation Council (GCC) (Gurtu & Johny, 2021).

1.3.4 The Sustainability Movement

As awareness of environmental and social issues grows, sustainability has become a priority in SCM. Modern supply chains focus on reducing waste, minimising carbon footprints, and ensuring ethical labour practices. Consumers and stakeholders are increasingly holding companies accountable for ensuring their operations are environmentally and socially responsible. European Union regulations under the Green Deal mandate carbon-neutral logistics corridors, while ASEAN's digital trade facilitation initiatives aim to reduce cross-border friction by 25% (ASEAN Secretariat, 2024).

1.4 Strategic Role of SCM in Business

SCM is more than just logistics; it is a strategic function that influences a business's overall success. Effective SCM enables companies to deliver quality products at lower costs, directly affecting profitability and market competitiveness. By aligning supply chain strategy with corporate objectives (see Figure 1.5), SCM functions as a growth enabler through cost leadership, differentiation, and market responsiveness (Chopra & Meindl, 2024).

1. **Cost Leadership:** SCM helps manage costs by improving efficiency and reducing waste. Lean manufacturing, demand forecasting, and optimal inventory management contribute to reducing cost of goods sold and TCO.
2. **Differentiation:** Agile supply chains support rapid product launches and customisation.
3. **Customer Satisfaction:** SCM impacts customer satisfaction by ensuring product availability, timely delivery, and quality. Efficient SCM can enhance customer loyalty and brand reputation by consistently meeting customer expectations.
4. **Agility and Resilience:** A responsive and resilient supply chain enables businesses to adapt to changes, manage disruptions, and capitalise on new opportunities. Agility is essential in a globalised market with unpredictable demand, while resilience helps firms recover quickly from unexpected disruptions, such as natural disasters or economic crises. Diversified sourcing and near-shoring mitigate geopolitical and climate risks.

Case Study – Apple's End-to-End Supplier Integration

Apple's coordination of suppliers across Taiwan, Vietnam, and India, coupled with real-time logistics visibility, trimmed iPhone launch-to-market times by 25%, sustaining premium positioning (Christopher, 2022).

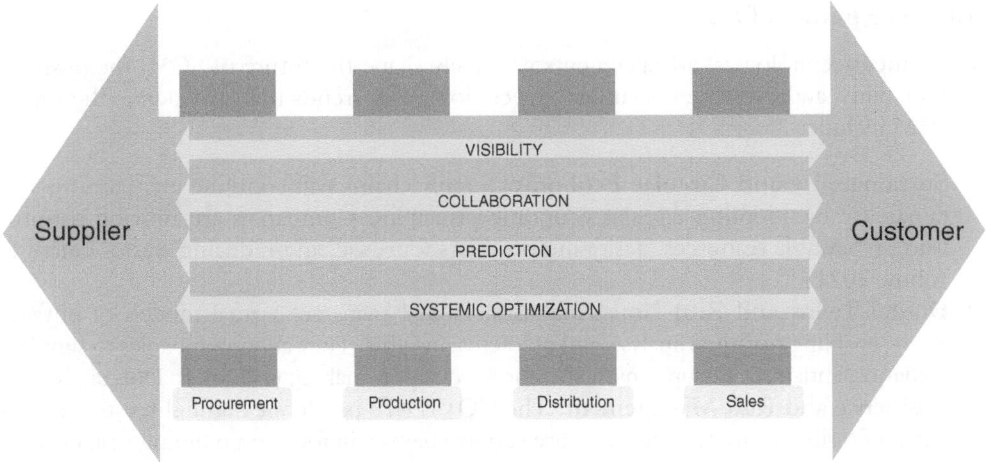

Figure 1.5 Strategic SCM Levers.

1.5 Technological Innovations in SCM

Technological advancements have revolutionised SCM, providing tools that enhance efficiency, accuracy, and decision-making. Emerging technologies, including blockchain for traceability, digital twins for scenario planning, and autonomous vehicles for last-mile delivery, are reshaping SCM capabilities. Concurrently, circular economy models in the Netherlands and Sweden champion product-life extension and closed-loop systems (Gurtu & Johny, 2021). From a global perspective, the GCC nations pilot solar-powered autonomous ports; South American agrifood exporters deploy blockchain to assure provenance.

Key technological innovations in SCM include:

1 **Automation and Robotics:** Automation reduces human error, speeds up repetitive tasks, and increases productivity. In manufacturing, robots perform tasks such as assembly and packaging, while warehouse automation supports order picking, sorting, and inventory management.
2 **IoT:** IoT technology enables real-time tracking of goods throughout the supply chain. Sensors on vehicles, containers, and equipment provide data on location, temperature, and condition, allowing for better control and visibility.
3 **Blockchain Technology:** Blockchain creates a transparent and secure record of transactions, making it ideal for tracking product origins, reducing fraud, and ensuring data integrity. It is especially useful for managing complex supply chains with multiple stakeholders (Min, 2019).
4 **AI and ML:** AI and ML assist in demand forecasting, predictive maintenance, and dynamic pricing. These technologies improve decision-making by analysing large volumes of data to identify patterns and trends.
5 **Data Analytics:** Data analytics plays a crucial role in SCM, providing insights into customer behaviour, supplier performance, and operational efficiency. Analytics enables better decision-making and more strategic planning across the supply chain (Wang et al., 2016).

1.6 The Future of SCM

Continued technological advancements will likely shape the future of SCM, the push for sustainability, and evolving consumer expectations. Key trends that may define the future of SCM include:

1. **Sustainability and Circular Economy:** Supply chains will continue emphasising sustainability by adopting circular economy principles. Companies are moving towards using renewable resources, designing products for reuse, and reducing waste (Gurtu & Johny, 2021).
2. **Digital Twins and Real-Time Analytics:** Digital twins are virtual models of physical assets, enabling real-time analysis and predictive insights. They allow companies to simulate scenarios, anticipate disruptions, and improve decision-making (Ivanov & Dolgui, 2020).
3. **Resilience and Risk Management:** The COVID-19 pandemic highlighted the importance of resilient supply chains. Future supply chains will focus on building resilience by diversifying suppliers, improving transparency, and creating contingency plans for potential disruptions (Ivanov & Das, 2020).
4. **Customisation and Personalisation:** As customer expectations shift towards personalised products and services, supply chains will need to become more flexible to accommodate these demands. Mass customisation and agile manufacturing will allow businesses to offer tailored products without sacrificing efficiency.
5. **Advanced Collaboration and Integration:** Collaboration across the supply chain will become more sophisticated, with integrated digital platforms enabling seamless communication between suppliers, manufacturers, and customers. Enhanced integration will foster stronger relationships and create value across the supply chain.

1.7 The Role of SCM in Business Success

SCM is essential for the success of modern businesses, directly impacting profitability, operational efficiency, and customer satisfaction. In a competitive and rapidly evolving marketplace, companies that optimise their supply chains are better positioned to respond to customer demands, reduce waste, and manage costs effectively. By aligning SCM with corporate strategy, businesses can secure a competitive advantage and drive long-term growth.

1.7.1 Enhancing Profitability and Reducing Costs

An efficient supply chain reduces costs by streamlining operations and eliminating redundancies. Cost reduction can be achieved through lean management practices, such as minimising inventory levels and implementing JIT production systems, which reduce warehousing costs and decrease waste. This focus on efficiency leads to significant savings, particularly in industries where margins are tight.

Case Study – Zara Fashion Retailer

Zara, a prominent fashion retailer, employs an agile supply chain that allows it to respond quickly to shifting trends. By keeping inventory levels low and reducing lead times, Zara can rapidly deliver trendy products to stores while minimising overproduction and excess stock. This lean, responsive model helps Zara reduce operational costs and maintain profitability, even in a highly competitive industry (Blanchard, 2022).

1.7.2 Building Strong Supplier Relationships

Successful SCM depends on strong partnerships with suppliers, as reliable suppliers ensure consistent quality and timely delivery of materials. Collaborative supplier relationships improve performance, as businesses and suppliers work together to optimise processes and respond to market changes. In industries like electronics, where product lifecycles are short, businesses with strong relationships with suppliers can expedite production and stay competitive.

Case Study – Apple's Supplier Relationships

Apple provides an example of the value of robust supplier relationships. The company's success hinges on its ability to launch new products efficiently, maintaining high quality and low costs. By working closely with its suppliers, Apple ensures that production schedules align with launch timelines, allowing the company to release products without delay. This approach has helped Apple become a leader in product innovation and market share (Blanchard, 2022).

1.7.3 Enhancing Customer Satisfaction

Customer satisfaction is a fundamental objective of SCM. By optimising logistics, inventory management, and customer service, businesses can meet customer expectations consistently, building trust and loyalty. A well-managed supply chain enables timely delivery, quality assurance, and accurate order fulfilment, which are all critical to customer satisfaction.

Case Study – Amazon

Companies like Amazon demonstrate how effective SCM can lead to customer satisfaction. Amazon's advanced logistics network and inventory management systems allow it to fulfil orders rapidly, even for customers in remote locations. The company's commitment to fast delivery and reliability has set a high standard for customer service in e-commerce, contributing to its dominance in the market (Christopher, 2016).

1.7.4 Leveraging Technology for Competitive Advantage

Technology plays a pivotal role in SCM, enabling businesses to enhance efficiency, make data-driven decisions, and maintain real-time visibility. Through tools such as AI, ML, and Big Data Analytics, companies can forecast demand accurately, manage inventory effectively, and respond to changes proactively. These tools provide companies with insights that help them anticipate trends, identify opportunities, and mitigate risks.

Case Study – Walmart

Walmart uses advanced data analytics to manage its supply chain. By analysing customer purchasing patterns, Walmart can forecast demand accurately and stock stores accordingly. This data-driven approach allows Walmart to reduce stockouts, enhance customer satisfaction, and maintain low prices, ultimately strengthening its market position (Hugos, 2018).

1.7.5 Adapting to Market Changes and Managing Risks

An agile supply chain is essential for adapting to market changes and managing risks. Global events, such as the COVID-19 pandemic, have highlighted the importance of resilient supply chains that can withstand disruptions. Businesses that proactively manage risks and adapt to changing conditions can mitigate the impact of supply chain disruptions and continue serving their customers.

Case Study – Toyota's Resilient Supply Chain

Toyota's response to supply chain disruptions illustrates the value of a resilient supply chain. During the 2011 earthquake and tsunami in Japan, Toyota's flexible supply chain allowed it to continue production by sourcing alternative parts and modifying production processes. Toyota's ability to adapt ensured that it could meet customer demand, despite significant disruptions (Ivanov & Dolgui, 2020).

1.8 The Role of Risk Management in SCM

SCM is not only about achieving efficiency but also about managing risks. In a globalised and interconnected economy, supply chains are increasingly exposed to various risks, including natural disasters, political instability, economic shifts, and global health crises. Effective risk management in SCM involves identifying, assessing, and mitigating these risks to ensure supply chains remain resilient and adapt to unexpected events. Global supply chains (GSCs) face risks from pandemics, climate events, cyber threats, and political instability. Robust risk management integrates supplier diversification, buffer inventories, and AI-enabled monitoring (Ivanov & Das, 2020).

1.8.1 Types of Risks in SCM

The types of risks encountered in SCM vary widely and can be grouped into several key categories:

1. **Operational Risks:** These include internal production, procurement, and logistics risks. Examples of operational risks are equipment failures, quality issues, and inefficiencies in production processes. Effective SCM must ensure that operations are streamlined and resilient to minimise these risks.
2. **Financial Risks:** Fluctuations in exchange rates, changes in commodity prices, and credit risks can all impact supply chains financially. Currency volatility, for instance, affects businesses that rely on overseas suppliers. Financial risk management includes using hedging strategies and diversifying sourcing options to mitigate these impacts (Waters, 2023).
3. **Strategic Risks:** Strategic risks arise from poor decision-making or flawed business strategies. An example is over-reliance on a single supplier or market, which increases vulnerability. Strategic risk management involves evaluating supply chain dependencies and seeking diversification to improve resilience (Ivanov & Dolgui, 2020).
4. **Environmental Risks:** Natural disasters, such as earthquakes, floods, and hurricanes, can severely disrupt supply chains. Companies in regions prone to these events must plan for such disruptions by developing contingency plans and ensuring alternative supply routes are available (Sheffi, 2020).

5 **Global Health Risks:** Pandemics, such as COVID-19, represent a significant risk. The pandemic exposed vulnerabilities in supply chains worldwide, leading to production, transport, and supply disruptions. Companies with resilient and adaptable supply chains, however, managed to minimise the impact (Sheffi, 2020).

Case Study – COVID-19 Pandemic and Supply Chain Resilience

The COVID-19 pandemic exemplifies the importance of risk management in SCM. Many companies experienced disruptions due to lockdowns, supply shortages, and logistical challenges. However, organisations with flexible supply chains were better positioned to adapt. In the pharmaceutical industry, for example, companies like Pfizer and Johnson & Johnson were able to maintain production and distribution by implementing flexible supply chain strategies. These companies diversified their supplier base, secured alternative logistics routes, and used real-time data to adjust production schedules (Sheffi, 2020).

By contrast, companies that relied heavily on a single geographic area for manufacturing, such as China, faced significant delays as factories were forced to close during the initial outbreak. This experience has prompted many companies to reassess their supply chains and consider reshoring, diversifying suppliers, or implementing dual-sourcing strategies to mitigate future risks.

1.8.2 Key Risk Management Strategies in SCM

There are several key strategies that businesses can adopt to enhance risk management in SCM:

1 **Supplier Diversification:** Relying on a single supplier or geographic area can increase vulnerability to disruptions. Diversifying suppliers across different regions reduces dependency on any single supplier and improves resilience.
2 **Dual Sourcing and Near-shoring:** Dual sourcing involves having two suppliers for critical components, while near-shoring moves production closer to the company's home market. Both strategies reduce the impact of global disruptions and improve supply chain agility (Ivanov & Dolgui, 2020).
3 **Inventory Buffering:** While lean inventory management reduces costs, maintaining a buffer inventory for critical components can prevent supply chain disruptions during unexpected events. This approach can be particularly useful for essential goods or high-demand items.
4 **Real-Time Monitoring and Data Analytics:** Leveraging data analytics and real-time monitoring enables companies to identify potential disruptions early and respond proactively. Technologies like the IoT and AI help companies gain visibility into their supply chains and predict potential risks before they materialise (Min, 2019).
5 **Collaborative Partnerships:** Building strong relationships with suppliers, logistics providers, and other partners fosters collaboration and improves information sharing. This allows for quicker responses to disruptions and strengthens the entire supply chain network.

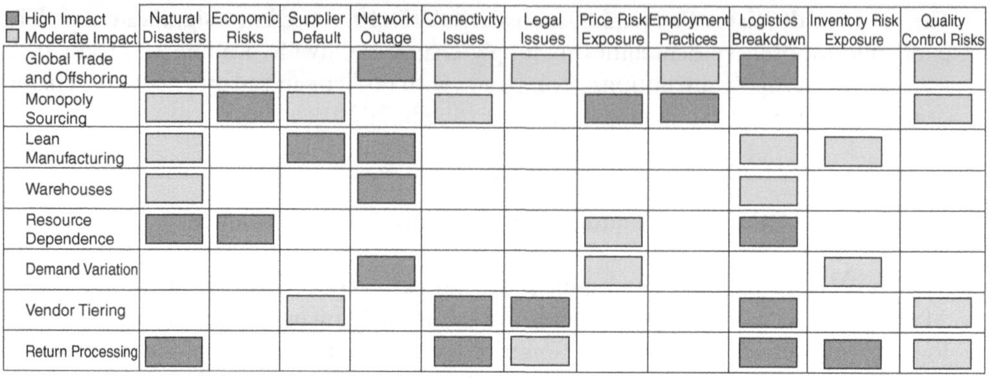

Figure 1.6 Risk Mitigation Matrix.

1.8.3 The Future of Risk Management in SCM

As the global business landscape continues to evolve, risk management in SCM will become even more critical. Future risk management strategies (see Figure 1.6) may involve increased investment in technologies like blockchain, which provides greater transparency, and digital twins, which enable companies to simulate potential disruptions and test response strategies. Additionally, companies are likely to emphasise sustainability and ethical sourcing more, recognising that environmental and social risks are integral to overall risk management.

The "digital supply chain twin" concept is also gaining traction. A digital twin is a virtual replica of a supply chain, allowing companies to model and predict the impact of various scenarios. This technology enables companies to develop contingency plans, test resilience, and enhance overall supply chain performance (Ivanov, 2021).

1.9 Key Concepts in SCM

SCM can be broken down into several core components that interact to support organisational objectives and customer satisfaction. These components include procurement, production, logistics, and distribution, each of which contributes to the overall efficiency and effectiveness of the supply chain.

1.9.1 Procurement

Procurement is the process of sourcing goods and services essential to a company's operations. This involves establishing a sourcing methodology, conducting market research, issuing a Request for Information (RFI) and a Request for Quotation (RFQ), selecting suppliers, negotiating contracts, managing the contracting phase, and implementing Supplier Relationship Management (SRM) (see Figure 1.7). Effective procurement strategies enable companies to secure reliable suppliers, reduce risks, and foster robust supplier relationships. A prominent example of effective procurement is Toyota's JIT system, which aims to minimise inventory levels by scheduling parts to arrive exactly when they are required in production (Liker, 2020). This model reduces excess inventory and ensures that production aligns closely with supplier deliveries, cutting down costs and enhancing operational efficiency.

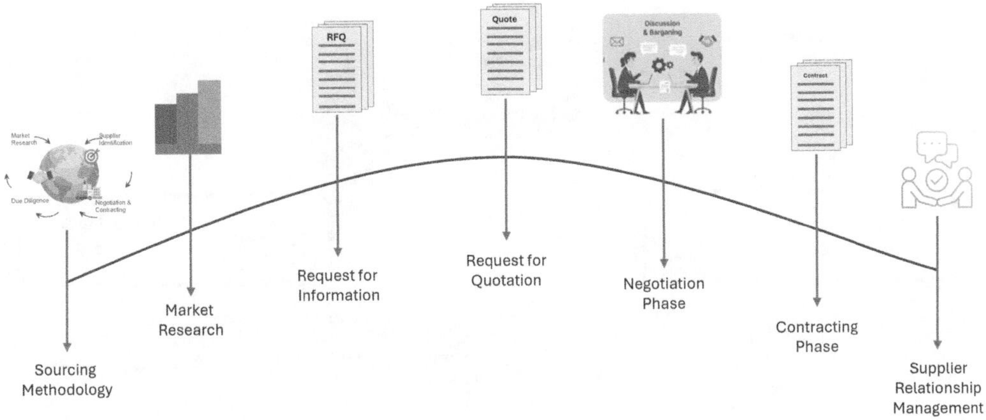

Figure 1.7 The Seven Steps of Procurement.

The significance of procurement within SCM is also evident in its impact on sustainability. Organisations are increasingly held accountable for their suppliers' environmental and ethical practices, especially in sectors such as retail and manufacturing. In Australia, companies are encouraged to engage in sustainable procurement, choosing suppliers who follow environmentally friendly practices and uphold labour standards (Australian Government, 2022). Sustainable procurement aligns with corporate social responsibility (CSR) goals and fosters brand loyalty among environmentally conscious consumers.

1.9.2 Production

Production in SCM involves transforming raw materials into finished goods that meet quality standards. Efficient production management strikes a balance between cost-effectiveness and the quality requirements expected by consumers. Lean manufacturing principles, pioneered by companies like Toyota, are widely adopted to eliminate waste, improve quality, and increase productivity (Womack & Jones, 1996). Lean principles focus on creating customer value by ensuring that each stage of the production process contributes meaningfully without waste.

Although smaller than many other industrialised nations, Australia's manufacturing sector has adopted lean principles to remain competitive, particularly in high-value sectors such as advanced manufacturing and food processing. In these industries, meeting consumer demand without overproduction is essential, and lean manufacturing allows companies to achieve this by minimising inefficiencies and optimising resource use (Australian Industry Group, 2020). A key component of the production cycle is the Sales and Operations Planning (S&OP) phase. To ensure the viability of the supply chain, representatives of the SCM processes must contribute to this planning activity.

1.9.3 Logistics

Logistics encompasses storing, transporting, and delivering goods, bridging the gap between production and distribution (see Figure 1.8). Effective logistics management ensures that products are delivered to customers in the right place, at the right time, and in optimal condition. In recent years, advancements in technology have transformed logistics operations. For example, Amazon's use of data analytics and fulfilment centres has

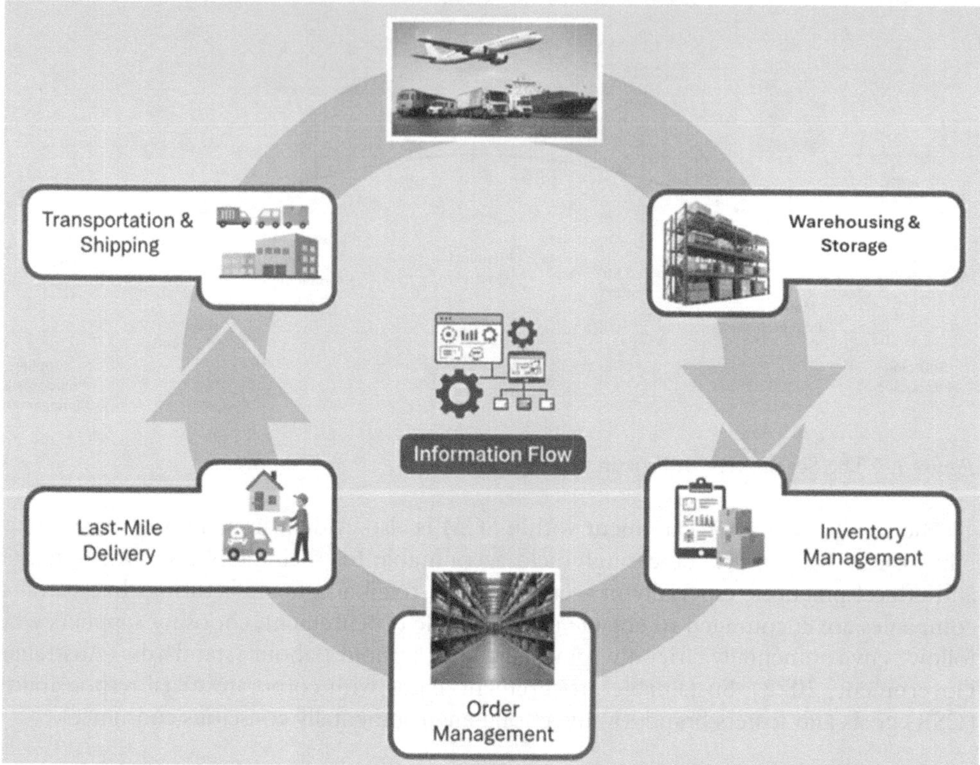

Figure 1.8 Logistics.

streamlined its global logistics, allowing the company to meet consumer demand swiftly and accurately (Stone, 2013). By leveraging real-time data and a vast distribution network, Amazon provides one of the most efficient delivery systems worldwide, setting a benchmark for other companies to follow.

Logistics is especially challenging for Australian businesses due to the country's large land area and relatively dispersed population centres. Efficient logistics solutions in Australia often require innovative approaches, such as regional distribution centres (DCs) and localised delivery networks, to overcome these geographic barriers and meet customer expectations (Lowe, 2021). Additionally, Australia's logistics sector is increasingly focused on sustainability, with companies investing in electric vehicles and carbon offset programmes to reduce their environmental impact.

1.9.4 Distribution

Distribution is the final stage of SCM, ensuring that finished products reach consumers through the appropriate channels. In a global market, distribution strategies vary widely depending on the industry, customer base, and geography. In Australia, e-commerce growth has transformed distribution, with online retail giants and local businesses needing efficient, customer-centric delivery options. As a result, companies often use a combination of 3PL providers and in-house solutions to optimise distribution and ensure timely delivery (Australian Competition and Consumer Commission, 2020).

The shift towards e-commerce has also highlighted the importance of last-mile delivery, the final step in the distribution process. Last-mile delivery can be costly and complex, especially in urban areas where traffic congestion may delay shipments. Companies are experimenting with alternative delivery models, such as drone deliveries and centralised pickup points, to overcome these challenges and enhance delivery efficiency (Hubner et al., 2013).

1.10 The Future Evolution of SCM

SCM has evolved significantly over the decades. Initially, SCM was viewed primarily as a logistical function aimed at optimising costs and ensuring reliable delivery. However, in the 21st century, SCM has shifted towards a more strategic role within organisations. Today, SCM focuses on cost efficiency and addresses risk management, customer satisfaction, and sustainability.

1.10.1 Globalisation and Technology

The forces of globalisation and technological advancement have profoundly impacted SCM. Globalisation has extended supply chains across continents, enabling companies to source materials from cost-effective regions and serve customers worldwide. This has increased competition and driven companies to adopt efficient SCM practices to maintain a competitive edge (Handfield & Nichols, 2002). Technology, particularly advancements in data analytics, AI, and automation, has further transformed SCM, allowing organisations to forecast demand accurately, optimise inventory, and swiftly respond to supply chain disruptions (Simchi-Levi et al., 2024).

1.11 Conclusion

In today's globalised and highly competitive market, SCM is indispensable for organisational success, spanning from procurement and production to logistics, distribution, and customer satisfaction. This chapter has outlined how each component plays a crucial role in ensuring that resources are effectively managed to create value for the end customer. By optimising these functions, SCM provides companies with a framework to maintain efficient operations, reduce costs, and improve responsiveness to market demands. As companies aim to adapt to an increasingly dynamic and uncertain environment, SCM offers strategic insights and frameworks for navigating challenges ranging from fluctuating consumer demand to economic shifts and environmental concerns.

The evolution of SCM from a logistics-focused approach to a strategic, integrated discipline reflects its critical role in modern business strategy. Over the decades, technological advancements, such as AI, blockchain, and the IoT, have revolutionised SCM practices, enhancing transparency, speed, and flexibility within supply chains. These innovations enable companies to better forecast demand, manage inventories, and coordinate across vast and intricate networks of suppliers and distributors. Additionally, the rise of data analytics has allowed businesses to make more informed, proactive decisions, reducing risks and supporting customer satisfaction.

In Australia, where unique logistical challenges are posed by its vast distances and regional dispersion, companies have embraced these advances to remain competitive in domestic and international markets. Australian supply chains increasingly focus on sustainable practices, aligning with global trends and responding to consumer demand for environmentally responsible business practices. This shift towards sustainable SCM reflects a broader movement within the discipline, with companies prioritising environmental impact, social responsibility, and ethical sourcing alongside profitability.

As SCM continues to adapt to global trends and technological changes, the emphasis on agility and resilience has become paramount. The COVID-19 pandemic underscored the importance of building resilient supply chains that can withstand disruptions and maintain continuity. Companies worldwide, and particularly in Australia, are now prioritising risk management strategies, such as supplier diversification, inventory buffering, and real-time monitoring, to protect against unforeseen challenges.

This chapter has articulated SCM's foundational definitions, key components, evolutionary trajectory, strategic significance, and the pivotal role of technological and risk-resilience innovations. With SCM at the intersection of efficiency, technology, and customer satisfaction, the discipline is set to remain integral to business success. Future chapters will delve into these components in detail, examining how companies can utilise SCM to achieve their strategic objectives, foster innovation, and enhance their long-term competitiveness. As businesses strive to align their operations with evolving consumer expectations and changing market conditions, the strategic significance of SCM will only grow, underscoring its crucial role in shaping a sustainable and resilient future for global commerce.

Q&A Section

Here is a short quiz to test your knowledge. The answers are provided in Appendix C.

1. What is the core purpose of SCM?
2. How does SCM contribute to reducing operational costs for businesses?
3. Why is flexibility necessary in SCM, particularly during global disruptions like the COVID-19 pandemic?
4. What is the JIT system, and how does it benefit companies like Toyota?
5. How does lean manufacturing support production efficiency in SCM?
6. What role does logistics play in SCM, and how does it affect customer satisfaction?
7. How has Amazon's logistics network contributed to its success?
8. In what ways can SCM help businesses align with sustainability goals?
9. What technologies are driving the evolution of modern supply chains?
10. How can businesses build resilient supply chains that are capable of adapting to unforeseen disruptions?

2 Key Frameworks, Models, and Theories in SCM

Learning Outcomes

By the end of this chapter, learners will be able to:

- Describe the Supply Chain Operations Reference (SCOR) model and its five core processes (Plan, Source, Make, Deliver, Return).
- Compare Lean, Agile, and Theory of Constraints (TOC) approaches and identify appropriate use cases.
- Apply systems thinking to trace how a decision in one node affects the whole chain.
- Analyse causes and consequences of the Bullwhip Effect in a multi-tier network.
- Select and justify the best framework(s) for a stated supply chain problem.

2.1 Introduction

SCM draws on interdisciplinary theories and frameworks to optimise end-to-end value creation. This chapter examines five foundational models: the SCOR Model, Lean, Agile, TOC, and the Bullwhip Effect, as well as Systems Thinking, demonstrating their practical applications and strategic relevance across global contexts. Understanding and applying these approaches enable businesses to improve efficiency, foster resilience, and secure competitive advantages in a challenging and rapidly evolving marketplace.

In the contemporary business landscape, SCM has emerged as an essential function for achieving operational efficiency, driving customer satisfaction, and fostering resilience in the face of global competition. As an interdisciplinary field, SCM draws on principles from operations, logistics, economics, and strategic management to create a streamlined flow of goods and services from suppliers to end consumers. The frameworks, models, and theories within SCM serve as guiding tools that organisations can apply to align supply chain processes with overarching business objectives while maintaining agility to respond to fluctuations in market conditions.

DOI: 10.4324/9781003740568-2

2.2 The SCOR Model

The SCOR Model is one of the most robust and universally recognised frameworks for analysing, improving, and benchmarking supply chain performance. Developed by the Supply Chain Council, now part of APICS (the Association for Supply Chain Management), the SCOR Model offers a structured methodology that integrates best practices, performance metrics, and process models. By dissecting supply chain activities into granular, actionable segments, the SCOR Model helps organisations align their operational capabilities with strategic business objectives. This section delves deeper into its five core components – Plan, Source, Make, Deliver, and Return – and explores their interdependencies, practical applications, and potential for driving competitive advantage. The SCOR Model is a unified taxonomy for cross-functional alignment, using KPIs such as perfect order fulfilment and cash-to-cash cycle time to benchmark operations.

2.2.1 Evolution and Purpose of the SCOR Model

The SCOR Model emerged in the 1990s as a response to the growing complexity of GSCs. Traditional SCM approaches, often siloed and reactive, were insufficient for addressing the intricacies of modern markets characterised by fluctuating demand, geopolitical instability, and rapidly advancing technologies. The SCOR Model, designed as a cross-industry standard, sought to bridge this gap by providing a comprehensive framework applicable across sectors.

At its core, the SCOR Model serves three primary purposes:

1 **Standardisation:** By offering a common language and structure for supply chain activities, the SCOR Model facilitates communication and collaboration among diverse stakeholders, including suppliers, manufacturers, and customers.
2 **Performance Benchmarking:** The framework includes KPIs that allow organisations to measure their efficiency against industry benchmarks.
3 **Process Optimisation:** Through its iterative approach, the SCOR Model enables CI by identifying inefficiencies, reducing waste, and enhancing agility (Bolstorff & Rosenbaum, 2017).

2.3 The Five Core Processes of the SCOR Model

Each of the SCOR Model's five processes (see Figure 2.1) represents a critical stage in the supply chain lifecycle, interwoven to ensure seamless flow from raw materials to end consumers. These processes provide a blueprint for operational excellence while remaining adaptable to the unique needs of individual organisations.

2.3.1 Plan

The planning stage is the strategic cornerstone of the SCOR Model. It involves forecasting demand, aligning resources, and setting objectives to balance supply and demand effectively. This phase encompasses several key activities:

1 **Demand Forecasting:** Leveraging historical data, market trends, and predictive analytics to estimate future demand accurately.
2 **Capacity Planning:** Assessing production capabilities and resource availability to prevent overproduction or underutilisation.
3 **Inventory Management:** Determining optimal stock levels to minimise holding costs while ensuring sufficient supply.

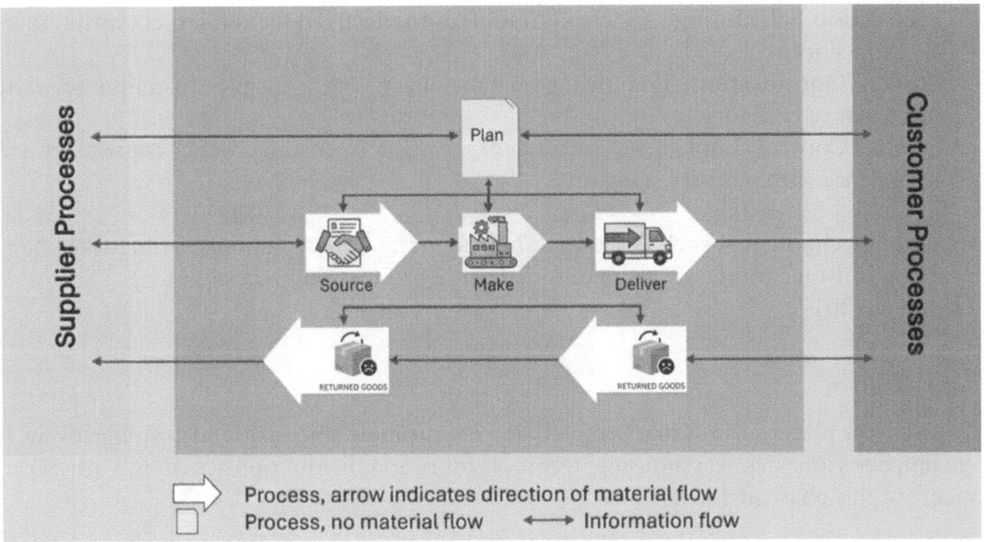

Figure 2.1 SCOR Plan, Make, Deliver Process.

Effective planning is critical for mitigating risks such as stockouts, overstocking, and supply chain disruptions. Advanced technologies, including AI and ML, are increasingly being employed to enhance the precision of planning activities (Chopra & Meindl, 2024).

2.3.2 *Source*

The sourcing phase focuses on acquiring the raw materials, components, or services necessary for production. It is characterised by SRM, procurement strategies, and quality assurance measures. Key considerations in this stage include:

1 **Supplier Selection:** Evaluating suppliers based on cost, quality, reliability, and sustainability.
2 **Contract Negotiation:** Establishing terms that align with organisational goals while fostering mutually beneficial partnerships.
3 **Compliance and Risk Management:** Ensuring adherence to regulatory standards and mitigating risks such as supplier insolvency or geopolitical instability.

Sourcing decisions have a significant impact on overall supply chain efficiency and cost structures. The integration of digital procurement platforms has transformed this phase, enabling real-time supplier collaboration and improved transparency (Moncza et al., 2015).

2.3.3 *Make*

The make phase transforms raw materials into finished goods through manufacturing, assembly, and quality assurance processes. This stage is central to value creation within the supply chain and includes:

1 **Production Scheduling:** Allocating resources to meet production targets within specified timelines.
2 **Process Optimisation:** Employing lean manufacturing principles to minimise waste and enhance efficiency.
3 **Quality Control:** Implementing stringent measures to ensure product consistency and compliance with industry standards.

Emerging technologies, such as the IoT and robotics, have revolutionised the make phase, enabling real-time monitoring and automation of production processes (Liao et al., 2017).

2.3.4 Deliver

The delivery phase ensures that products reach customers efficiently and cost-effectively. It encompasses logistics, warehousing, transportation, and distribution activities. Critical elements of this phase include:

1 **Order Management:** Processing customer orders accurately and promptly.
2 **Transportation Planning:** Selecting optimal shipping methods to balance speed, cost, and environmental impact.
3 **Customer Service:** Maintaining open lines of communication to address queries and ensure satisfaction.

The advent of e-commerce and the rise of omnichannel retailing have heightened the importance of agility and responsiveness in the delivery phase. Technologies like route optimisation software and blockchain for supply chain visibility are driving innovations in this area (Christopher, 2016).

2.3.5 Return

The return phase addresses reverse logistics, including product returns, repairs, and recycling. While often overlooked, this stage is vital for managing customer satisfaction and sustainability. Key aspects include:

1 **Return Policies:** Establishing clear guidelines to facilitate hassle-free returns.
2 **Product Refurbishment:** Repairing and reselling returned items to minimise waste.
3 **Recycling Initiatives:** Implementing programmes to recover materials and reduce environmental impact.

Effective return management not only enhances customer loyalty but also aligns with the growing emphasis on circular economy practices (Govindan et al., 2015).

2.4 Integration and Interdependencies

The SCOR Model's five processes are not isolated; they are deeply interconnected, creating a seamless flow of activities across the supply chain. For instance:

1. Planning decisions influence sourcing strategies, as accurate forecasts enable better supplier negotiations.
2. Efficient manufacturing depends on the timely sourcing of materials and robust planning.
3. Delivery schedules must align with production timelines to meet customer expectations.
4. Return processes feed back into planning by providing insights into product performance and customer behaviour.

These interdependencies underscore the importance of adopting a holistic approach to SCM, where decisions in one area have a ripple effect across the entire network.

2.5 SCOR Model in Practice: Case Studies

Several organisations have successfully implemented the SCOR Model, achieving remarkable improvements in supply chain performance. For example:

Procter & Gamble (P&G) utilised the SCOR framework to streamline its GSC, reducing lead times by 30% and inventory levels by 20% (APICS, 2017).

Dell Technologies adopted SCOR-based metrics to enhance its build-to-order model, enabling rapid response to customer demands while minimising excess inventory (Chopra & Meindl, 2024).

Boeing integrated SCOR metrics into its 787 Dreamliner production, reducing cycle time by 12% through standardised supplier scorecards and real-time order tracking across US and Japanese facilities (APICS, 2017).

These examples highlight the model's adaptability and effectiveness across diverse industries.

2.6 Challenges and Limitations

Despite its strengths, the SCOR Model is not without challenges. Critics argue that:

1. Its generic nature may require significant customisation for niche industries.
2. Implementation can be resource-intensive, necessitating robust data infrastructure and skilled personnel.
3. The framework's focus on operational efficiency may sometimes overlook broader strategic goals (Bolstorff & Rosenbaum, 2017).

Organisations must address these limitations by tailoring the model to their unique contexts and complementing it with other strategic tools.

2.7 The Future of the SCOR Model

The SCOR Model continues to evolve, integrating emerging trends such as digital transformation, sustainability, and resilience. Future iterations will need to incorporate advanced analytics, blockchain, and AI to enhance decision-making and agility. Additionally, the growing emphasis on sustainable supply chain practices will likely lead to the inclusion of environmental and social metrics within the SCOR framework.

2.8 Conclusion

The SCOR Model remains a cornerstone of modern SCM, offering a proven methodology for enhancing efficiency, agility, and customer satisfaction. By dissecting supply chain activities into the Plan, Source, Make, Deliver, and Return phases, the model provides a comprehensive roadmap for operational excellence. However, its successful implementation requires a nuanced understanding of interdependencies, a commitment to CI, and a willingness to adapt to evolving market dynamics. As organisations navigate the complexities of GSCs, the SCOR Model will undoubtedly continue to serve as an invaluable tool for achieving competitive advantage and sustainable growth.

The SCOR Model is a widely recognised framework developed by the Supply Chain Council to help organisations evaluate and optimise supply chain performance. As a comprehensive roadmap, the SCOR Model offers a structured approach for enhancing supply chain processes across multiple stages, from procurement to product delivery.

2.9 Lean SCM

Lean SCM embodies lean manufacturing principles, tailored to address the complexities of modern supply chains. Originating from the Toyota Production System (TPS), Lean SCM seeks to eliminate waste, optimise processes, and deliver superior value to customers. This approach, often associated with industries characterised by stable demand, has broader applications due to its versatility and emphasis on efficiency. This section explores the theoretical foundations of Lean SCM, its methodologies, applications across various industries, and its transformative impact on GSCs.

2.9.1 Historical Context and Theoretical Foundations

The origins of Lean SCM can be traced back to post-World War II Japan, where Toyota revolutionised manufacturing through practices designed to maximise value and minimise waste. Inspired by the principles of jidoka (automation with a human touch) and JIT production, the TPS laid the groundwork for lean practices in SCM. In the 1990s, these concepts gained international prominence through the works of Womack, Jones, and Roos in their seminal book *The Machine That Changed the World* (Womack et al., 1990).

Lean SCM is grounded in the idea of value stream optimisation, where every activity in the supply chain is scrutinised to determine its contribution to customer value. Non-value-adding activities, or "waste" (muda), are systematically eliminated, resulting in streamlined processes and enhanced operational efficiency.

2.9.2 Principles of Lean SCM

Lean SCM operates on several foundational principles, each integral to achieving a waste-free, value-driven supply chain. These principles are intertwined and collectively drive the CI ethos that defines lean practices.

The first principle emphasises value creation from the customer's perspective. Understanding customer needs and expectations is essential for aligning supply chain activities with the ultimate goal of delivering products or services that meet or exceed customer satisfaction. This involves not only reducing costs but also enhancing product quality and delivery reliability.

The second principle, waste elimination, is at the core of Lean SCM. Waste can manifest in various forms, including overproduction, excess inventory, defects, and unnecessary transportation. By identifying and eliminating these inefficiencies, organisations can reduce costs and improve supply chain responsiveness.

CI, also known as Kaizen, represents the third principle. This philosophy fosters a culture where employees at all levels are encouraged to identify areas for improvement and implement incremental changes. Over time, these small adjustments aggregate into substantial gains in efficiency and effectiveness.

Finally, the principle of pull-driven systems underpins JIT inventory practices. Instead of producing goods based on forecasted demand, lean supply chains produce and replenish stock in response to actual customer orders. This minimises excess inventory, reduces holding costs, and aligns production schedules with market demand.

2.9.3 The Eight Types of Waste in Lean Manufacturing

According to *Engineering with Management* (Engineering with Management, 2025), "The basic purpose to implement lean manufacturing is to identify and minimize waste". The concept of waste in operational contexts, particularly within lean manufacturing principles, fundamentally pertains to any non-value-added activity (NVA) from the customer's perspective. These NVA activities consume resources without directly contributing to the value of the final product or service as perceived by the end-user.

The following is an explanation of the eight distinct categories of such waste (see Figure 2.2):

Figure 2.2 The Eight Types of Waste in Manufacturing.

1 **Transportation Waste:** This refers to the movement of materials from one location to another. While seemingly inherent in many processes, excessive or unnecessary movement adds no direct value to the product and can include activities such as material transit between production and inspection stages, material transfer within storage areas, or the movement of finished goods from the factory to distribution points. From a customer's viewpoint, this movement incurs cost without enhancing product utility.
2 **Inventory Waste:** This category encompasses stored materials or goods across various stages, including raw materials, work in progress (WIP), and finished goods. Elevated inventory levels are a significant factor in locking up liquidity and can negatively impact the cash-to-cash cycle and revenue generation. Examples include storing a large quantity of raw materials for a delayed order, WIP waiting for assembly, or finished goods held in a warehouse in anticipation of future demand. It is crucial that inventory reduction positively impacts the dispatch of finished goods to customers for it to affect financial cycles.
3 **Motion Waste:** This type of waste involves the movement of personnel within a workstation or premises. Although often perceived as minor, the cumulative effect of seemingly small, inefficient movements can significantly impede overall output. Instances include a retail shop owner's continuous movement to retrieve items for customers, or a worker moving between departments to locate necessary items or within their immediate workspace. Systematic monitoring of such movements can reveal opportunities for substantial time savings.
4 **Waiting Waste:** This refers to delays in a process, where a resource (e.g., machine, material, or person) is idle due to a preceding bottleneck or issue. This can manifest as a machine waiting for materials or manpower, personnel waiting for consumable items, or materials awaiting processing at a workstation. Ineffective line balancing and badly planned maintenance downtime within a production process are common antecedents to waiting waste.
5 **Overproduction Waste:** Defined as producing more than the customer's immediate requirement. This often leads to an increase in finished goods inventory, which, according to lean principles, is considered an incorrect approach even under low-load conditions. Producing products like bearings or ice cream without specific customer orders or clear future demand exemplifies this waste.
6 **Over-processing Waste:** This occurs when additional value is added to a product beyond what the customer requires or is willing to pay for. This can involve performing unnecessary steps or applying excessive treatments during production, thereby internally increasing costs. For instance, a car manufacturing industry might apply more paint coating than necessary in certain areas, or an electroplating method might result in a coating thicker than customer specifications.
7 **Defect Waste:** Pertains to the production of goods that do not meet customer requirements, often necessitating rework or rejection. Defects can arise from errors in machinery, human error, or system malfunctions. The impact of defects is more significant when discovered externally by the customer. Effective management of defect waste relies on meticulous data capture and thorough root cause analysis. Examples include products not meeting customer specifications, a consumer discovering a poor-quality product at home (external defect), or defects identified during the dispatch stage (internal defect).
8 **Unutilised Human Talent Waste:** This represents the failure to leverage the diverse skills and talents of the workforce effectively. Organisations often struggle with identifying and appropriately allocating tasks based on the unique capabilities of their human assets. Mitigating this waste involves developing skill matrices, assigning tasks based on these skills, setting targeted goals, establishing review mechanisms, and conducting root cause analysis for performance gaps.

Understanding these categories is crucial for any organisation committed to optimising processes and maximising value delivery, much like a skilled chef meticulously prepares each ingredient to contribute optimally to the final dish, avoiding any unnecessary steps or excess that detracts from the perfect flavour.

2.9.4 Key Methodologies in Lean SCM

Several methodologies and tools form the backbone of Lean SCM, enabling organisations to apply its principles effectively.

Value Stream Mapping (VSM) is a diagnostic tool used to visualise and analyse the flow of materials and information across the supply chain. By identifying value-adding and non-value-adding activities, organisations can pinpoint inefficiencies and devise strategies for improvement.

JIT practices align inventory levels with real-time demand, reducing the need for large stockpiles and ensuring resources are allocated efficiently. This approach demands high levels of coordination with suppliers and robust communication systems to prevent stock-outs and disruptions.

Total Quality Management (TQM) and Six Sigma are complementary methodologies often integrated into Lean SCM. While TQM focuses on fostering a culture of quality across all organisational processes, Six Sigma employs data-driven techniques to reduce variability and eliminate defects.

2.9.5 Applications of Lean SCM across Industries

While Lean SCM is particularly effective in industries with predictable demand, its principles and methodologies are adaptable to diverse contexts. The automotive industry, exemplified by Toyota, remains the gold standard for lean practices. Toyota's integration of JIT, CI, and stringent quality control has enabled it to achieve unparalleled efficiency and customer satisfaction.

In the retail sector, companies like Walmart have adopted lean principles to optimise inventory management and streamline distribution networks. By leveraging data analytics and real-time inventory tracking, Walmart minimises waste while ensuring product availability.

The healthcare industry has also embraced Lean SCM to improve patient outcomes and reduce operational costs. Hospitals and clinics use VSM to identify bottlenecks in patient care processes and implement solutions that enhance efficiency without compromising quality.

Similarly, the food and beverage industry relies on Lean SCM to navigate challenges such as perishability and fluctuating demand. Companies like Nestlé employ JIT practices to reduce waste and maintain product freshness, while adhering to strict quality standards.

2.9.6 Benefits of Lean SCM

The benefits of Lean SCM extend beyond cost savings, offering organisations a competitive edge in dynamic markets. By eliminating waste and optimising processes, lean supply chains achieve greater agility and responsiveness, enabling organisations to adapt quickly to changing customer needs and market conditions. This is particularly valuable in industries where consumer preferences evolve rapidly or where supply chain disruptions are prevalent.

Lean SCM also contributes to environmental sustainability by reducing resource consumption and waste generation. For example, JIT practices minimise excess inventory and associated storage costs, while recycling and reusing materials align with circular economy principles. These efforts not only enhance organisational efficiency but also bolster CSR initiatives.

Moreover, Lean SCM fosters a culture of collaboration and innovation. By engaging employees at all levels in CI efforts, organisations unlock new ideas and approaches to problem-solving, driving long-term growth and resilience.

Case Study – Nike's Lean Transformation in Vietnam

At its Ho Chi Minh City facility, Nike implemented Lean cell manufacturing and daily Kaizen events, cutting production lead times by 30% and improving defect rates by 25% (Imai, 1986).

2.9.7 *Challenges and Limitations*

Despite its numerous advantages, Lean SCM is not without challenges. Implementing lean practices requires significant investment in training, infrastructure, and technology. Organisations must also overcome resistance to change, as lean transformations often involve shifts in organisational culture and processes.

Additionally, lean supply chains are highly dependent on supplier collaboration and coordination. Disruptions at any stage of the supply chain can have cascading effects, particularly in JIT systems with minimal buffer inventory. The COVID-19 pandemic underscored these vulnerabilities, as GSCs faced unprecedented disruptions due to lockdowns and transportation restrictions.

Lean SCM may also face limitations in industries with volatile demand patterns. In such contexts, maintaining low inventory levels can increase the risk of stockouts, leading to lost sales and customer dissatisfaction.

2.9.8 *The Role of Technology in Lean SCM*

Technological advancements have significantly enhanced the implementation and effectiveness of Lean SCM. Tools such as IoT devices, cloud computing, and advanced analytics provide real-time visibility into supply chain operations, enabling organisations to identify inefficiencies and respond proactively.

For instance, IoT sensors can monitor inventory levels and track the movement of goods across the supply chain, facilitating JIT practices. Predictive analytics, powered by AI, can improve demand forecasting accuracy, reducing the risk of overproduction or understocking.

Automation technologies, including robotics and autonomous vehicles, further streamline supply chain processes by reducing manual labour requirements and improving operational efficiency. These innovations complement lean principles by enabling organisations to achieve more with fewer resources.

2.9.9 *The Future of Lean SCM*

As GSCs become increasingly complex and interconnected, Lean SCM will continue to evolve. Future developments are likely to emphasise sustainability, resilience, and digital transformation. Organisations will need to strike a balance between lean efficiency and the need for flexibility and redundancy to mitigate risks.

The integration of circular economy principles into Lean SCM represents a promising avenue for reducing environmental impact. By prioritising recycling, remanufacturing, and resource optimisation, organisations can achieve sustainable growth while adhering to lean principles.

Digital technologies will also play a central role in the future of Lean SCM. Blockchain, for example, offers enhanced traceability and transparency, enabling organisations to track the origin and movement of goods across the supply chain. This is particularly valuable in industries where product authenticity and ethical sourcing are critical.

2.9.10 Conclusion

Lean SCM represents a paradigm shift in how organisations approach efficiency, quality, and value creation. By adopting principles such as waste elimination, CI, and customer-centricity, lean supply chains achieve superior performance and adaptability. However, successful implementation requires a nuanced understanding of the challenges and opportunities associated with lean practices. As GSCs continue to face disruptions and complexities, Lean SCM will remain a cornerstone of operational excellence, offering a roadmap for sustainable and resilient SCM.

2.10 Agile SCM

Agile SCM has emerged as a critical paradigm for addressing the complexities and uncertainties of modern markets. Unlike traditional supply chain models that prioritise efficiency, Agile SCM is defined by its focus on adaptability and responsiveness. This approach is particularly relevant in industries characterised by rapidly changing customer preferences, short product lifecycles, and volatile demand patterns. By leveraging flexibility, collaboration, and advanced technologies, agile supply chains enable organisations to thrive in dynamic environments and maintain a competitive edge. This section explores the theoretical foundations, methodologies, and practical applications of Agile SCM, with a focus on its transformative impact on industries like fashion, technology, and consumer goods.

2.10.1 Origins and Conceptual Framework

The concept of agility in SCM emerged during the 1990s as a response to the limitations of traditional supply chains in addressing market volatility. While lean supply chains excel in stable environments through waste reduction and process optimisation, their rigidity can render them vulnerable to disruptions and demand fluctuations. Agile SCM addresses this gap by prioritising speed, flexibility, and customer-centricity.

At its core, Agile SCM is built on the ability to sense, respond to, and adapt to changes in market conditions. This involves close collaboration with suppliers and customers, real-time demand forecasting, and flexible production systems. Unlike lean supply chains, which operate on a "push" model based on demand forecasts, agile supply chains typically employ a "pull" model, where actual market signals drive production and inventory decisions.

2.10.2 Principles of Agile SCM

Agile SCM operates on several key principles that guide its implementation and define its distinct characteristics.

The first principle emphasises customer-centricity, with a strong focus on understanding and responding to customer needs. Agile supply chains prioritise the delivery of value to customers through tailored products and services that align with their preferences and expectations.

The second principle is flexibility, which manifests across all stages of the supply chain. Flexible production systems enable organisations to scale operations up or down quickly in response to changes in demand, while diverse supplier networks enhance resilience and adaptability.

The third principle involves integration and collaboration across the supply chain. Agile supply chains rely on seamless communication and cooperation among stakeholders, including suppliers, manufacturers, distributors, and retailers. This ensures the alignment of goals and the efficient exchange of information, enabling real-time decision-making.

Finally, the principle of technology-driven responsiveness underscores the role of advanced tools and systems in supporting agility. Technologies such as big data analytics, AI, and blockchain enhance visibility, improve forecasting accuracy, and enable organisations to respond rapidly to market shifts.

As described earlier, a lean supply chain focuses on efficiency, cost reduction, and minimising waste. On the other hand, an agile supply chain emphasises flexibility and responsiveness, particularly in industries where demand is highly variable (see Figure 2.3). As the world becomes more unpredictable, many companies are adopting hybrid approaches, combining the best of both strategies.

2.10.3 Methodologies and Practices in Agile SCM

The implementation of Agile SCM involves a range of methodologies and practices that facilitate its principles and objectives.

Real-time Demand Forecasting is a cornerstone of agile supply chains. By leveraging advanced analytics and ML, organisations can generate accurate predictions of customer demand based on real-time data. This reduces reliance on static forecasts and minimises the risk of overproduction or stockouts.

Collaborative Supplier Networks are another critical component of Agile SCM. Companies cultivate relationships with multiple suppliers, fostering trust and mutual dependence. This allows for quick adjustments in sourcing decisions and enhances supply chain resilience in the face of disruptions.

Lean vs Agile Supply Chain: Key Differences

	Lean Supply Chain	Agile Supply Chain
Operational Focus	Efficiency, waste reduction, cost savings	Flexibility, responsiveness to market changes
Inventory Management	Just-in-time (JIT), minimal inventory	Higher levels of inventory to meet sudden demand
Production Approach	Standardised, long production runs	Short, customised production runs based on demand
Customer Demand	Best suited for stable, predictable demand	Best for unpredictable, highly variable demand
Lead Time	Longer lead times due to JIT systems	Shorter lead times, adaptable to real-time demand
Cost Consideration	Focused on minimising costs and maximising efficiency	Willing to accept higher costs for increased flexibility
Risk Management	Risks tied to supply chain disruptions due to rigidity	More adaptable to disruptions but may have higher costs

Figure 2.3 Lean vs Agile.

Postponement Strategies are widely used in Agile SCM to delay final product assembly or customisation until customer demand becomes clear. This approach, often referred to as "mass customisation", balances efficiency with responsiveness, allowing organisations to meet diverse customer needs while minimising inventory costs.

Rapid Prototyping and Iterative Development are particularly relevant in industries like fashion and technology. These practices enable organisations to bring new products to market quickly, respond to customer feedback, and refine offerings based on real-world data.

2.10.4 Applications across Industries

Agile SCM has found widespread application across various industries, each leveraging its principles and practices to address unique challenges and opportunities.

In the fashion industry, Zara exemplifies the power of agile supply chains. The Spanish retailer has revolutionised the industry with its ability to design, produce, and deliver new styles within weeks. Zara's agile supply chain integrates real-time data from retail stores, enabling the company to adjust production schedules and inventory levels based on customer preferences. This rapid response capability allows Zara to capitalise on emerging trends and maintain high inventory turnover, giving it a significant competitive advantage (Christopher, 2016).

The technology sector also benefits from Agile SCM, particularly in the production of consumer electronics. Companies like Apple and Dell employ agile practices to navigate short product lifecycles and frequent technological advancements. For example, Dell's build-to-order model relies on close collaboration with suppliers and customers, enabling the company to customise products and minimise excess inventory (Chopra & Meindl, 2024).

In the consumer goods industry, P&G demonstrates the potential of Agile SCM to enhance supply chain flexibility and customer responsiveness. P&G uses advanced analytics and digital platforms to monitor consumer behaviour, enabling real-time adjustments to production and distribution strategies.

2.10.5 Benefits of Agile SCM

The benefits of Agile SCM extend across operational, financial, and strategic dimensions, making it an invaluable approach for modern businesses.

One of the primary advantages is enhanced responsiveness to market changes. Agile supply chains enable organisations to adapt quickly to shifts in customer demand, economic conditions, or competitive pressures, reducing the risk of obsolescence and lost sales.

Agile SCM also promotes resilience by building flexibility into supply chain operations. This is particularly important in the face of disruptions such as natural disasters, geopolitical conflicts, or pandemics. For instance, during the COVID-19 pandemic, companies with agile supply chains were better equipped to navigate disruptions and maintain business continuity (Ivanov & Dolgui, 2020).

Furthermore, Agile SCM fosters innovation by creating a framework for rapid product development and iterative improvement. This accelerates time-to-market for new products, enhances customer satisfaction, and strengthens competitive positioning.

Finally, Agile SCM supports sustainable practices by reducing waste and enabling more efficient resource utilisation. By aligning production and inventory decisions with actual demand, organisations can minimise overproduction, reduce energy consumption, and decrease their environmental footprint.

2.10.6 Challenges and Limitations

Despite its advantages, Agile SCM is not without challenges. One of the main obstacles is the complexity of implementation, as agility requires significant investment in technology, infrastructure, and training. Organisations must also overcome cultural resistance to change, as agile practices often involve shifts in organisational mindset and processes.

Additionally, Agile SCM relies heavily on supplier collaboration and integration, which can be challenging to achieve in fragmented supply chains. Building trust and ensuring alignment among diverse stakeholders is a time-consuming process that requires ongoing effort.

Another limitation is the potential trade-off between agility and cost efficiency. Agile supply chains prioritise flexibility over standardisation, which can lead to higher operational costs in some cases. Organisations must carefully balance these considerations to ensure the long-term viability of their supply chain strategies.

2.10.7 Future Directions for Agile SCM

The future of Agile SCM is closely tied to advancements in technology and the increasing emphasis on sustainability. Emerging technologies such as IoT, blockchain, and advanced robotics are expected to enhance the speed and accuracy of agile supply chains, enabling organisations to achieve new levels of responsiveness and efficiency.

Sustainability will also play a central role in shaping the evolution of Agile SCM. As consumers and regulators place greater emphasis on environmental and social responsibility, organisations will need to integrate sustainable practices into their agile supply chains. This may involve adopting circular economy principles, prioritising ethical sourcing, and reducing carbon emissions.

2.10.8 Conclusion

Agile SCM represents a transformative approach to managing supply chains in dynamic and uncertain environments. By emphasising flexibility, collaboration, and technology-driven responsiveness, agile supply chains enable organisations to navigate market volatility, enhance customer satisfaction, and achieve a competitive advantage. However, successful implementation requires a deep understanding of its principles and methodologies, as well as a commitment to overcoming the associated challenges. As industries continue to evolve, Agile SCM will remain a critical driver of innovation, resilience, and sustainable growth.

2.11 The TOC

The TOC, introduced by Eliyahu M. Goldratt, is a powerful management philosophy aimed at optimising system performance by addressing limiting factors, or bottlenecks, that constrain productivity. Unlike conventional management strategies that often focus on incremental improvements across all areas, TOC emphasises targeted interventions on critical constraints to maximise overall system throughput. The philosophy's practical and theoretical implications extend across industries, particularly manufacturing, logistics, and project management, offering organisations a systematic approach to achieving operational excellence.

2.11.1 Origins and Conceptual Framework

Eliyahu M. Goldratt first introduced TOC in his 1984 book, *The Goal: A Process of Ongoing Improvement*. Presented as a novel approach to management, TOC sought to address inefficiencies stemming from overlooked constraints within complex systems. Goldratt proposed that a system's performance is dictated not by the sum of its parts but by its weakest link, much like a chain is only as strong as its weakest link. This foundational principle forms the basis for TOC's focus on identifying and managing bottlenecks.

TOC operates on the premise that every system has at least one constraint that limits its capacity to achieve its goals. These constraints can take various forms, including physical bottlenecks in manufacturing, policy constraints in organisational decision-making, or market constraints in demand fulfilment. By systematically addressing these constraints, organisations can achieve significant improvements in throughput, profitability, and efficiency.

To move nearer to your goal or even to achieve it, it is fundamental to understand the company constraints. The ability to recognise a constraint is crucial for organisational progress and effective strategic management.

An established methodology, known as the Five Focusing Steps (see Figure 2.4), is specifically designed to help organisations find and address these constraints. This structured approach assists in systematically managing limitations that hinder the attainment of company objectives. The Five Focusing Steps comprise the following distinct stages:

1 Identify
2 Exploit
3 Subordinate
4 Elevate
5 Avoid Inertia

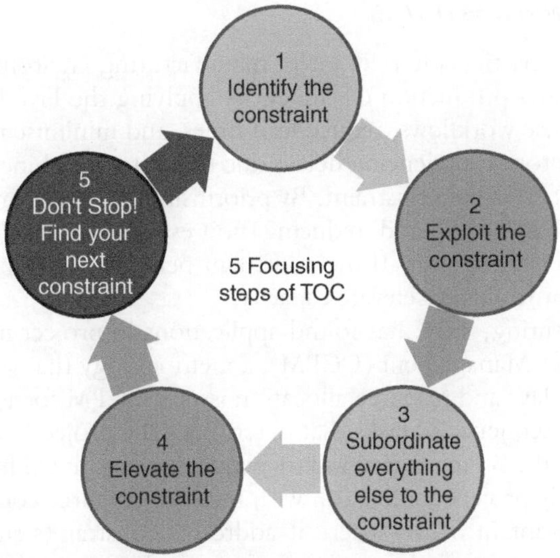

Figure 2.4 Five Focusing Steps.

By systematically applying this framework, organisations can pinpoint the most critical restrictive factors within their operations and strategically manage them. This systematic process aims to enhance overall efficiency and enable sustained progress towards defined goals, as understanding and addressing constraints directly contribute to moving nearer to or achieving an organisation's objectives.

2.11.2 The Five Focusing Steps of TOC

TOC's methodology revolves around a structured process known as the Five Focusing Steps, which provides a practical framework for identifying and managing constraints.

The first step is to identify the system's constraint. This involves pinpointing the resource, process, or factor that limits overall performance. Constraints may manifest as physical limitations, such as a slow machine on a production line, or intangible barriers, such as restrictive company policies.

Once the constraint is identified, the second step is to exploit it. This entails maximising the efficiency of the constraint to ensure it is operating at its full potential. For instance, in a manufacturing context, this might involve eliminating downtime or ensuring that the bottlenecked resource is prioritised in production scheduling.

The third step is to subordinate all other processes to the constraint. This means aligning the rest of the system to support the constraint's operation. For example, non-bottleneck resources might operate at reduced capacity to prevent overwhelming the constraint with excess input.

The fourth step focuses on elevating the constraint. If the constraint's efficiency has been maximised but it remains a limiting factor, organisations should invest in increasing its capacity. This might involve acquiring additional machinery, hiring more staff, or implementing new technologies.

Finally, the fifth step is to repeat the process by identifying and addressing new constraints as they arise. TOC views improvement as an ongoing journey, recognising that resolving one constraint often shifts the bottleneck to another part of the system.

2.11.3 Practical Applications of TOC

TOC's principles are particularly relevant in manufacturing environments, where bottlenecks frequently hinder production efficiency. By applying the Five Focusing Steps, manufacturers can optimise workflows, reduce lead times, and minimise resource wastage.

For instance, a factory experiencing delays due to limited machine capacity might identify the machine as its primary constraint. By prioritising its operation, scheduling maintenance during off-peak hours, and reducing non-essential downtime, the factory can significantly improve throughput. If the constraint persists, the company might invest in additional equipment to further elevate capacity.

Beyond manufacturing, TOC has found applications in project management through Critical Chain Project Management (CCPM), a methodology that adapts TOC principles to address project delays and resource allocation issues. CCPM focuses on identifying the critical chain, or the sequence of tasks that determines the project's duration and protecting it from disruptions. By managing task dependencies and introducing project buffers, CCPM ensures timely project completion with minimal resource conflict.

TOC is also relevant in SCM, where it addresses constraints such as transportation delays, inventory shortages, and capacity limitations. For example, logistics companies might use TOC to optimise delivery routes or streamline warehouse operations, ensuring that resources are allocated to address critical bottlenecks.

2.11.4 Benefits of Implementing TOC

The implementation of TOC offers numerous benefits, ranging from enhanced operational efficiency to improved decision-making. One of its most significant advantages is the ability to achieve substantial performance improvements through targeted interventions. By focusing resources and efforts on the system's most critical constraint, TOC eliminates inefficiencies and maximises productivity without requiring extensive changes across the entire system.

TOC also promotes a culture of CI. Its iterative approach encourages organisations to assess their processes and identify new opportunities for optimisation regularly. This proactive mindset fosters adaptability and resilience, enabling organisations to respond effectively to changing market conditions and operational challenges.

Furthermore, TOC enhances strategic decision-making by providing a clear framework for prioritising initiatives. By identifying and addressing constraints, organisations can allocate resources more effectively, avoiding the pitfalls of overinvestment in non-critical areas.

2.11.5 Challenges and Limitations of TOC

Despite its strengths, TOC is not without its challenges. One of the primary limitations is its reliance on accurate constraint identification. Misidentifying the constraint can lead to misguided efforts and wasted resources. Organisations must, therefore, invest in robust diagnostic tools and processes to ensure accurate analysis.

Another challenge is the potential for resistance to change. TOC often requires shifts in organisational culture and practices, which may encounter pushback from employees or stakeholders accustomed to traditional approaches. Effective change management strategies and leadership commitment are essential to overcoming these barriers.

Additionally, TOC's focus on constraints can sometimes overshadow broader strategic considerations. While addressing bottlenecks is critical for short-term performance improvements, organisations must also consider long-term goals and market dynamics to ensure sustained success.

2.11.6 Case Studies in TOC Implementation

Several organisations have successfully implemented TOC, demonstrating its practical value across industries.

In the manufacturing sector, a well-documented example is Boeing's application of TOC principles in its production facilities. Faced with delays in aircraft assembly, Boeing identified bottlenecks in its supply chain and production processes. By exploiting and elevating these constraints, the company reduced lead times and improved delivery schedules (Goldratt, 2004).

In retail, TOC has been employed by companies like Walmart to optimise inventory management and streamline supply chain operations. By addressing constraints in DCs and transportation networks, Walmart improved product availability while minimising excess inventory and associated costs.

Dell pinpointed its order-fulfilment process as a bottleneck and introduced dynamic WIP limits, boosting throughput by 18% and reducing customer wait times by 22% in its Texas and Penang plants (Goldratt, 2004).

2.11.7 *The Future of TOC*

As industries continue to evolve, TOC is likely to remain a relevant and valuable framework for operational excellence. Advances in technology, such as AI and data analytics, have the potential to enhance TOC's effectiveness by enabling more accurate constraint identification and real-time monitoring.

Furthermore, the growing emphasis on sustainability presents new opportunities for applying TOC principles. By addressing environmental constraints, such as energy consumption and waste generation, organisations can align their operations with sustainability goals while maintaining profitability.

2.11.8 *Conclusion*

The TOC offers a powerful approach to optimising system performance by focusing on critical bottlenecks. Its structured methodology, encapsulated in the Five Focusing Steps, provides a practical framework for achieving significant improvements in throughput, efficiency, and profitability. While challenges such as accurate constraint identification and resistance to change must be addressed, TOC's potential benefits make it a valuable tool for organisations across industries. As businesses navigate an increasingly complex and dynamic landscape, TOC will continue to play a central role in driving innovation, resilience, and sustainable growth.

2.12 The Bullwhip Effect

The Bullwhip Effect (see Figure 2.5) represents a significant challenge in SCM, where small fluctuations in consumer demand at the retail level can lead to disproportionate and magnified variations in orders up the supply chain. This phenomenon disrupts the flow of goods and information, leading to inefficiencies such as excess inventory, stockouts, increased costs, and reduced customer satisfaction. First introduced in detail by Lee, Padmanabhan, and Whang in the late 1990s, the Bullwhip Effect remains a critical focus

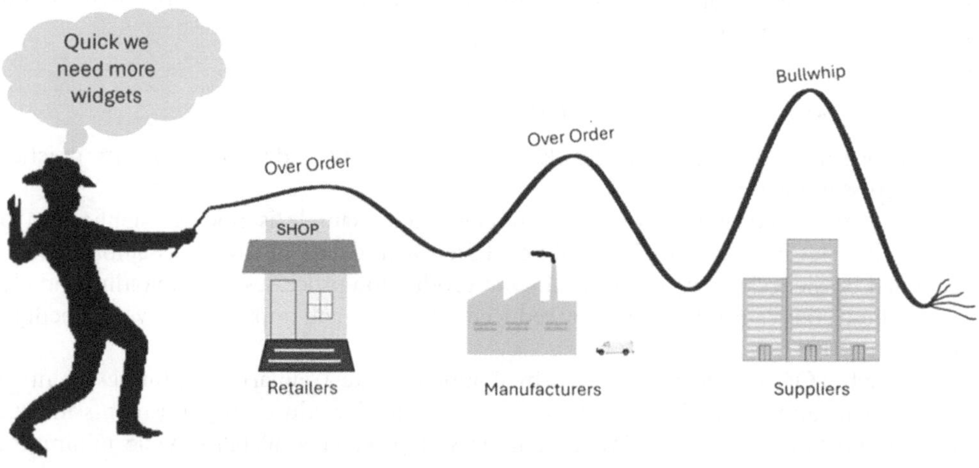

Figure 2.5 The Bullwhip Effect.

Note: Small changes in demand can produce a whip-like effect upstream.

for academics and practitioners alike, given its implications for operational efficiency and profitability (Lee et al., 1997).

2.12.1 Causes of the Bullwhip Effect

Understanding the root causes of the Bullwhip Effect is essential for addressing its adverse impacts. The phenomenon arises from a combination of behavioural and operational factors that interact across different supply chain levels.

A primary cause of the Bullwhip Effect is demand forecasting errors. Retailers and downstream supply chain participants often rely on historical sales data to predict future demand, which can lead to over- or under-ordering. These errors are compounded as forecasts move upstream to manufacturers and suppliers, amplifying demand variability at each stage.

Order batching further exacerbates the Bullwhip Effect. Many companies place large, infrequent orders to take advantage of economies of scale in transportation or production. While this reduces per-unit costs in the short term, it creates artificial peaks and troughs in demand, which upstream suppliers interpret as changes in consumer behaviour.

Price fluctuations, driven by promotions, discounts, or market dynamics, also contribute to the Bullwhip Effect. Temporary price reductions can prompt customers to purchase in bulk, distorting demand patterns and complicating forecasting efforts. Once the promotion ends, demand often drops sharply, creating challenges for suppliers attempting to manage production schedules and inventory.

Another critical factor is the lack of effective communication and collaboration across supply chain partners. Disjointed or siloed information systems result in delayed or incomplete data sharing, causing supply chain members to act on outdated or inaccurate information. This misalignment reinforces the amplification of demand variability.

2.12.2 Impacts of the Bullwhip Effect

The consequences of the Bullwhip Effect (see Figure 2.6) extend across operational, financial, and customer-facing dimensions. For businesses, amplified demand variability leads to inefficiencies such as overstocking and stockouts. Overstocking results in higher holding costs, increased risk of obsolescence, and tied-up working capital. On the other hand, stockouts result in missed sales opportunities, eroded customer trust, and potential loss of market share.

From a cost perspective, the Bullwhip Effect drives up operational expenses. Frequent production adjustments, expedited shipping, and overtime labour requirements to meet fluctuating demand all contribute to higher costs. Additionally, suppliers and manufacturers may incur penalties for failing to fulfil contractual obligations or delivering products outside agreed timelines.

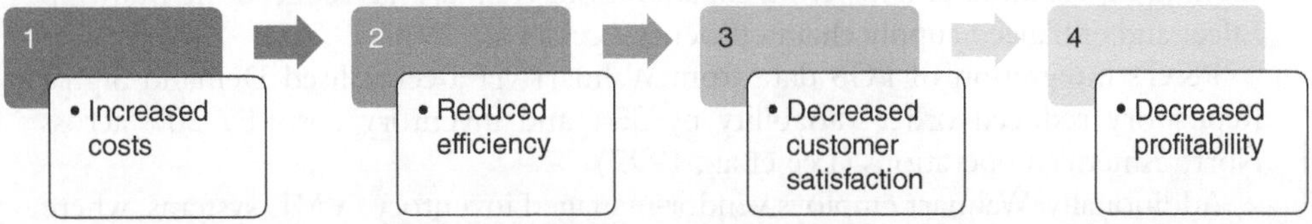

Figure 2.6 Impacts of the Bullwhip Effect.

The Bullwhip Effect also undermines supply chain resilience and agility. As companies struggle to align supply with demand, they become less responsive to market changes and less capable of navigating disruptions. This rigidity impacts the entire supply chain's ability to compete effectively in dynamic environments.

2.12.3 Mitigating the Bullwhip Effect

Despite its pervasive impacts, the Bullwhip Effect can be mitigated through targeted strategies that address its root causes. These strategies focus on improving demand forecasting accuracy, enhancing communication and collaboration, and implementing advanced technologies.

Collaborative forecasting and planning are among the most effective ways to combat the Bullwhip Effect. Techniques such as Collaborative Planning, Forecasting, and Replenishment (CPFR) enable supply chain partners to share real-time data and develop joint demand forecasts. This shared approach reduces uncertainty and aligns expectations across all supply chain levels.

Another key strategy involves improving communication and data visibility. By integrating information systems and adopting technologies like cloud computing and blockchain, companies can facilitate seamless data exchange and ensure that all stakeholders have access to accurate, up-to-date information. Improved transparency reduces the likelihood of overreaction to demand changes and helps synchronise supply chain activities.

JIT inventory management practices can also play a role in mitigating the Bullwhip Effect. By maintaining low inventory levels and replenishing stock based on actual demand, companies can reduce variability and minimise the impact of order batching. However, JIT strategies require robust supplier relationships and reliable transportation networks to succeed.

Dynamic pricing and demand smoothing techniques can further help mitigate demand variability caused by promotions. For example, companies can use loyalty programmes or gradual discounts to incentivise consistent purchasing behaviour, thereby stabilising demand patterns over time.

Case Study – Walmart's Approach

Walmart provides a compelling example of how to mitigate the Bullwhip Effect through advanced technologies and collaborative practices. As one of the world's largest retailers, Walmart relies on a vast network of suppliers and DCs to meet customer demand efficiently. To address demand variability, Walmart has invested heavily in data analytics and supply chain integration.

Using advanced forecasting tools, Walmart captures real-time sales data from its retail stores and shares this information with suppliers through its Retail Link platform. This transparency enables suppliers to adjust production schedules and inventory levels based on actual consumer demand rather than forecasted projections. By aligning expectations and fostering collaboration, Walmart has reduced the Bullwhip Effect and enhanced supply chain efficiency (Lee et al., 1997).

P&G's integration of POS data from Walmart via a centralised Demand Signal Repository reduced order variability by 35% and inventory costs by 20% across North American operations (Lee et al., 1997).

Additionally, Walmart employs vendor-managed inventory (VMI) systems, where suppliers take responsibility for managing stock levels at Walmart's warehouses and stores. This approach streamlines inventory replenishment and reduces the need for frequent order adjustments, further minimising demand amplification.

2.12.4 Broader Industry Implications

The lessons learned from Walmart's success in mitigating the Bullwhip Effect are applicable across various industries. For instance, in the automotive sector, companies like Toyota have adopted lean supply chain practices and real-time communication systems to align production with actual demand. Similarly, in the consumer electronics industry, firms such as Dell use build-to-order models and demand-driven manufacturing to minimise inventory fluctuations and improve supply chain responsiveness.

The adoption of Industry 4.0 technologies, such as IoT sensors, AI, and predictive analytics, is also transforming SCM. These technologies enable organisations to detect demand changes early, simulate different scenarios, using digital twins, and implement proactive measures to mitigate potential disruptions.

2.12.5 Challenges and Limitations

While the strategies discussed above are effective, they are not without challenges. Implementing collaborative forecasting and data-sharing systems requires significant investment in technology and infrastructure. Additionally, fostering trust and alignment among supply chain partners can be a time-consuming process, particularly in fragmented or competitive industries.

Organisational inertia and resistance to change may also hinder the adoption of new practices. Companies accustomed to traditional SCM approaches may struggle to embrace the transparency and collaboration required to address the Bullwhip Effect.

2.12.6 Conclusion

The Bullwhip Effect is a pervasive issue that undermines supply chain efficiency, increases costs, and erodes customer satisfaction. By addressing its root causes: demand forecasting errors, order batching, price fluctuations, and communication gaps, organisations can mitigate its impacts and enhance operational performance. Through collaborative forecasting, advanced data analytics, and innovative practices like VMI, companies like Walmart have demonstrated the potential for overcoming demand variability and achieving supply chain excellence. As industries continue to embrace digital transformation and interconnected technologies, the opportunities for mitigating the Bullwhip Effect and fostering resilient, agile supply chains will only grow.

2.13 Systems Thinking in SCM

Systems Thinking offers a transformative approach to SCM by encouraging organisations to view their supply chains as dynamic, interconnected systems rather than as isolated, linear processes. By understanding the relationships and interdependencies between components, Systems Thinking enables businesses to make decisions that optimise the entire supply chain rather than focusing solely on individual segments. This approach is particularly valuable in today's complex global markets, where disruptions in one area can have cascading effects across the entire network.

Systems Thinking treats the supply chain as an interconnected ecosystem, emphasising feedback loops and holistic optimisation rather than siloed improvements. This perspective underpins initiatives in the circular economy and sustainable SCM (Sterman, 2000).

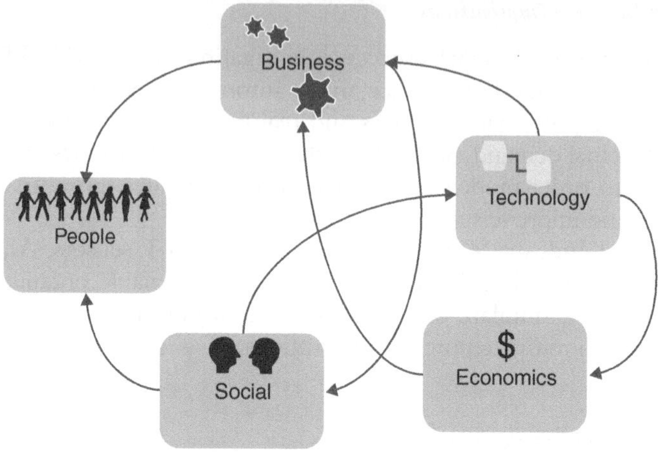

Figure 2.7 Systems Thinking Feedback Loops.

2.13.1 Theoretical Foundations of Systems Thinking

Systems Thinking emerged from the broader field of systems theory, which examines how components within a system interact and influence one another. In a supply chain context, Systems Thinking highlights the interplay between sourcing, production, distribution, and customer demand, recognising that changes in one area can ripple through the entire network. This interconnected perspective contrasts with traditional management approaches that often treat supply chain activities as discrete and independent.

A key principle of Systems Thinking is feedback loops (see Figure 2.7), which describe how outputs of a system influence its inputs. Positive feedback loops amplify changes, while negative feedback loops stabilise the system by counteracting fluctuations. Understanding these dynamics helps supply chain managers anticipate and address potential imbalances, ensuring smoother operations and greater resilience (Sterman, 2000).

Another critical concept is leverage points, which represent strategic areas within a system where small changes can lead to significant improvements. Identifying and addressing these leverage points allows organisations to optimise resource use, reduce inefficiencies, and enhance overall performance.

2.13.2 Benefits of Systems Thinking in SCM

Adopting a Systems Thinking approach offers numerous benefits for SCM. One of the most significant advantages is improved decision-making. By considering the broader system-wide implications of their actions, supply chain managers can avoid decisions that solve localised problems but create inefficiencies or disruptions elsewhere in the network. For example, cutting costs in transportation without considering its impact on inventory levels or customer service can undermine overall supply chain performance.

Systems Thinking also enhances collaboration and coordination across supply chain partners. Recognising the interconnected nature of supply chains encourages businesses to share information, align objectives, and work together to achieve mutual benefits. This collaborative mindset is particularly valuable in addressing challenges such as demand variability, capacity constraints, and supply disruptions.

Another benefit is greater adaptability to changing market conditions. Systems Thinking helps organisations understand how external factors, such as economic shifts or geopolitical events, interact with internal processes. This holistic perspective enables businesses to anticipate and respond to disruptions more effectively, building resilience and maintaining competitive advantage.

Finally, Systems Thinking supports sustainability by promoting resource efficiency and reducing waste. By optimising the entire supply chain rather than individual segments, organisations can minimise their environmental footprint and contribute to broader sustainability goals.

2.13.3 Practical Applications of Systems Thinking

Systems Thinking has been successfully applied in various industries to enhance supply chain performance. One notable example is P&G, a global leader in consumer goods. P&G integrates Systems Thinking into its SCM by coordinating activities across sourcing, production, and distribution. This holistic approach allows the company to optimise resource use, reduce costs, and improve supply chain reliability. For instance, P&G uses advanced analytics to model the interdependencies between its manufacturing facilities and DCs, enabling it to make strategic decisions that benefit the entire network (Senge, 2006).

Another example is Toyota, which incorporates Systems Thinking principles into its renowned TPS. By viewing the production process as a cohesive system, Toyota identifies and addresses inefficiencies holistically. This approach has enabled the company to achieve high levels of operational efficiency, product quality, and customer satisfaction.

In the healthcare sector, hospitals and pharmaceutical companies use Systems Thinking to improve SCM for medical supplies and equipment. For instance, by mapping the flow of critical items such as vaccines or surgical instruments, healthcare organisations can identify bottlenecks and implement solutions that ensure timely delivery to patients.

2.13.4 Challenges of Implementing Systems Thinking

While Systems Thinking offers significant benefits, implementing this approach is not without challenges. One of the primary obstacles is the complexity of supply chains, particularly in global networks with multiple stakeholders and diverse processes. Mapping and analysing these systems require substantial expertise, resources, and time.

Another challenge is resistance to change. Traditional management approaches often prioritise short-term gains and localised efficiency, which may conflict with the long-term, holistic perspective of Systems Thinking. Overcoming this resistance requires strong leadership, effective communication, and a clear demonstration of the value of a systems-based approach.

Additionally, achieving the level of collaboration and information sharing required for Systems Thinking can be difficult, particularly in competitive or fragmented industries. Building trust and alignment among supply chain partners is essential for realising the benefits of a systems perspective.

Finally, the dynamic nature of supply chains adds to the complexity of implementing Systems Thinking. External factors such as market volatility, regulatory changes, and technological advancements can disrupt established processes and necessitate continuous adaptation.

2.13.5 The Role of Technology in Enabling Systems Thinking

Technological advancements have played a pivotal role in facilitating the adoption of Systems Thinking in SCM. Tools such as big data analytics, AI, and digital twin simulations enable organisations to model, analyse, and optimise complex supply chain systems.

Big data analytics provides insights into supply chain performance by analysing vast amounts of data from diverse sources, such as customer orders, inventory levels, and transportation routes. These insights help organisations understand interdependencies and identify leverage points for improvement.

AI and ML algorithms enhance decision-making by predicting future trends and simulating the impact of various scenarios on the supply chain. For example, AI can forecast demand fluctuations and recommend adjustments to production schedules, ensuring alignment with system-wide objectives.

Digital twin technology creates virtual replicas of supply chain systems, allowing organisations to test and refine strategies in a risk-free environment. By simulating different scenarios, businesses can evaluate the potential impacts of their decisions and optimise processes accordingly.

2.13.6 The Future of Systems Thinking in SCM

As supply chains continue to grow in complexity, the importance of Systems Thinking will only increase. Future developments are likely to focus on integrating sustainability, resilience, and digital transformation into systems-based approaches.

Sustainability will remain a central concern, with organisations leveraging Systems Thinking to balance economic, environmental, and social objectives. This includes reducing carbon emissions, minimising waste, and promoting circular economy principles.

Resilience will also be a key priority, as supply chains face growing risks from climate change, geopolitical tensions, and other disruptions. Systems Thinking provides a framework for identifying vulnerabilities and developing strategies to mitigate risks, ensuring continuity and stability.

Finally, digital transformation will enable deeper and more sophisticated applications of Systems Thinking. Emerging technologies such as blockchain, IoT, and quantum computing will enhance data transparency, connectivity, and analytical capabilities, further empowering organisations to manage their supply chains as integrated systems.

2.13.7 Conclusion

Systems Thinking represents a paradigm shift in SCM, offering a holistic perspective that prioritises interconnectedness, collaboration, and long-term optimisation. By recognising the interdependencies within supply chains, organisations can make strategic decisions that enhance efficiency, resilience, and sustainability. While challenges such as complexity and resistance to change must be addressed, the benefits of Systems Thinking make it an invaluable approach for navigating the demands of modern supply chains. As technology continues to evolve and global markets become increasingly dynamic, Systems Thinking will remain a cornerstone of effective SCM.

Q&A Section

Here is a short quiz to test your knowledge. The answers are provided in Appendix C.

1. What is the SCOR Model used for?
2. How does Lean SCM benefit businesses?
3. What is the main focus of Agile SCM?
4. What is TOC?
5. How does the Bullwhip Effect impact supply chains?
6. What is Systems Thinking in SCM?
7. What role does JIT play in Lean SCM?
8. How does Zara use Agile SCM?
9. What is the importance of VSM in Lean SCM?
10. Why is flexibility important in SCM?

3 Supply Chain Management as a Competitive Advantage

Learning Outcomes

By the end of this chapter, learners will be able to:

- Explain how SCM can be used to achieve cost leadership and differentiation.
- Assess the contribution of technology and sustainability to competitive advantage.
- Develop a simple strategic alignment map linking supply chain levers to corporate objectives.
- Critique a company's SCM approach and recommend strategic changes to improve market position.
- Propose measurable KPIs to track SCM performance against strategic goals.

3.1 Introduction

SCM has evolved from a functional logistics exercise into a strategic capability that can confer sustainable competitive advantage. In this chapter, we examine how organisations deploy cost leadership, differentiation, strategic alignment, technology, and sustainability to build and maintain competitive positions. Each section integrates real-world case studies drawn from diverse geographical contexts to illustrate theoretical constructs in practice (Figure 3.1).

In the contemporary business environment, SCM plays a pivotal role in driving competitive advantage. No longer confined to a support function, SCM now serves as a strategic enabler that can significantly influence a company's market position and profitability. Effective supply chain strategies enable businesses to reduce costs, enhance efficiency, and exceed customer expectations, providing a foundation for sustainable competitive advantage. This chapter delves into the two primary strategies companies use – cost leadership and differentiation – while exploring the critical roles of technology and sustainability in amplifying these advantages.

DOI: 10.4324/9781003740568-3

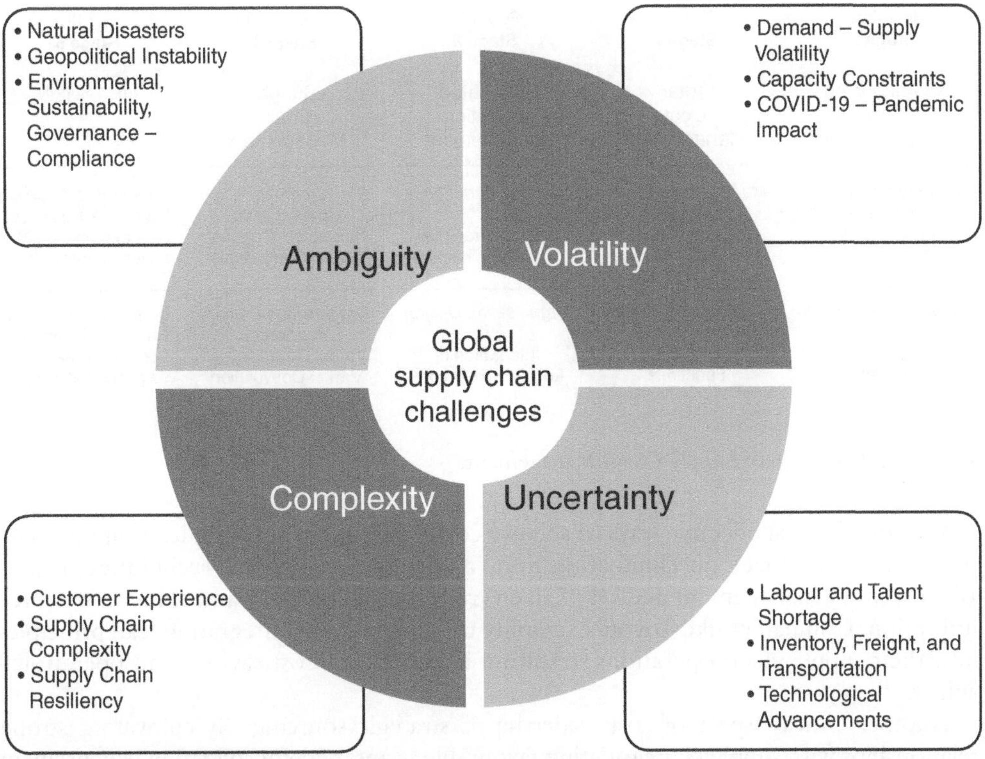

Figure 3.1 Global Supply Chain Challenges.

3.1.1 The Evolution of SCM

Traditionally, supply chains were viewed as linear, operational processes focused on the movement of goods from suppliers to customers. However, the increasing complexity of global markets, coupled with heightened competition and shifting consumer expectations, has transformed SCM into a dynamic and strategic discipline. Organisations now recognise that their ability to manage supply chain activities efficiently and innovatively can determine their success in an increasingly interconnected and volatile market (Figure 3.2).

The integration of SCM into core business strategy aligns with Michael Porter's concept of competitive advantage, which is rooted in cost leadership and differentiation. These strategies highlight how SCM can drive value creation and provide a sustainable edge over competitors. By focusing on efficiency and customer-centric innovation, businesses can achieve superior performance, market positioning, and resilience in the face of disruption (Porter, 2008).

3.1.2 Cost Leadership and Supply Chain Efficiency

Cost leadership as a strategy emphasises operational efficiency, aiming to deliver products or services at the lowest possible cost without compromising quality. Within the realm of SCM, this involves optimising processes, reducing waste, and leveraging economies of scale to achieve cost advantages.

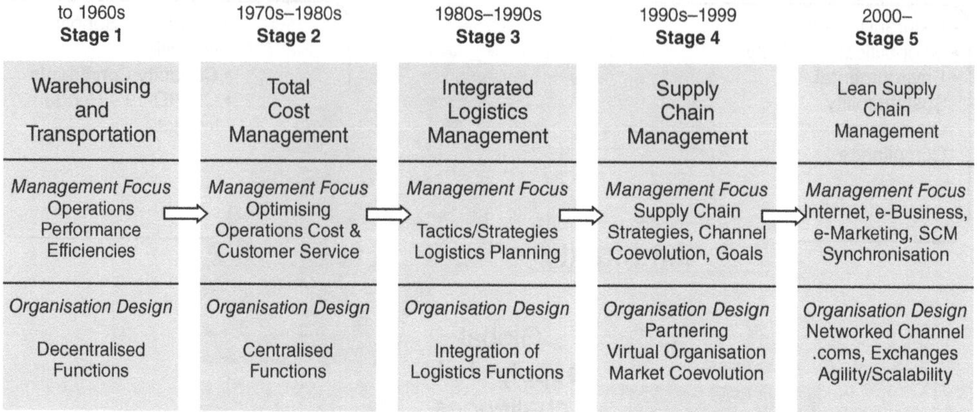

Figure 3.2 Evolution of Supply Chain Management.

One of the most effective ways to achieve cost leadership is through lean supply chain practices, which focus on eliminating non-value-adding activities. Techniques such as JIT inventory management and CI (Kaizen) reduce holding costs and enhance resource utilisation. Companies like Toyota exemplify this approach by integrating lean principles into their supply chain operations, resulting in significant cost savings and operational agility.

Another critical aspect of cost leadership is strategic sourcing. By cultivating strong relationships with suppliers, negotiating favourable terms, and consolidating procurement activities, organisations can reduce input costs while maintaining high-quality standards. For instance, Walmart has achieved cost leadership by leveraging its extensive supplier network and advanced inventory management systems. The company's ability to negotiate bulk purchasing agreements and optimise logistics has allowed it to offer consistently low prices to customers (Chopra & Meindl, 2024).

Technology also plays a vital role in enabling cost leadership within SCM. Automation, AI, and predictive analytics enhance process efficiency, reduce errors, and enable data-driven decision-making. For example, Amazon's use of robotics in its warehouses has streamlined order fulfilment processes, reducing labour costs and improving order accuracy.

3.1.3 Differentiation and Supply Chain Innovation

While cost leadership focuses on efficiency, differentiation emphasises innovation and customer value. This strategy involves creating unique offerings that set a company apart from its competitors. In the context of SCM, differentiation can be achieved by prioritising quality, customisation, and superior customer service.

Quality management is a cornerstone of differentiation in supply chains. By implementing rigorous quality control measures and partnering with reliable suppliers, organisations can ensure that their products meet or exceed customer expectations. Apple, for instance, differentiates itself through its meticulously designed supply chain, which prioritises quality and innovation at every stage. The company's close collaboration with suppliers and commitment to high standards enable it to deliver premium products that command brand loyalty and premium pricing (Christopher, 2016).

Customisation is another powerful avenue for differentiation. By adopting flexible manufacturing and distribution systems, businesses can offer tailored products and services that cater to individual customer preferences. Companies like Dell have successfully implemented build-to-order models, allowing customers to customise their products while maintaining efficiency and cost-effectiveness.

Superior customer service further enhances differentiation by fostering trust and loyalty. Supply chains that prioritise responsiveness and reliability can build long-term relationships with customers. For instance, Zappos, an online retailer, distinguishes itself through its exceptional customer service, supported by a well-integrated and agile supply chain. This approach has helped the company cultivate a strong reputation and loyal customer base.

3.1.4 The Role of Technology in Strengthening Competitive Advantage

Technology has emerged as a transformative force in SCM, enabling organisations to achieve both cost leadership and differentiation. Advanced tools and systems enhance visibility, coordination, and efficiency across supply chain activities, creating new opportunities for innovation and competitive advantage (see Figure 3.3).

One of the most impactful technologies in SCM is big data analytics. By analysing vast amounts of data from various sources, businesses can gain valuable insights into customer behaviour, demand patterns, and operational performance. These insights inform strategic decision-making, optimise resource allocation, and improve demand forecasting accuracy.

Automation and robotics are also revolutionising supply chain operations. Automated systems streamline repetitive tasks, reduce labour costs, and enhance precision in areas such as inventory management, order fulfilment, and quality control. For example, Ocado, a UK-based online grocery retailer, uses robotics and AI-driven systems to manage its warehouse operations, achieving unparalleled efficiency and scalability.

The IoT enhances supply chain visibility by enabling real-time tracking and monitoring of goods. IoT devices provide actionable data on inventory levels, transportation conditions, and equipment performance, allowing organisations to respond proactively to potential disruptions.

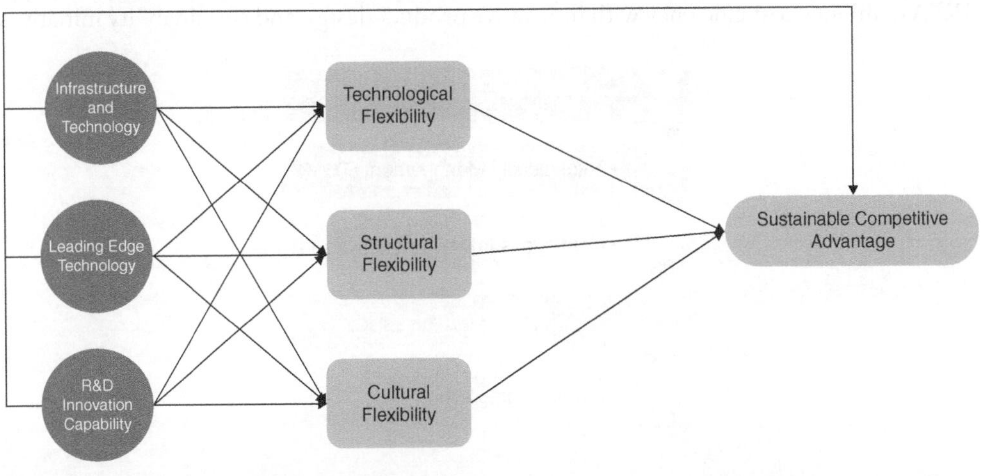

Figure 3.3 Technology in Competitive Advantage.

Blockchain technology further strengthens SCM by improving transparency and traceability. By providing a secure and immutable record of transactions, blockchain enables businesses to verify the authenticity of products, monitor compliance, and enhance trust among supply chain partners.

3.1.5 Sustainability as a Competitive Differentiator

Sustainability has become an essential consideration for modern supply chains, reflecting the growing importance of environmental and social responsibility. Integrating sustainability into SCM not only addresses ethical concerns but also serves as a powerful differentiator in competitive markets.

Sustainable supply chains prioritise resource efficiency, waste reduction, and ethical sourcing. These practices align with consumer preferences for environmentally friendly products and contribute to long-term cost savings. For instance, Unilever's Sustainable Living Plan incorporates sustainability into every aspect of its supply chain, from sourcing raw materials to reducing greenhouse gas emissions. This approach has enhanced the company's reputation, strengthened stakeholder relationships, and driven financial performance (Unilever, 2023).

Circular economy principles represent another avenue for sustainability in SCM. By designing products and processes that facilitate recycling, remanufacturing, and reuse, businesses can minimise waste and extend the lifecycle of materials. Companies like Patagonia have embraced circular economy practices, offering repair and recycling programmes that align with their brand values and resonate with environmentally conscious consumers.

Governments and regulatory bodies are also driving the adoption of sustainable supply chains by introducing policies and incentives that encourage responsible practices. Compliance with these regulations enhances a company's credibility and reduces the risk of reputational damage.

3.1.6 The Interplay between Cost Leadership, Differentiation, and Sustainability

While cost leadership and differentiation are often viewed as distinct strategies, they are not mutually exclusive (see Figure 3.4). Businesses can achieve a competitive advantage by integrating elements of both approaches into their supply chain strategies. For example, IKEA combines cost efficiency with innovative product design and sustainability initiatives.

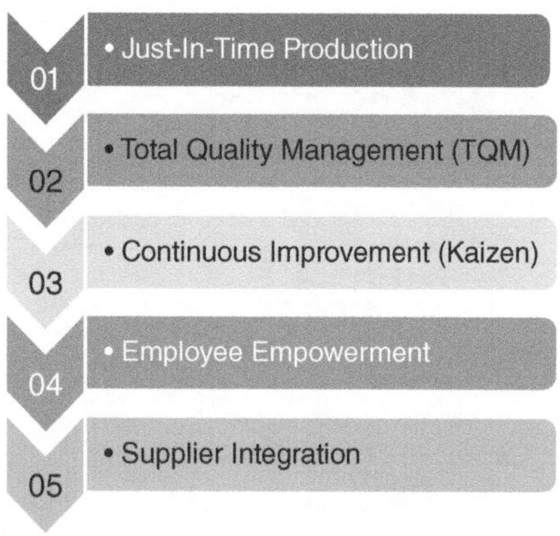

Figure 3.4 Cost Leadership Strategies.

The company's flat-pack furniture reduces production and transportation costs while appealing to customers seeking affordable and eco-friendly solutions.

Sustainability further complements both cost leadership and differentiation by aligning economic performance with environmental and social goals. Sustainable practices not only reduce costs through resource efficiency but also enhance brand loyalty and market differentiation by meeting the expectations of socially conscious consumers.

3.1.7 Conclusion

SCM has evolved into a strategic imperative for achieving competitive advantage in today's dynamic business landscape. By adopting cost leadership and differentiation strategies, organisations can optimise efficiency, drive innovation, and exceed customer expectations. The integration of advanced technologies and sustainability further enhances these advantages, providing a foundation for resilience and long-term success. As markets continue to evolve, the ability to leverage SCM strategically will remain a defining characteristic of industry leaders.

3.2 Cost Leadership in SCM

Cost leadership is a fundamental strategy in business that seeks to position a company as the lowest-cost producer within its industry. In the context of SCM, cost leadership revolves around optimising various supply chain processes – procurement, production, distribution, and beyond – to reduce operational expenses and deliver products to consumers at competitive prices. This strategy is particularly advantageous in industries where products are largely not differentiated, and purchasing decisions are heavily influenced by price. By adopting cost leadership strategies within SCM, companies can attract price-sensitive customer segments, expand their market share, and sustain profitability in highly competitive markets.

3.2.1 The Concept of Cost Leadership in SCM

The cost leadership strategy in SCM aligns with Michael Porter's generic strategies framework, which identifies cost leadership as one of three primary ways companies achieve competitive advantage. The focus of cost leadership is to minimise costs across the supply chain while maintaining acceptable product quality. By achieving economies of scale, leveraging efficient processes, and streamlining operations, organisations can reduce their overall cost structure and gain a pricing advantage over competitors (Porter, 1985).

In practice, cost leadership in SCM involves meticulous analysis and optimisation of each stage of the supply chain. From sourcing raw materials to delivering finished goods, companies seek to eliminate waste, improve efficiency, and harness technological advancements to reduce costs. These efforts not only improve profitability but also enable businesses to offer lower prices to customers, thereby strengthening their competitive position.

3.2.2 Key Drivers of Cost Leadership in SCM

Several factors contribute to the successful implementation of cost leadership strategies within SCM. These include efficient procurement practices, streamlined production processes, optimised logistics and distribution systems, and the strategic use of technology.

One of the primary drivers of cost leadership is effective procurement. Companies that establish strong relationships with suppliers, negotiate favourable terms, and consolidate purchasing activities can significantly reduce input costs. For instance, Walmart, a global leader in cost leadership, employs sophisticated procurement strategies to secure low prices from suppliers. By purchasing in bulk and using its vast distribution network, Walmart minimises costs and passes these savings on to its customers (Chopra & Meindl, 2020).

Streamlined production processes also play a critical role in achieving cost leadership. By adopting lean manufacturing principles, organisations can eliminate waste, optimise resource utilisation, and enhance operational efficiency. Toyota's implementation of the TPS exemplifies this approach. By focusing on CI, standardisation, and waste reduction, Toyota has achieved significant cost savings while maintaining high-quality standards.

Optimised logistics and distribution systems further enhance cost leadership by reducing transportation and inventory holding costs. Companies that leverage advanced route planning, WMS, and JIT inventory practices can minimise operational expenses and improve supply chain responsiveness. Amazon's use of robotics and data analytics in its fulfilment centres has revolutionised logistics, enabling the company to deliver products quickly and cost-effectively.

Technology is another crucial enabler of cost leadership in SCM. Automation, AI, and big data analytics streamline processes, reduce errors, and enable data-driven decision-making. For example, predictive analytics tools help companies forecast demand more accurately, reducing the risk of overproduction or stockouts. Similarly, IoT devices enhance supply chain visibility, enabling real-time monitoring of inventory levels, transportation conditions, and equipment performance.

3.2.3 *Benefits of Cost Leadership in SCM*

The adoption of cost leadership strategies within SCM yields numerous benefits, ranging from increased profitability to enhanced market competitiveness. One of the most significant advantages is the ability to attract price-sensitive customer segments. By offering lower prices than competitors, companies can expand their customer base and increase market share. This is particularly relevant in industries such as retail, fast-moving consumer goods (FMCG), and automotive, where cost plays a decisive role in purchasing decisions.

Cost leadership also strengthens a company's resilience to market fluctuations and economic downturns. By maintaining a low-cost structure, organisations can sustain profitability even when demand declines or input costs rise. For instance, during periods of economic recession, cost-leading companies are better positioned to retain customers and maintain financial stability.

Another benefit is the potential for reinvestment in other strategic areas. Cost savings achieved through efficient SCM can be reinvested in research and development (R&D), marketing, or customer service, further enhancing a company's competitive position. For example, Samsung leverages cost leadership in its supply chain to fund innovation in product development, enabling the company to compete effectively in both price-sensitive and premium segments of the consumer electronics market.

3.2.4 *Challenges of Cost Leadership in SCM*

While cost leadership offers significant advantages, its implementation is not without challenges. One of the primary risks is the potential for compromised quality. In pursuit of cost reductions, companies may inadvertently cut corners, leading to lower-quality products or services. Maintaining a balance between cost efficiency and product quality is essential to avoid damaging brand reputation and customer trust.

Another challenge is the vulnerability to supply chain disruptions. Cost leadership strategies often rely on lean operations and minimal buffer inventory, which can increase susceptibility to disruptions caused by natural disasters, geopolitical tensions, or supply shortages. For instance, the COVID-19 pandemic exposed the fragility of many cost-optimised supply chains, prompting companies to re-evaluate their risk management practices.

The pressure to continuously reduce costs can also lead to strained relationships with suppliers and employees. Aggressive cost-cutting measures may result in lower supplier margins, delayed payments, or increased workload for employees, potentially harming morale and long-term partnerships.

Finally, the pursuit of cost leadership can limit a company's ability to differentiate itself through innovation or customer experience. By focusing primarily on cost reduction, organisations may neglect opportunities to invest in unique value propositions, leaving them vulnerable to competitors that prioritise differentiation.

3.2.5 Case Studies in Cost Leadership

Several companies have successfully implemented cost leadership strategies in their supply chains, demonstrating the potential for operational excellence and competitive advantage.

Walmart is a quintessential example of cost leadership in SCM. The company's relentless focus on efficiency has enabled it to become one of the largest and most profitable retailers in the world. Walmart's supply chain strategies include bulk purchasing, centralised distribution, and advanced inventory management systems. By optimising these processes, Walmart consistently offers low prices to its customers while maintaining strong financial performance (Chopra & Meindl, 2020).

Another notable example is Ryanair, a budget airline that has achieved cost leadership through efficient operations and stringent cost control. Ryanair's supply chain strategies include standardising its fleet to reduce maintenance costs, using secondary airports to lower landing fees, and negotiating favourable contracts with suppliers. These measures have enabled Ryanair to offer low fares while remaining highly profitable.

Toyota's implementation of the TPS also highlights the benefits of cost leadership in SCM. By eliminating waste, standardising processes, and fostering a culture of CI, Toyota has achieved significant cost savings while maintaining high product quality. This approach has made Toyota a global leader in the automotive industry and a benchmark for lean supply chain practices.

Nestlé's centralised regional distribution in Latin America reduced per-unit logistics costs by 12% through consolidated freight and shared warehousing facilities across Mexico, Brazil, and Argentina (Nestlé, 2024).

3.2.6 The Future of Cost Leadership in SCM

As supply chains become increasingly complex and technology-driven, the future of cost leadership will be shaped by innovation and digital transformation (see Figure 3.5). Emerging technologies such as blockchain, AI, and predictive analytics will further enhance cost optimisation efforts by improving visibility, efficiency, and decision-making.

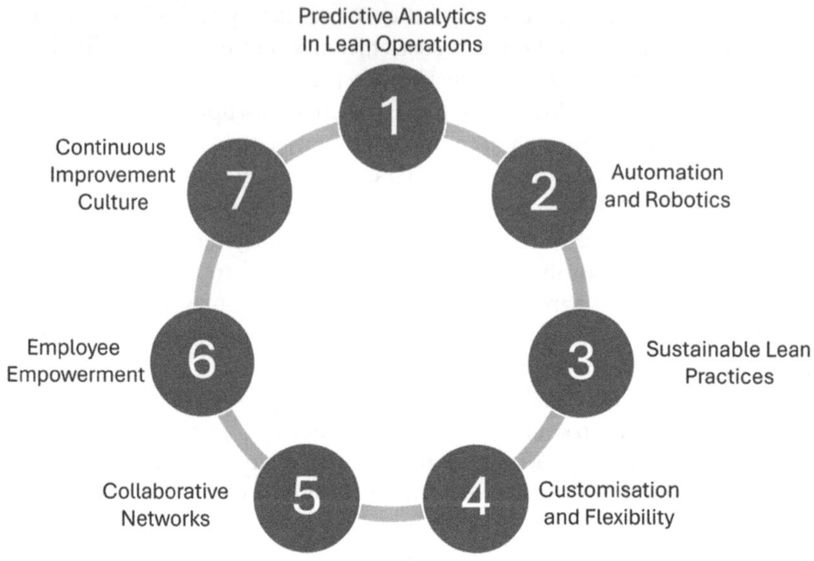

Figure 3.5 Future Trends in Lean Operations.

Sustainability will also play a critical role in the evolution of cost leadership. Companies that integrate sustainable practices into their supply chains can achieve long-term cost savings while meeting the expectations of environmentally conscious consumers. For example, renewable energy sources, waste reduction initiatives, and circular economy principles can reduce operational costs and enhance brand reputation.

3.2.7 Conclusion

Cost leadership is a powerful strategy that enables organisations to achieve a competitive advantage by minimising costs across the supply chain. Through efficient procurement, streamlined production, optimised logistics, and the strategic use of technology, companies can deliver products at lower prices without compromising quality. While challenges such as supply chain disruptions and quality risks must be addressed, the benefits of cost leadership, including increased profitability, market share, and resilience, make it a cornerstone of effective SCM. As technology and sustainability continue to reshape the business landscape, cost leadership will remain a vital strategy for organisations seeking to thrive in a competitive and dynamic environment.

3.3 Key Tactics for Achieving Cost Leadership in SCM

Cost leadership in SCM hinges on adopting and mastering specific tactics that enable organisations to reduce operational expenses while maintaining or enhancing the quality of their products and services. This strategy requires a comprehensive and systematic approach that integrates efficient procurement, process optimisation, and distribution efficiency. By excelling in these areas, companies can achieve significant cost savings, gain a competitive edge, and deliver value to customers in price-sensitive markets. This section explores these key tactics in detail, drawing on real-world examples and theoretical insights to illustrate their implementation and impact.

Implementing Lean Six Sigma across sourcing and manufacturing can yield significant savings. In Australia, Woolworths Group leveraged collaborative planning with major suppliers, sharing demand forecasts to optimise order quantities and cut stockouts by 30% (Woolworths Group, 2023).

3.3.1 Efficient Procurement

Procurement plays a central role in determining the cost structure of a supply chain, as raw materials and components often represent a substantial portion of total expenses. Efficient procurement involves building strong relationships with suppliers to negotiate favourable terms, ensure reliable delivery, and implement joint cost-saving initiatives. Collaboration with suppliers fosters mutual trust and understanding, enabling both parties to align their goals and optimise the supply chain for efficiency.

One key aspect of efficient procurement is strategic sourcing, which involves identifying and partnering with suppliers that offer the best balance of cost, quality, and reliability. By consolidating purchasing activities and leveraging economies of scale, organisations can secure discounts and reduce administrative costs. Additionally, supplier performance management tools help track and evaluate supplier reliability, quality, and delivery timelines, ensuring consistent performance.

For example, Walmart has excelled in procurement by fostering long-term partnerships with its suppliers. The company's approach involves negotiating bulk purchase agreements, implementing VMI systems, and leveraging its extensive distribution network to streamline logistics. These practices not only reduce raw material costs but also improve supply chain responsiveness and reliability (Lee, 2004).

Technology further enhances procurement efficiency by automating processes, improving visibility, and enabling data-driven decision-making. Digital procurement platforms, such as e-sourcing and e-auctions, facilitate competitive bidding, while AI algorithms analyse market trends and supplier performance to identify cost-saving opportunities.

3.3.2 Process Optimisation

Process optimisation is another critical tactic for achieving cost leadership in SCM. It focuses on streamlining production and operational processes to minimise labour, energy, and material costs while enhancing quality and efficiency (see Figure 3.6). Techniques such as Lean Manufacturing, Six Sigma, and TQM are widely used to eliminate waste, reduce variability, and improve overall productivity.

Lean Manufacturing, a methodology rooted in the TPS, emphasises the elimination of non-value-adding activities. By identifying and addressing inefficiencies, organisations can optimise resource utilisation and reduce production costs. For instance, implementing JIT inventory practices ensures that materials and components are delivered only when needed, reducing holding costs and minimising excess inventory.

Six Sigma complements Lean Manufacturing by focusing on reducing process variability and improving quality. Through rigorous data analysis and process monitoring, Six Sigma identifies defects and root causes, enabling organisations to implement targeted improvements. The combination of Lean and Six Sigma, often referred to as Lean Six Sigma, has become a popular framework for achieving cost leadership in SCM.

Process optimisation is not limited to manufacturing; it also extends to other supply chain functions, such as inventory management and demand planning. By leveraging

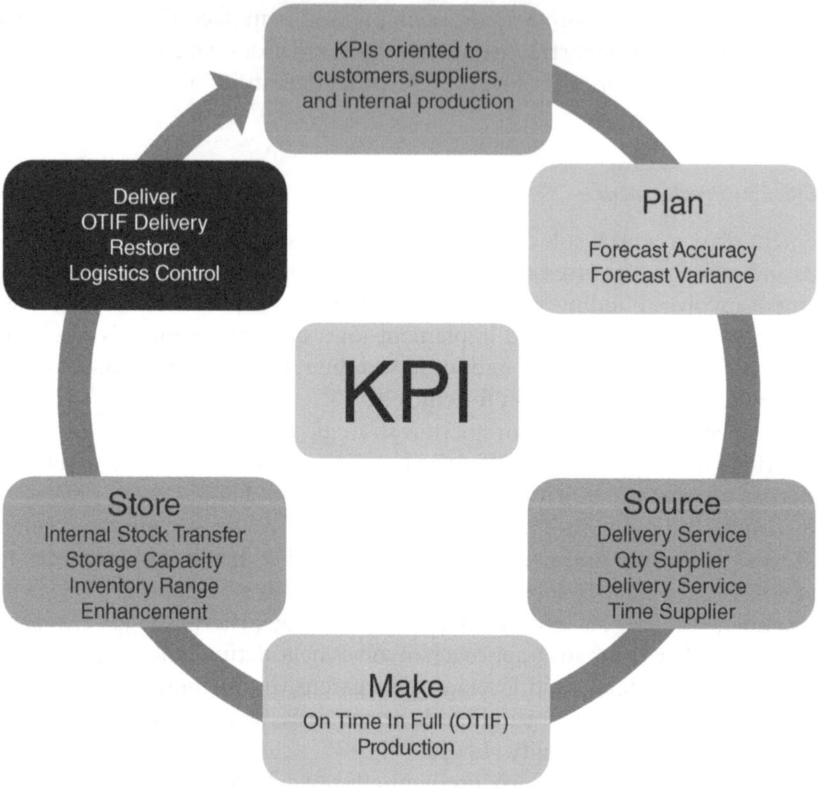

Figure 3.6 Process Optimisation in SCM.

predictive analytics and advanced planning systems, companies can align production schedules with demand forecasts, reducing overproduction and underutilisation of resources.

An example of successful process optimisation is Toyota's implementation of TPS principles. The company's focus on standardisation, CI, and waste reduction has enabled it to achieve significant cost savings while maintaining high-quality standards. This approach has solidified Toyota's position as a global leader in the automotive industry and a benchmark for process excellence (Christopher, 2016).

3.3.3 Distribution Efficiency

Distribution efficiency is a critical component of cost leadership in SCM, as transportation, warehousing, and handling costs can significantly impact overall expenses. Optimising logistics involves streamlining distribution networks, improving route planning, and adopting advanced inventory management practices to minimise costs and enhance service levels.

One effective tactic is decentralised warehousing, where companies strategically locate warehouses closer to key markets. This approach reduces transportation costs and delivery times while improving customer satisfaction. Additionally, automated WMS enhance operational efficiency by optimising storage layouts, streamlining order picking, and reducing labour requirements.

Route optimisation is another important aspect of distribution efficiency. By using advanced routing algorithms and real-time traffic data, companies can identify the most cost-effective delivery routes, reducing fuel consumption and transportation expenses. For example, logistics companies like FedEx and DHL leverage route optimisation technologies to minimise costs and improve delivery reliability.

Inventory management also plays a crucial role in achieving distribution efficiency. Techniques such as demand-driven replenishment and collaborative inventory planning enable organisations to maintain optimal stock levels, reducing holding costs and minimising stockouts. Amazon's use of predictive analytics and robotics in its fulfilment centres has revolutionised inventory management, allowing the company to achieve high levels of efficiency and scalability.

3.3.4 The Role of Technology in Enabling Cost Leadership

Technology serves as a critical enabler of cost leadership in SCM, providing the tools and capabilities needed to enhance efficiency across procurement, production, and distribution processes. Digital transformation has introduced a range of innovations, including AI, IoT, blockchain, and big data analytics, that empower organisations to optimise their supply chains and achieve cost savings.

AI and ML algorithms enable data-driven decision-making by analysing historical and real-time data to identify cost-saving opportunities. For instance, predictive analytics tools forecast demand with greater accuracy, allowing companies to optimise production schedules and inventory levels.

IoT devices enhance supply chain visibility by providing real-time data on inventory levels, transportation conditions, and equipment performance. This transparency enables organisations to respond proactively to potential disruptions and ensure smooth operations.

Blockchain technology improves traceability and transparency in procurement and logistics, reducing the risk of fraud and ensuring compliance with regulatory requirements. By providing a secure and immutable record of transactions, blockchain facilitates trust and collaboration among supply chain partners.

Big data analytics provides valuable insights into supply chain performance, helping organisations identify inefficiencies and implement targeted improvements. For example, advanced analytics tools can pinpoint bottlenecks in production or distribution processes, enabling companies to address issues and reduce costs.

3.3.5 CI and Adaptability

Achieving and sustaining cost leadership requires a commitment to CI and adaptability. As market conditions, customer preferences, and technological advancements evolve, organisations must remain agile and proactive in identifying new opportunities for cost reduction. This involves regularly reviewing supply chain processes, benchmarking performance against industry standards, and fostering a culture of innovation and collaboration (Figure 3.7).

CI also extends to sustainability initiatives, which align cost leadership with environmental and social responsibility. By reducing energy consumption, minimising waste, and adopting circular economy principles, organisations can achieve long-term cost savings while enhancing their reputation and meeting stakeholder expectations.

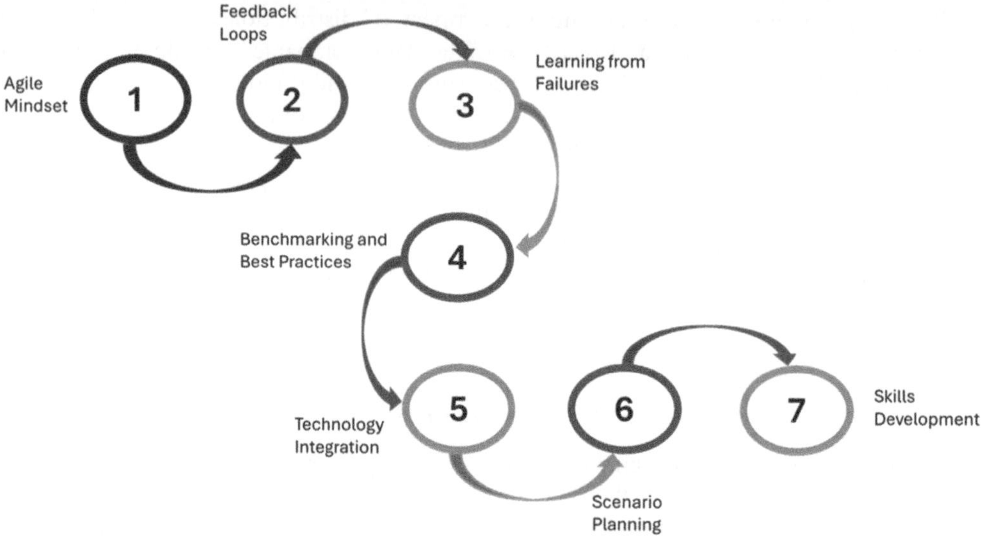

Figure 3.7 Continuous Improvement and Adaptability.

3.3.6 Conclusion

Cost leadership in SCM is a strategic imperative for organisations seeking to compete effectively in price-sensitive markets. By focusing on efficient procurement, process optimisation, and distribution efficiency, companies can reduce operational expenses, deliver value to customers, and gain a competitive edge. Technology plays a pivotal role in enabling these tactics, providing the tools and insights needed to optimise supply chain performance. However, achieving cost leadership requires a CI mindset, adaptability, and a commitment to balancing cost efficiency with quality and sustainability. As global markets continue to evolve, the ability to execute cost leadership strategies will remain a critical determinant of business success.

3.4 Differentiation in SCM

In competitive markets, differentiation is a key strategy for businesses seeking to stand out. Differentiation involves offering unique value propositions that go beyond price competition, including superior quality, innovative product features, and exceptional customer service. Differentiation strategies emphasise unique offerings, service excellence, and rapid responsiveness. Zara's agile replenishment model, drawing real-time POS data from European, Asian, and North American stores, enables bi-weekly restocking and trend-driven design launches, reducing lead times to market from months to weeks (Blanchard, 2022). In Japan, Sony's premium electronics line employs blockchain for provenance tracking, enabling authenticated resale markets and bolstering brand value (Sony, 2024). In SCM, differentiation plays a pivotal role in enabling businesses to tailor their supply chains to deliver these unique offerings effectively.

3.4.1 Understanding Differentiation in SCM

Differentiation strategies in SCM aim to enhance a company's competitive edge by creating value for customers that competitors cannot easily replicate. This requires a shift from

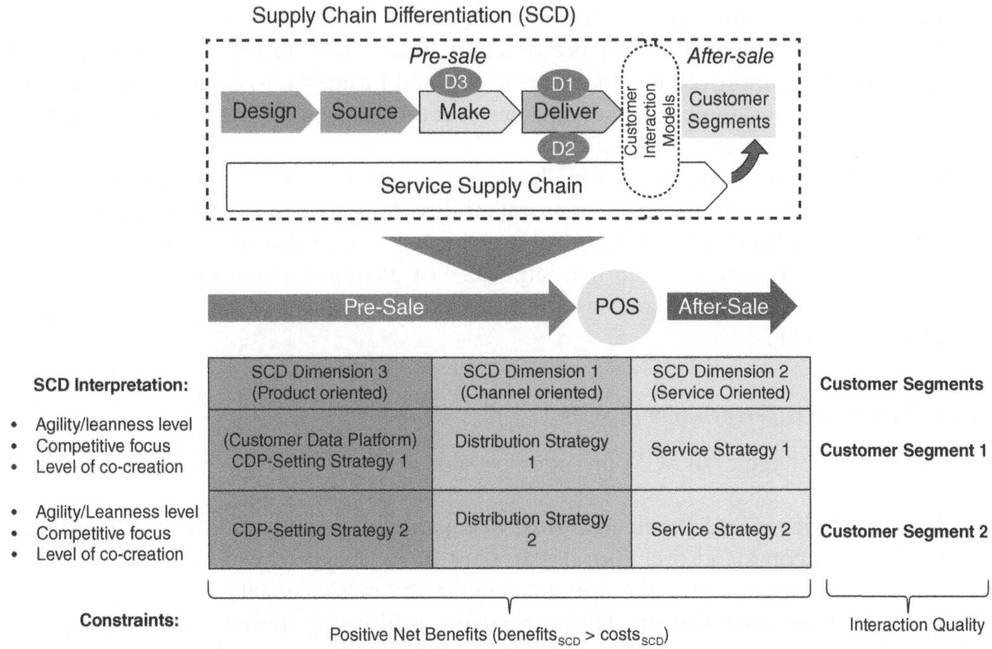

Figure 3.8 Supply Chain Differentiation.

cost-focused operations to value-focused strategies, prioritising quality, innovation, and customer satisfaction. Supply chains that support differentiation must be adaptable, innovative, and closely aligned with a company's strategic goals.

In their 2016 paper, "Supply Chain Differentiation: Background, Concept and Examples", Hofmann and Knébel claim to provide a "...framework that brings together the most relevant factors...of supply chain differentiation" (Hofmann & Knébel, 2016) (see Figure 3.8).

3.4.2 Key Approaches to Differentiation in SCM

There are several approaches to achieving differentiation within supply chain operations:

1 **Innovation in Product:** Design companies focusing on product innovation develop unique and specialised designs that address specific customer needs. For example, Apple Inc. seamlessly integrates its hardware and software, ensuring a superior user experience. Apple's supply chain prioritises flexibility and responsiveness to changes in design and customer demand, maintaining high-quality standards throughout the production process (Fisher, 1997).

2 **Enhanced Customer Service:** Exceptional customer service, such as fast delivery, flexible return policies, and personalised interactions, enhances the customer experience and builds brand loyalty. Companies with supply chains that prioritise service excellence can retain customers even in highly competitive markets. For instance, Amazon's same-day delivery option and efficient order tracking system demonstrate how SCM supports a superior customer experience (Christopher, 2016).

3 **Advanced Technology Integration:** Leveraging technologies such as the IoT, AI, and blockchain can significantly enhance differentiation. These technologies enable better quality control, improved product traceability, and insights into customer preferences. IoT sensors, for example, allow companies to monitor product conditions during transit, ensuring quality and reliability.
4 **Sustainability as Differentiation:** Increasingly, customers are drawn to companies that demonstrate commitment to sustainability. Supply chains that focus on reducing waste, lowering carbon footprints, and adopting ethical sourcing practices can differentiate a business in the marketplace. For example, Patagonia's focus on sustainability in its supply chain has strengthened its reputation and customer loyalty (Harland, 2024).

3.4.3 Benefits of Differentiation in SCM

Differentiation strategies in SCM provide several key benefits:

1 **Premium Pricing and Profit Margins:** Companies that successfully differentiate their offerings can command premium prices. Customers are often willing to pay more for products and services that offer unique benefits or superior quality.
2 **Increased Customer Loyalty Differentiation:** Addressing specific needs and expectations fosters stronger customer relationships. Enhanced customer loyalty drives repeat business and generates positive word-of-mouth referrals.
3 **Enhanced Brand Equity:** A differentiated supply chain contributes to a company's reputation and brand equity. Companies that consistently deliver on their promises of quality and service strengthen their market position.

3.4.4 Case Studies of Differentiation in SCM

1 **Apple Inc.:** Apple's emphasis on innovative product design and seamless integration of hardware and software has established it as a leader in the technology sector. Its supply chain ensures high standards of quality and timely delivery, contributing to the brand's premium positioning (Fisher, 1997).
2 **Zara:** Zara's supply chain exemplifies responsiveness and innovation. The company's ability to design, produce, and deliver new fashion trends to stores within weeks enables it to differentiate itself in the competitive fast-fashion industry (Blanchard, 2022).

3.4.5 Challenges of Differentiation in SCM

While differentiation offers numerous benefits, it also poses challenges:

1 **Higher Costs:** Differentiated supply chains often require significant investment in advanced technologies, quality control measures, and customer service infrastructure.
2 **Complexity in Operations:** Meeting the diverse needs of customers and maintaining flexibility can increase operational complexity. Companies must carefully manage these complexities to avoid inefficiencies.
3 **Risk of Imitation:** Competitors may attempt to replicate differentiation strategies, making it essential for companies to innovate and improve continuously.

3.4.6 Future Trends in Differentiation

As markets evolve, the scope for differentiation in SCM will expand, particularly in areas such as personalisation and sustainability. Companies are increasingly leveraging data analytics and AI to offer customised products and experiences. Sustainability will also remain a significant driver of differentiation, as consumers demand greater transparency and accountability in supply chains. The so-called "Triple Bottom Line" is ever increasingly driving business strategy, and for good reason. The general public and investors are analysing a company's sustainability efforts from a holistic view, based on Environmental, Social, and Governance (ESG) factors, also known as the Triple Bottom Line.

3.4.7 Conclusion

Differentiation is a powerful strategy in SCM, enabling businesses to deliver unique value to customers and establish a competitive advantage. By focusing on innovation, customer service, technology, and sustainability, companies can develop supply chains that align with their strategic objectives. As markets continue to evolve, the ability to adapt and innovate will remain critical for differentiation in SCM.

3.5 Strategic Alignment in SCM

Strategic alignment links SCM objectives with corporate vision and market positioning. Unilever's Sustainable Agriculture Programme aligns procurement in India, Brazil, and Nigeria with its global sustainability targets, embedding social impact and traceability metrics into supplier scorecards. This approach has reduced raw material cost volatility by 10% and improved yields by 8% (Unilever, 2023). Aligning with digital transformation strategies, Samsung Electronics integrates its SCM platforms with enterprise systems across Korea, Vietnam, and the United States, ensuring real-time visibility and decision support (Samsung, 2024).

Strategic alignment is the synchronisation of supply chain activities with a company's overarching business strategy. It ensures that every component of the supply chain, from procurement and production to logistics and distribution, contributes to achieving the organisation's competitive goals. In a world where market dynamics and customer expectations are constantly evolving, strategic alignment is critical to maintaining competitiveness and achieving long-term success. It is the engine room of Modern Supply Chain Management theory.

3.5.1 The Concept of Strategic Alignment

Strategic alignment in SCM involves tailoring supply chain processes to support the core competencies and objectives of the business. Whether a company focuses on cost leadership, differentiation, or sustainability, its supply chain must be designed to reinforce these strategic priorities. For example:

Companies prioritising cost efficiency must optimise their supply chains to minimise expenses, often by leveraging economies of scale or adopting lean practices.

Businesses focusing on innovation require agile supply chains capable of rapid adaptation to changing market demands and technological advancements.

Companies committed to sustainability must integrate environmentally friendly practices, such as reducing carbon footprints, into their supply chains (Sabet et al., 2017).

3.5.2 *Importance of Strategic Alignment in SCM*

Strategic alignment fosters a coherent and goal-oriented approach to SCM, allowing businesses to:

1 **Enhance Efficiency:** Aligning supply chain processes with business objectives streamlines operations, reducing redundancies and improving resource utilisation.
2 **Boost Customer Satisfaction:** Strategically aligned supply chains are better equipped to meet customer expectations for quality, timeliness, and sustainability.
3 **Drive Competitive Advantage:** By aligning supply chain capabilities with strategic priorities, businesses can differentiate themselves in the marketplace and build a resilient competitive edge.

For instance, Amazon has aligned its supply chain with a customer-centric strategy. Its emphasis on fast delivery and convenience drives investments in advanced logistics and predictive analytics, allowing the company to consistently exceed customer expectations (Christopher, 2016).

3.5.3 *Key Components of Strategic Alignment*

Achieving strategic alignment in SCM requires focusing on several key components (see Figure 3.9):

1 **Core Competencies:** Businesses must identify their unique strengths and ensure that their supply chains amplify these competencies. For example, Toyota's lean manufacturing system enhances its reputation for operational excellence by minimising waste and optimising efficiency (Blanchard, 2022).
2 **Collaboration across Functions:** Cross-functional collaboration between SCM, marketing, and operations ensures that all departments work towards shared strategic goals. Effective communication and coordination reduce silos and align efforts across the organisation.
3 **Sustainability and Ethics:** With growing consumer demand for environmentally and socially responsible practices, businesses must align their supply chains with sustainability goals. Incorporating ethical sourcing and green logistics enhances brand reputation while reducing environmental impact (Harland, 2024).
4 **Technology and Innovation:** Digital transformation plays a pivotal role in strategic alignment. Advanced technologies such as AI, Blockchain, and Big Data Analytics enable businesses to optimise operations, predict trends, and ensure transparency across the supply chain.

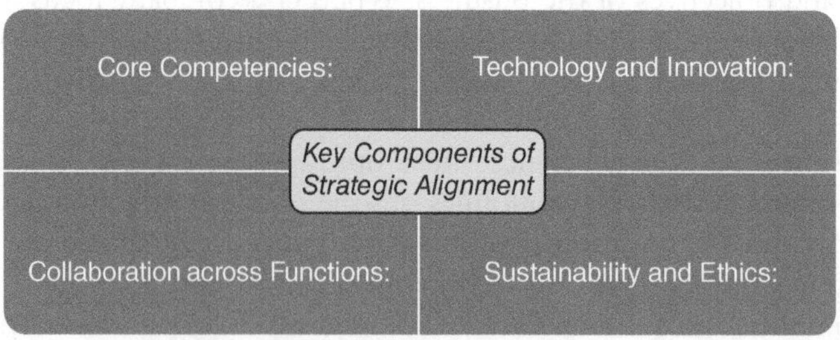

Figure 3.9 Key Components of Strategic Alignment.

3.5.4 Challenges in Achieving Strategic Alignment

While the benefits of strategic alignment are significant, businesses often face challenges in achieving it:

1. **Dynamic Market Conditions:** Rapid shifts in consumer preferences, technological advancements, and economic fluctuations require businesses to adapt their strategies continuously. Maintaining alignment in such a dynamic environment is complex.
2. **Operational Complexity:** Large organisations with GSCs may struggle to align diverse operations across regions and functions. Ensuring consistency and cohesion demands robust communication and governance structures.
3. **Balancing Priorities:** Companies often face conflicting demands, such as balancing cost efficiency with sustainability. Effective decision-making and resource allocation are critical to managing these trade-offs.

3.5.5 Case Studies of Strategic Alignment

1. **Unilever – Sustainable Supply Chain Strategy:** Unilever has integrated sustainability into its supply chain to align with its corporate vision of reducing environmental impact. The company sources materials responsibly, reduces waste, and invests in eco-friendly technologies. This alignment enhances Unilever's appeal to environmentally conscious consumers (Harland, 2024).
2. **Apple – Innovation-Driven Supply Chain:** Apple's supply chain aligns seamlessly with its innovation-focused strategy. By maintaining close relationships with suppliers and adopting cutting-edge manufacturing technologies, Apple ensures high-quality products that resonate with its premium brand image (Fisher, 1997).
3. **Zara – Agile Supply Chain for Fast Fashion:** Zara's supply chain exemplifies alignment with a strategy of speed and responsiveness. The company's ability to design, produce, and deliver new fashion trends within weeks supports its competitive positioning in the fast-fashion industry (Blanchard, 2022).

3.5.6 Future Trends in Strategic Alignment

Looking ahead, the role of strategic alignment in SCM will become even more critical as businesses navigate complex global markets. Key trends include:

1. **Increased Personalisation:** Supply chains will become more customer-focused, enabling businesses to deliver tailored products and services that meet specific needs.
2. **Digital Integration:** Enhanced digital integration across supply chains will improve visibility, streamline operations, and enable real-time decision-making.
3. **Focus on Circular Economy:** Strategic alignment with circular economy principles will encourage businesses to design supply chains that minimise waste and promote the reuse of resources.

3.5.7 Conclusion

Strategic alignment in SCM is essential for achieving business success in today's competitive landscape. By ensuring that supply chain activities support core competencies and strategic goals, businesses can enhance efficiency, customer satisfaction, and market competitiveness.

As markets evolve, the ability to adapt and innovate will be crucial for maintaining alignment and achieving long-term success.

3.6 Technology as a Driver of Competitive Advantage

The relentless march of technological innovation has irrevocably transformed the landscape of SCM. This digital revolution has opened up a plethora of opportunities for businesses to enhance efficiency, make data-driven decisions, and elevate customer experiences. Technology has emerged as a formidable force, propelling companies towards cost leadership and differentiation, fostering the development of innovative, responsive, and transparent supply chains.

Emerging technologies, such as AI, IoT, blockchain, and robotics, are enabling predictive analytics, automated operations, and transparent networks. For example, Siemens' Amberg Electronics Plant in Germany deploys over 1,200 IoT sensors coupled with AI-driven maintenance algorithms, achieving a 99.9% quality rate and a 20% throughput increase (Siemens AG, 2024). In the Middle East, DP World's autonomous port terminals in Dubai use robotics and digital twins to simulate cargo flows, cutting berth turnaround by 25% (DP World, 2024).

The Technology Adoption Curve, also known as the Technology Adoption Lifecycle or Innovation Curve, describes how a new technology spreads through a population over time. In the context of SCM, this curve illustrates how different companies or individuals adopt and integrate new technologies within their supply chain operations. Understanding this curve helps in predicting adoption rates, identifying potential challenges, and developing effective strategies for technology implementation (see Figure 3.10).

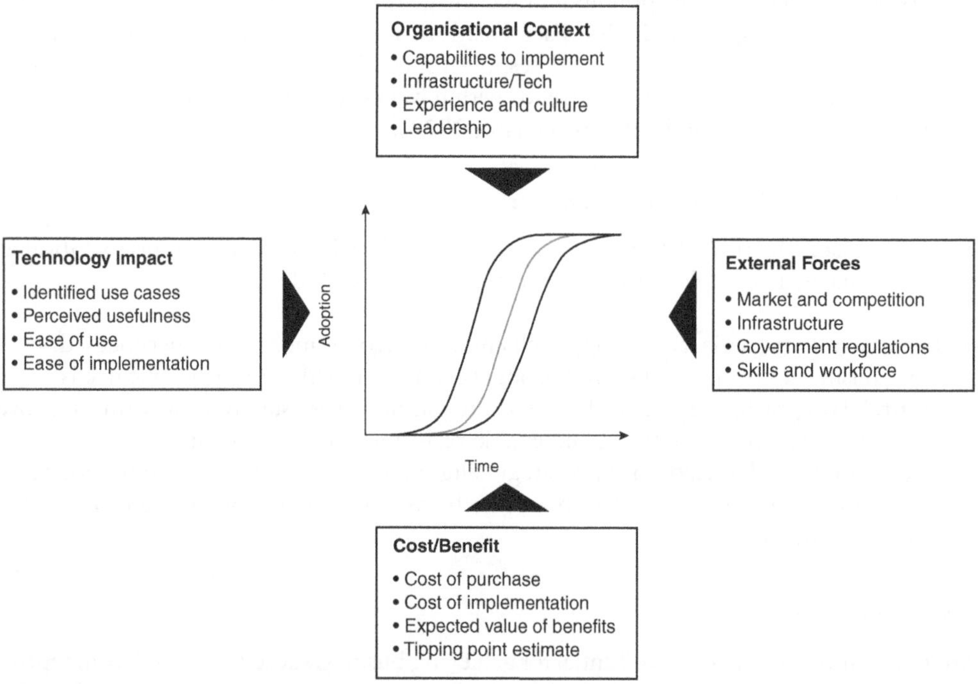

Figure 3.10 Technology Adoption Curve.

3.6.1 Key Technological Drivers of Competitive Advantage in SCM

1. **Big Data Analytics:** Big Data Analytics has become a cornerstone of modern SCM. By harnessing the power of vast datasets, companies can uncover hidden patterns, optimise inventory levels, and refine demand forecasting models. This data-driven approach leads to more efficient operations, reducing the risk of stockouts and overstocking, and ultimately improving customer satisfaction.
2. **AI:** AI has revolutionised SCM by automating routine tasks, enabling real-time decision-making, and facilitating rapid responses to dynamic market conditions. AI-powered systems can analyse complex datasets, identify trends, and predict future outcomes, empowering businesses to make informed decisions that drive growth and profitability.
3. **IoT:** The IoT has ushered in a new era of connectivity, enabling businesses to track and monitor assets, equipment, and inventory in real time. By integrating IoT devices into their supply chains, companies can gain unprecedented visibility, enhance transparency, and proactively address potential disruptions. This increased visibility fosters trust among supply chain partners, strengthens relationships, and ultimately improves overall performance.
4. **Blockchain Technology:** Blockchain technology has the potential to revolutionise SCM by providing a secure, transparent, and immutable record of transactions. This technology can be used to track the movement of goods, verify the authenticity of products, and ensure compliance with regulations. By eliminating intermediaries and reducing paperwork, blockchain can streamline supply chain processes, reduce costs, and enhance trust among supply chain partners.

Case Study – Amazon's Technological Prowess

Amazon, the e-commerce behemoth, stands as a testament to the power of technology in SCM. The company leverages AI and ML to forecast demand, optimise inventory levels, and schedule deliveries with precision. By employing robotics and automation in its warehouses, Amazon has significantly increased efficiency and reduced operational costs. This technological prowess enables the company to deliver products rapidly and reliably, delighting customers and solidifying its position as a market leader.

3.6.2 Technology as a Competitive Advantage

Technology has emerged as a critical differentiator in SCM, enabling companies to:

1. **Leverage Data for Insights:** By harnessing the power of Big Data Analytics, businesses can gain valuable insights into customer behaviour, market trends, and operational performance.
2. **Optimise Processes:** AI and automation can streamline supply chain processes, reduce errors, and improve efficiency.
3. **Build Customer Trust:** Transparent and reliable supply chains, facilitated by technologies like blockchain and IoT, can enhance customer confidence and loyalty.
4. **Foster Innovation:** By embracing emerging technologies, companies can develop innovative solutions that disrupt the market and create new opportunities.

3.6.3 Conclusion

Technology has become an indispensable tool for businesses seeking to achieve a competitive advantage in SCM. By harnessing the power of Big Data Analytics, AI, IoT, and blockchain, companies can create more efficient, responsive, and customer-centric supply chains. As technology continues to evolve, businesses must adapt and innovate to stay ahead of the curve.

3.7 The Role of Sustainable SCM in Competitive Advantage

In today's environmentally conscious world, sustainable SCM (see Figure 3.11) has emerged as a critical driver of competitive advantage. By adopting sustainable practices, businesses can minimise their environmental impact, enhance their brand reputation, and attract environmentally conscious consumers.

Sustainability transcends compliance and can differentiate brands. IKEA's renewable energy partnership in China and Eastern Europe powers 90% of its manufacturing facilities, reducing carbon emissions by 35% and securing long-term energy cost stability (IKEA, 2023). In Scandinavia, Ørsted sources 100% green energy for offshore wind turbine logistics, integrating cradle-to-cradle principles to minimise waste (Ørsted, 2024).

3.7.1 Key Components of Sustainable SCM

1 **Reducing Waste:** Implementing waste reduction strategies, such as recycling, composting, and zero-waste initiatives, can significantly reduce a company's environmental footprint. Adopting energy-efficient technologies, optimising transportation routes, and reducing packaging materials can help to lower carbon emissions and mitigate climate change. Sourcing materials from responsible suppliers who adhere to ethical and environmental standards can help to minimise the negative impacts of production.
2 **Social Sustainability:** Fair Labour practices, such as ensuring fair wages, safe working conditions, and ethical labour practices throughout the supply chain, can help build a positive brand image and attract socially responsible consumers.

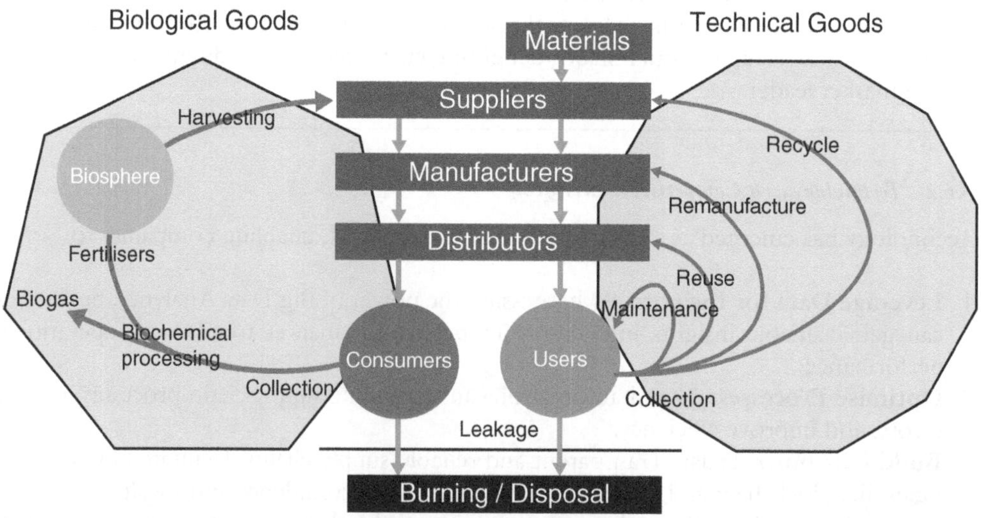

Figure 3.11 Sustainable Supply Chain.

3 **Community Development:** Engaging with local communities and supporting social initiatives can strengthen relationships and contribute to sustainable development.
4 **Economic Sustainability:** Long-term profitability means investing in sustainable practices that can lead to long-term cost savings and improved profitability.
5 **Risk Management:** Businesses can enhance their resilience and protect their bottom line by mitigating environmental and social risks.

3.7.2 The Benefits of Sustainable SCM

Consumers are increasingly seeking out brands that prioritise sustainability. By adopting sustainable practices, companies can differentiate themselves from competitors and build a strong, positive brand reputation. Customers who value sustainability are more likely to choose brands that align with their values. Companies can foster customer loyalty and drive repeat business by demonstrating a commitment to sustainability.

Sustainable practices, such as energy efficiency and waste reduction, can lead to significant cost savings. By identifying and addressing potential environmental and social risks, companies can protect their reputation and avoid costly legal and reputational damage. Adhering to environmental and social regulations can help companies avoid fines and penalties. Investing in sustainable innovation can lead to the development of new products and services that meet the needs of environmentally conscious consumers.

3.8 Key Sustainable SCM Practices

Sustainable SCM has evolved into a critical component of modern business strategy. By adopting sustainable practices, companies can minimise their environmental impact, enhance their brand reputation, and gain a competitive edge. This section delves into key sustainable SCM practices and explores how companies can implement them to achieve long-term success.

3.8.1 Green Procurement

Green procurement involves sourcing materials and services from suppliers who are committed to sustainable practices. By selecting suppliers that prioritise environmental and social responsibility, companies can reduce their overall environmental impact and enhance their brand reputation. When implementing green procurement, consider the following key factors:

1 **Supplier Selection:** Carefully evaluate suppliers based on their environmental and social performance.
2 **Performance Measurement:** Develop KPIs to monitor supplier sustainability performance.
3 **Collaboration:** Foster strong relationships with suppliers to encourage CI and innovation.

3.8.2 Eco-efficient Logistics

Eco-efficient logistics optimises transportation routes, reduces fuel consumption, and minimises emissions. By adopting sustainable logistics practices, companies can reduce their carbon footprint and improve their overall environmental performance. Key strategies for eco-efficient logistics include:

1 **Mode Selection:** Choose the most environmentally friendly mode of transport, such as rail or water, whenever possible.
2 **Route Optimisation:** Utilise advanced technologies, such as route optimisation software, to identify the most efficient routes and reduce fuel consumption.
3 **Consolidation:** Consolidate shipments to reduce the number of vehicles on the road and minimise emissions.
4 **Fuel Efficiency:** Invest in fuel-efficient vehicles and technologies to reduce fuel consumption.

3.8.3 Waste Minimisation

Waste minimisation involves reducing, reusing, and recycling materials throughout the supply chain. Companies can save costs, conserve resources, and reduce their environmental impact by implementing effective waste reduction strategies. Key waste minimisation practices include:

1 **Design for Environment:** Design products with sustainability in mind, minimising the use of materials and energy.
2 **Recycling and Reuse:** Implement recycling programmes and reuse materials whenever possible.
3 **Waste Reduction:** Reduce waste generation through efficient operations and lean manufacturing principles.

Case Study – Patagonia

Patagonia, a leading outdoor apparel company, is a prime example of a company that has successfully integrated sustainability into its business model. The company has a long history of environmental activism and has implemented a range of sustainable practices, including:

1 **Fair Trade Certified Sourcing:** Patagonia sources materials from Fair Trade Certified suppliers, ensuring fair wages and safe working conditions for workers.
2 **Recycled Materials:** The company uses recycled materials in its products, reducing the demand for virgin resources.
3 **Carbon Neutral Operations:** Patagonia has committed to carbon neutrality and offsets its carbon emissions through investments in renewable energy and carbon reduction projects.
4 **Repair and Reuse:** Patagonia encourages customers to repair and reuse their products, extending their lifespan and reducing waste.

By prioritising sustainability, Patagonia has built a loyal customer base and established itself as a leader in the outdoor apparel industry.

Case Study – Unilever's Sustainable SCM

Unilever, a multinational consumer goods company, is a leading example of a company that has successfully integrated sustainability into its supply chain. The company has implemented a range of sustainable practices, including:

1. **Sustainable Sourcing:** Unilever sources sustainable palm oil and other key ingredients.
2. **Water Stewardship:** The company has committed to reducing water usage and improving water quality.
3. **Climate Change Mitigation:** Unilever is working to reduce its carbon footprint and develop low-carbon products.
4. **Social Impact:** The company is committed to improving the livelihoods of smallholder farmers and promoting fair labour practices.

By adopting these sustainable practices, Unilever has strengthened its brand reputation and attracted environmentally conscious consumers.

3.8.4 The Benefits of Sustainable SCM

Sustainable SCM offers numerous benefits for businesses, including:

1. **Enhanced Brand Reputation:** By demonstrating a commitment to sustainability, companies can enhance their brand reputation and attract environmentally conscious consumers.
2. **Increased Customer Loyalty:** Customers who value sustainability are more likely to choose brands that align with their values.
3. **Reduced Costs:** Sustainable practices, such as energy efficiency and waste reduction, can lead to significant cost savings.
4. **Risk Mitigation:** By identifying and addressing potential environmental and social risks, companies can protect their reputation and avoid costly legal and reputational damage.
5. **Innovation and Competitive Advantage:** Investing in sustainable innovation can lead to the development of new products and services that meet the needs of environmentally conscious consumers.

3.8.5 The Future of Sustainable SCM

As consumer awareness of sustainability grows, the demand for sustainable products and services will continue to increase. Companies that fail to adopt sustainable practices risk losing market share and damaging their reputation. By embracing sustainable SCM, businesses can not only contribute to a more sustainable future but also gain a competitive edge.

Looking ahead, future-focused SCM strategies will prioritise climate resilience, traceability, and closed-loop innovation. Firms will increasingly be expected to report not only on carbon emissions but also on biodiversity impacts, water use, and social equity outcomes. Regulators in the European Union, Australia, and Canada are leading the way with mandatory ESG disclosures that influence GSC compliance. This is often referred to as the "Triple Bottom Line".

Additionally, consumer-facing technologies such as QR code tracking and digital product passports are enabling buyers to verify origin, labour conditions, and carbon intensity at the POS. Businesses that invest in traceable, low-impact supply networks will be well-positioned to attract ethically conscious consumers and institutional investors. Ultimately, sustainability will shift from being a reputational add-on to a central pillar of supply chain competitiveness.

3.8.6 Conclusion

By integrating cost leadership, differentiation, strategic alignment, technology, and sustainability, SCM becomes a multi-dimensional source of competitive advantage. These interrelated levers are not simply operational tools, but strategic enablers that shape how organisations respond to dynamic market demands, global disruptions, and evolving stakeholder expectations.

The case studies presented throughout this chapter highlight how businesses across the world are innovating within their supply chains to reduce costs, increase speed to market, deliver unique customer experiences, and meet pressing environmental and social goals. Whether through AI-enabled predictive analytics, blockchain traceability, agile restocking, or renewable energy-powered logistics, these organisations demonstrate that SCM excellence can serve as a linchpin for long-term success.

Furthermore, as supply chains become more global and interdependent, the ability to orchestrate these competitive levers across cultural, regulatory, and geopolitical contexts will define the next generation of industry leaders. Companies that fail to integrate these principles risk falling behind in an era where supply chain agility, visibility, and accountability are not optional but expected.

In the next chapter, we explore the complexities of managing truly GSCs, focusing on resilience, regulatory compliance, and the strategic importance of building adaptive, risk-resilient supply networks.

Q&A Section

Here is a short quiz to test your knowledge. The answers are provided in Appendix C.

1 What are the two primary strategies for achieving competitive advantage that the document centres on?
2 Name three key practices that a company would use in its supply chain to achieve Cost Leadership.
3 What are three ways a company can use its supply chain to achieve Differentiation?
4 According to the document, what are the two strategic enablers that amplify competitive advantage in SCM?
5 What are Lean Supply Chain Practices designed to eliminate, and what is one example technique mentioned?
6 The document mentions that an agile supply chain, drawing real-time POS data to enable bi-weekly restocking and trend-driven design launches, is characteristic of which company?

7 What three factors make up the "Triple Bottom Line" that is increasingly driving business strategy?
8 How does Blockchain technology strengthen SCM?
9 Give two examples of how Process Optimisation can be achieved in SCM to support cost leadership.
10 What is the central aim of Strategic Alignment in SCM?

4 Global Supply Chains

Learning Outcomes

By the end of this chapter, learners will be able to:

- Identify structural and operational challenges unique to GSCs.
- Assess the impact of regulatory, cultural, and logistical factors on international operations.
- Design a high-level contingency for a cross-border disruption (e.g., port closure).
- Compare options for regionalisation vs global scale in a given scenario.
- Evaluate trade-offs between cost, speed, and geopolitical risk in network design.

4.1 Introduction

GSCs connect manufacturers, suppliers, logistics providers, and customers across multiple continents, forming the backbone of modern commerce (see Figure 4.1). By spreading sourcing and production globally, firms can tap into lower-cost labour, specialised skills, and new markets, improving efficiency and profitability. However, global networks also introduce complexity: products now travel through many countries and regulations, increasing exposure to disruptions, compliance challenges, and cultural differences.

The global nature of these chains means that a problem in one region (such as a natural disaster or political crisis) can have cascading effects worldwide. For example, the 2011 earthquake and tsunami in Japan, which caused widespread factory shutdowns, immediately impacted automotive and electronics supply chains around the world. Likewise, the COVID-19 pandemic underscored this interconnection: mass lockdowns halted production in key hubs and caused a worldwide ripple effect on inventory shortages and logistics delays. Today's multinational companies must therefore manage global risks proactively while reaping the rewards of international specialisation.

4.1.1 Key Advantages of GSCs

One of the primary advantages of GSCs is the ability to source materials and components from regions where labour costs are lower or where unique resources are abundant. For example, textile manufacturers may procure cotton from India or Egypt due to the

DOI: 10.4324/9781003740568-4

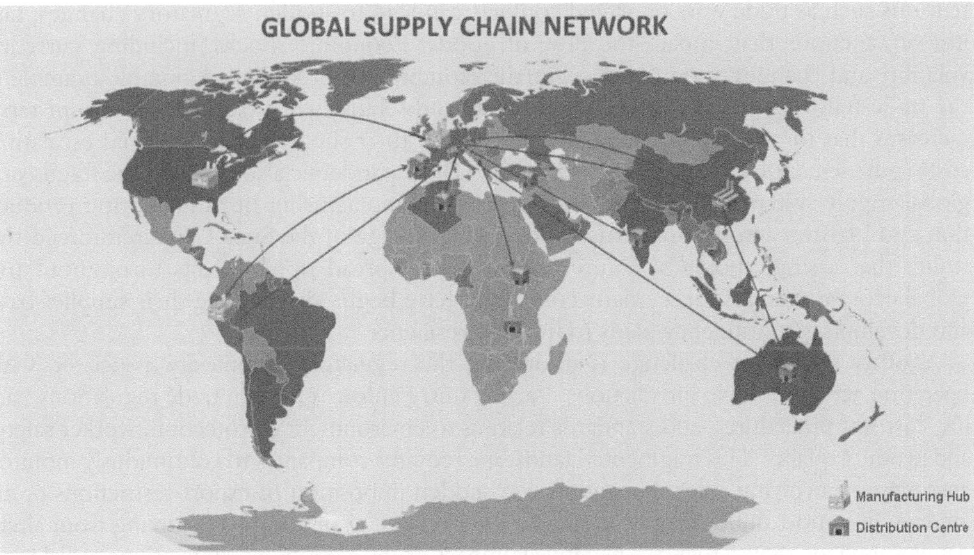

Figure 4.1 Global Supply Chains.

favourable climate and established agricultural infrastructure. At the same time, electronics firms may source rare earth metals from China, which dominates global production. This geographical flexibility allows companies to manage input costs effectively and maintain competitive pricing.

GSCs also grant firms access to specialised expertise and advanced technologies that are often concentrated in specific countries. Taiwan, for instance, is a global leader in semiconductor manufacturing, while Germany is renowned for its precision engineering and automotive innovation. By tapping into these localised capabilities, companies can incorporate cutting-edge components and processes into their products, enhancing quality, performance, and overall market competitiveness.

Another strategic benefit is the opportunity to reach new customer markets by positioning production closer to major demand centres. Establishing manufacturing or distribution hubs in key regions such as North America, Europe, or Southeast Asia not only shortens delivery times but also helps companies better understand and respond to local consumer preferences. This proximity improves service levels, fosters customer loyalty, and can also reduce tariffs or import duties when producing within trade zones.

Finally, GSCs enable companies to spread their sourcing activities across multiple regions, thereby diversifying risk. Relying on a single country or supplier creates vulnerability to disruptions such as natural disasters, political instability, or trade restrictions. By developing a multi-sourced network, organisations can respond more flexibly to unforeseen events, ensuring continuity of supply and maintaining resilience in the face of global uncertainty.

4.1.2 Key Challenges of GSCs

Managing international supply networks introduces a range of complex challenges, chief among them being supply chain disruptions. Natural disasters such as earthquakes, floods, and hurricanes can abruptly halt production or transportation in key regions. Geopolitical tensions such as trade wars or armed conflicts can lead to sudden regulatory changes, tariffs, or sanctions that impact the flow of goods. Economic shocks, including currency volatility and changes in trade policy, further compound these risks. A notable example is the trade tensions between the United States and China, which resulted in abrupt tariff increases that forced many companies to redesign their supply chains to avoid escalating costs (pdfs.semanticscholar, 2022). The COVID-19 pandemic also revealed the fragility of global supply systems, with lockdowns in major manufacturing hubs disrupting production and logistics across continents. The 2021 blockage of the Suez Canal reinforced the reality that a single point of failure can have widespread ripple effects throughout the global economy. In response, many companies have begun diversifying their supplier base and developing contingency plans to increase resilience.

Another significant challenge is navigating the regulatory complexity associated with operating across multiple jurisdictions. Each country enforces its own trade regulations, tariffs, customs procedures, and standards relating to environmental protection, worker safety, and product quality. This fragmented landscape requires companies to continuously monitor and adapt to evolving rules. For instance, a sudden imposition of export restrictions or an increase in import duties may necessitate a swift rerouting of goods or sourcing from alternative suppliers, moves that can negatively impact profit margins and operational efficiency. Furthermore, compliance with differing regulatory frameworks, such as food safety standards in the European Union, chemical regulations in the United States, or labour protections in Southeast Asia, demands tailored approaches in each market. Companies must invest in robust compliance teams and legal advisory functions to manage this complexity effectively.

Cultural and linguistic differences further complicate the management of GSCs. Engaging with suppliers, customers, and partners across different countries entails navigating diverse languages, business etiquette, and societal norms. Communication styles vary significantly: while some cultures value direct and explicit communication, others rely heavily on context and implicit understanding, which can easily lead to misinterpretations if not carefully managed. Decision-making processes also differ, where some organisations prioritise swift, data-driven decisions, while others may prefer a consensus-based approach that involves extended consultation and relationship-building. These differences can affect negotiations, contract terms, and conflict resolution. To bridge these cultural gaps, successful global firms invest in cross-cultural training for their managers and often rely on local representatives or intermediaries who possess deep knowledge of regional customs and expectations. Such efforts enhance collaboration, reduce friction, and build stronger international partnerships.

Case Study – Automotive Industry

Major automakers like Toyota and Volkswagen illustrate both the strengths and vulnerabilities of global chains. Toyota's famous JIT system relies on precisely timed deliveries of parts from suppliers in Asia, North America, and Europe. This system drives efficiency but became a liability when the 2011 Japan earthquake hit. Toyota subsequently built extra SS for critical components and diversified suppliers geographically to improve resilience. Similarly, during the COVID-19 crisis, many automakers realised the risk of over-concentration in one region (e.g., China or Mexico) and have since moved some production to alternative sites.

4.1.3 The Role of Technology in Managing GSCs

Technology has played a crucial role in enabling the growth and complexity of GSCs. Some of the key technologies that are transforming the way companies manage their supply chains include:

1. **Big Data Analytics and AI:** By analysing large datasets from suppliers, logistics, and sales, companies can identify patterns and predict demand shifts. Predictive analytics help companies adjust inventory proactively, reducing stockouts or overstocks (for example, by forecasting holiday demand spikes). AI-powered platforms automate routine planning tasks, optimise transport routes in real time, and quickly identify anomalies (such as unusual supplier delays). Studies show AI-driven forecasting can improve service levels while lowering costs (Ghosh, 2022).
2. **IoT:** IoT devices (sensors, trackers) provide real-time location and condition data on goods and vehicles. For instance, refrigerated containers with IoT sensors can report temperature and location throughout a transoceanic voyage, alerting managers immediately if a delay is likely. This visibility greatly improves responsiveness: companies can reroute shipments or contact customers pre-emptively when they see an emerging delay.
3. **Blockchain and Distributed Ledgers:** Blockchain provides a secure, tamper-proof ledger for recording transactions and product movements. This technology enables end-to-end traceability across complex, multi-party networks. A prominent example is IBM and Maersk's TradeLens platform, which uses blockchain to share shipping information among carriers, ports, and customs. TradeLens has demonstrated how a shared ledger reduces paperwork, speeds up documentation, and increases trust between global partners.
4. **Advanced SCM Software:** Integrated SCM platforms can orchestrate planning and execution across regions, incorporating real-time data from all partners. Such software automates order processing, manages multimodal transportation, and integrates supplier networks into one system. By using these tools, companies like Amazon and Walmart optimise inventory distribution across their global networks, ensuring products are replenished at the right time and place (Kamath, 2018).

Case Study – Technology in Action

Many logistics and industrial firms, including FedEx and DHL, have adopted integrated IoT-enabled sensor tracking and AI analytics in recent years. For example:

DHL's SmartSensor technology monitors temperature, humidity, and location of sensitive shipments in real time, using AI-driven insights to optimise routing, reduce delays, and improve risk management (Analytics Insights, 2025; Three Group Solutions, 2025).

FedEx has publicly detailed its AI-powered predictive platforms that combine live sensor data with ML models to anticipate disruptions and reroute shipments proactively, achieving reductions in delivery delays (AI Expert Network, 2024).

Walmart, through its collaboration with IBM's Food Trust platform, enables full traceability of produce like mangoes and pork. By scanning packaging QR codes, consumers and regulators can trace the product's journey to source farms. This system has reduced recall response times from around a week to just seconds (Ellahi et al., 2023).

Carrefour, working with IBM, has implemented blockchain traceability for items such as milk, eggs, and salmon, allowing end-to-end transparency via consumer-scannable QR codes in European markets (Westerlund et al., 2021).

4.1.4 *Building Resilient GSCs*

Companies should adopt a proactive approach to building resilience to mitigate the risks associated with GSCs. To withstand the uncertainties of international trade, the leading organisations employ a variety of resilience strategies.

4.1.4.1 *Supplier Diversification*

Rather than relying on a single supplier or country, successful companies source from multiple geographies. This spreads risk: if one region faces a disruption (e.g., a factory fire or strike), an alternate supplier elsewhere can fill the gap. Global technology firms often have parallel factories in Asia and Europe for key components. Diversification can also improve leverage in negotiations, as suppliers compete for business.

4.1.4.2 *Near-shoring and Local Sourcing*

Some companies shift production closer to their major markets. By manufacturing in nearby countries or even domestically (near-shoring), companies reduce long-distance transit risks, tariffs, and lead times. For example, many American companies have opened plants in Mexico or the United States to serve North American customers more quickly. In response to supply chain strains, the European Union is encouraging "reshoring" industries to rebuild critical capacity within Europe. Local sourcing can also improve compliance with local regulations and strengthen relationships with regional partners.

4.1.4.3 *Strategic Inventory Buffers*

Traditionally, firms kept minimal inventory to lower costs. Now, many are holding extra "safety stock" of essential parts or finished goods to guard against stockouts. For instance, an automotive original equipment manufacturer might maintain a buffer inventory of semiconductors after experiencing chip shortages. Advanced analytics help determine the optimal buffer size: just enough to cover potential delays without incurring excessive carrying costs. This balance is critical; too much inventory ties up capital, but too little leaves the chain brittle and exposed.

4.1.4.4 *Collaborative Partnerships*

Building trust and communication with suppliers and logistics partners is vital. Companies share forecasts and production plans with key suppliers and engage in joint problem-solving. For example, a consumer electronics firm may collaborate with its PCB supplier to co-invest in capacity upgrades, ensuring supply continuity. Shared performance metrics and regular supply chain reviews (often called Supplier Relationship Management, or SRM) create transparency. Collaborative networks can also spur innovation (e.g., joint R&D on new packaging methods to reduce costs).

4.1.4.5 *Leveraging Technology for Resilience*

All the tools mentioned above play a role in agility. Real-time data allows a company to detect a disruption early and execute contingency plans (for instance, rerouting a shipment when a port closure is detected). AI can run "what-if" simulations to test how a disruption in one country would affect the entire network. In summary, digital systems provide visibility and early warning, enabling faster recovery from disruptions.

4.1.5 *Case Studies*

4.1.5.1 *Suez Canal Disruption and Diversification of Shipping Routes*

The blockage of the Suez Canal during the *Ever Given* incident illustrated global vulnerability to single-route disruptions. Many shipping operators began rerouting vessels around the Cape of Good Hope, representing a shift to alternate transit corridors to maintain supply continuity. Business analyses and logistics reports affirm that such route diversification became a common resilience tactic among global firms post-2021 (FreightAmigo, 2025).

4.1.5.2 *Shift of Production from China to Southeast Asia during COVID-19*

Apparel production faced severe concentration risk during COVID-19 when major manufacturing countries shut down. Many companies responded by shifting production from China to alternative sourcing locations such as Bangladesh and Vietnam, diversifying risk and maintaining continuity. This realignment is well documented in studies analysing the impact of the pandemic on apparel supply chains (Castañeda-Navarrete et al., 2021).

4.1.5.3 *Adoption of 3D Printing for Accelerating Response to Fashion Trends*

The fashion industry has increasingly adopted 3D printing and digital prototyping technologies to reduce lead times, support rapid design iteration, and localise production closer to demand. Research and industry reports document how brands are using 3D modelling and printing to prototype items rapidly, enhancing time-to-market agility (Anamika, 2025).

4.1.6 *International and Regional Perspectives*

GSCs play out differently across regions. Asia remains the manufacturing hub: China, Japan, South Korea, and Southeast Asian nations supply a large share of electronics, textiles, and consumer goods. Europe excels in high-precision engineering (automotive, aerospace) and strongly emphasises regulatory compliance and sustainability; the EU's Green Deal and Circular Economy initiatives are pushing companies to reduce carbon footprints and improve labour standards in their chains. North America focuses on high-tech and agricultural products; recent policies (like the USMCA trade pact and domestic manufacturing incentives) are encouraging more onshoring.

In Latin America and Africa, many industries are still building local capacity; these regions often export raw materials (minerals, crops) and import finished goods. However, regional trade agreements, such as AfCFTA in Africa, aim to integrate local markets and grow intra-regional supply chains. Because of these differences, a strategy that works in one context may not transfer directly to another. For instance, a company expanding in Asia might prioritise low-cost production and long supplier networks, while the same organisation in Europe might emphasise automation and compliance from the start. A truly GSC manager must understand these international nuances and adapt practices accordingly.

4.1.7 Summary

GSCs offer immense benefits, efficiency, specialisation, and market reach, while also requiring sophisticated management of risk and complexity. Disruptions can now arise from any corner of the world, so organisations must blend diversification, technology, and collaboration to build resilient networks. Advances in AI, IoT, and blockchain are empowering supply chain professionals with greater visibility and agility. By studying real-world cases and continuously learning from global events, managers can design supply chains that not only survive shocks but also seize international growth opportunities.

4.2 Structural and Operational Challenges

Global supply networks are distinguished by their scale, geographic dispersion, and interdependence. These characteristics create efficiencies through specialisation and scale, but also transmit shocks rapidly across tiers. The principal operational challenges are supply chain disruptions, regulatory complexity, and cultural differences (see Table 4.1).

4.2.1 Supply Chain Disruptions

The efficiency afforded by tightly coupled global networks often comes at the cost of vulnerability. Natural disasters (earthquakes, floods, hurricanes), geopolitical events (trade disputes, sanctions, armed conflict), and exogenous economic shocks (currency crises,

Table 4.1 Global Supply Chain Risk Matrix

	Supply Disruption Risks			
	Stakeholder Crisis	*Strategic Crisis*	*Operational Crisis*	*Financial Crisis*
Organisational Signals	• Ownership changes in the supplier company and the successor has no interest in running the business per se; • High employee turnover in the supplier company; • Supplier's order books	• Lack of information regarding supplier's inventory; • Higher prices are voluntarily paid to keep the supplier alive; • Supply is insecure; • No disaster planning at key suppliers	• Frequent obsolescence of parts; • Plant fire/plant shut down or any similar unprecedented situation; • Loss of volume/product mix flexibility; • Capacity issues; • No production stock available for ramp-up phase	• Lack of information regarding supplier's insurance (ex ante contract signing); • Supplier request for reduced payment terms, factoring etc; • Profit slump (although it is not always transparent); • Invitation to talks with banks (*it is already too late by then*)

(*Continued*)

Table 4.1 (Continued)

	Supply Disruption Risks			
	Stakeholder Crisis	*Strategic Crisis*	*Operational Crisis*	*Financial Crisis*
Environmental Signals	• Changes in Political landscape; • Changes in regulations; • Changing import/ export customs rules; • Natural hazards; • Labour/ transportation strikes	• Disruptions via technology levers	• External disturbances like political movements causing disruption in the supply chain	• Factors like economic crisis that impact each and every member of the supply chain causing disruptions in the flow of materials, information and/ or money (*for example, the USA imposing broad tariffs*)
Network-related Signals	• Supplier is (over) dominated by competitors	• Single/sole sourcing market conditions; • Supplier is highly dependent on a handful of suppliers and/or customers	• Lack of flexibility in the suppliers' supply network; • Frequent stock-outs within the network	• A major player within the supply chain is facing financial distress

rapid tariff changes) can interrupt production and logistics flows with little warning. The aggregation in output at regional clusters, an outcome of agglomeration economics, means a localised disruption can create global bottlenecks.

Case Study – Automotive Sector Resilience

The 2011 Tohoku earthquake and tsunami in Japan exposed the fragility of JIT systems that depended on single-source suppliers for specialised components. Global automakers suffered widespread part shortages; in response, manufacturers instituted multi-tier supply-mapping initiatives, increased SSs for critical parts, and invested in secondary supplier development in alternative geographies. This pragmatic shift illustrates how catastrophic events can convert abstract risk assessments into concrete supply chain redesigns.

Case Study – Maritime Chokepoints

The blockage of the Suez Canal in 2021 by a grounded container ship disrupted flows between Asia and Europe, creating immediate port congestion and longer transit times. Several carriers temporarily rerouted vessels around the Cape of Good Hope, increasing voyage lengths and freight costs. The episode prompted many organisations to reassess their modal and route-selection strategies and to formalise contingency routing in continuity plans.

Case Study – Pandemic Lockdowns

The COVID-19 pandemic underscored the interconnectedness and vulnerability of GSCs. Widespread lockdowns and restrictions disrupted operations and logistics on a global scale, leading companies to reassess their dependence on single suppliers or regions. Many companies have since implemented strategies to mitigate similar future disruptions, including diversifying suppliers, building local sources, and establishing contingency plans (Ivanov & Das, 2020).

4.2.2 Regulatory Complexity

Managing operations across multiple jurisdictions requires continuous adaptation to a mosaic of tariffs, customs procedures, product standards, and emerging sustainability regulations. Regulatory changes can be sudden and material; export controls, anti-dumping duties, and sanctions regimes can force immediate supplier substitution or reconfiguration of logistics, often at substantial cost.

Adapting to regulatory changes requires companies to maintain up-to-date knowledge of local laws, establish robust compliance frameworks, and often work closely with regulatory bodies. For instance, changing tariffs or new trade restrictions can alter sourcing and distribution decisions, impacting profitability and competitive positioning (Schneider-Petsinger, 2021).

Case Study – Food Retail Traceability

European food safety regulation and heightened consumer expectations have compelled multinational retailers to invest in traceability systems. Several chains piloted distributed-ledger (blockchain) solutions to capture immutable provenance data for fresh produce; when combined with rapid analytics, these systems shortened recall times and improved regulatory reporting.

4.2.3 Cultural and Linguistic Differences

Cross-border operations require sensitivity to diverse business norms, communication styles, and decision-making protocols. Misunderstandings can create inefficiencies, misaligned expectations, and even contract disputes. Effective global managers cultivate cultural literacy, appoint local leadership, and institutionalise governance mechanisms that reconcile differing business practices.

1. **Communication Styles:** Cultures vary in their communication preferences; some cultures value direct communication, while others adopt a more diplomatic or indirect approach. Misunderstandings can arise when these preferences clash.
2. **Business Practices:** Business protocols differ widely, from how meetings are conducted to expectations around contracts and agreements. For example, while Western cultures

may prioritise speed and directness in negotiations, other cultures may value relationship-building and consensus. It is absolutely critical that companies that operate globally familiarise themselves with the local practices and protocols.

3 **Decision-Making Processes:** Decision-making approaches also vary, with some cultures favouring individual decision-making, while others prefer collaborative or hierarchical methods.

Because of these differences, a strategy that works in one context may not transfer directly to another. For instance, a company expanding in Asia might prioritise low-cost production and long supplier networks, while the same organisation in Europe might emphasise automation and compliance from the start. A truly GSC manager must understand these international nuances and adapt practices accordingly. Companies can bridge these cultural gaps by investing in cross-cultural training, hiring local experts, and promoting open communication channels to better understand and adapt to regional nuances. Recognising and respecting cultural differences not only improves collaboration but also builds trust among global partners (Basu, 2023).

4.3 Conclusion

GSCs offer immense benefits, efficiency, specialisation, and market reach, but also require sophisticated management of risk and complexity. Disruptions can now arise from any corner of the world, so companies must blend diversification, technology, and collaboration to build resilient networks. Advances in AI, IoT, and blockchain are empowering supply chain professionals with greater visibility and agility. By studying real-world cases and continuously learning from global events, managers can design supply chains that not only survive shocks but also seize international growth opportunities.

Q&A Section

Here is a short quiz to test your knowledge. The answers are provided in Appendix C.

1 What is a GSC?
2 What are the primary sources of disruption in GSCs?
3 How did the COVID-19 pandemic impact GSCs?
4 Why is regulatory compliance challenging in GSCs?
5 What cultural differences can impact GSCs?
6 How does big data analytics support GSCs?
7 What is the role of blockchain in supply chains?
8 Why is supplier diversification important for resilience?
9 What is the advantage of localisation or near-shoring?
10 How do collaborative partnerships benefit SCM?

5 Demand Forecasting and Planning

Learning Outcomes

By the end of this chapter, learners will be able to:

- Explain the role of demand forecasting and planning in SCM.
- Differentiate between qualitative and quantitative forecasting methods and their uses.
- Apply basic forecasting technique(s) to a simple demand dataset and interpret accuracy metrics.
- Identify common sources of forecast error and propose mitigation tactics.
- Recommend how advanced analytics (ML/SCA) could improve forecast performance for a sample product.

5.1 Introduction

Demand forecasting and planning are foundational elements of SCM, enabling organisations to anticipate market demand, allocate resources effectively, and streamline operations. By accurately predicting customer needs, businesses can avoid excess inventory, reduce stockouts, and optimise production schedules. Integrating demand forecasting with planning aligns supply chain processes with strategic objectives, enhancing operational efficiency and customer satisfaction.

This chapter examines the key methodologies used in demand forecasting – qualitative and quantitative techniques – and discusses the role of technology in refining these processes. Furthermore, it explores the critical importance of demand planning and addresses the challenges organisations face when forecasting demand in an increasingly dynamic market. By blending theoretical perspectives with practical insights, this chapter underscores the strategic value of demand forecasting and planning in modern SCM.

5.2 The Role of Demand Forecasting in SCM

Demand forecasting serves as the cornerstone of effective SCM. When organisations can predict future demand accurately, they can align inventory, production, and procurement decisions with market needs. This coordination improves resource allocation, reduces waste, and enhances customer satisfaction. For example, a multinational consumer goods

DOI: 10.4324/9781003740568-5

company with production facilities in Asia and DCs in Europe can use demand forecasts to synchronise production runs across factories, ensuring products are produced in the right quantities and delivered to each region on time. Such coordinated forecasting allows the company to minimise transportation costs and maintain high service levels globally.

An illustrative case is a global technology manufacturer that consolidated demand data from customers in the Americas, Europe, and Asia. By centralising and analysing sales and web-traffic data, the company generated more reliable forecasts, improving production planning and reducing lead times in its Asian and European factories (Destino et al., 2022) (dotData, 2022). The result was smoother operations and significantly fewer costly stock-outs. In another example, a FMCG company integrated forecasting across its entire supply chain, enabling demand signals in one region (like rising demand for beverage products in Africa) to adjust production runs in another (such as bottling lines in Europe). This global coordination improved efficiency and responsiveness to customer needs.

5.3 The Importance of Accurate Demand Forecasting

Accurate demand forecasting has a profound impact on supply chain performance. When forecasts closely match actual demand, organisations maintain inventory levels that align with market needs. This minimises holding costs, such as warehousing, insurance, and obsolescence, and frees up working capital (Manokhin, 2025). Industry studies indicate that even a 10–20% improvement in forecast accuracy can reduce inventory costs by roughly 5% (Manokhin, 2025) (see Figure 5.1). Small gains in accuracy thus translate to significant cost savings.

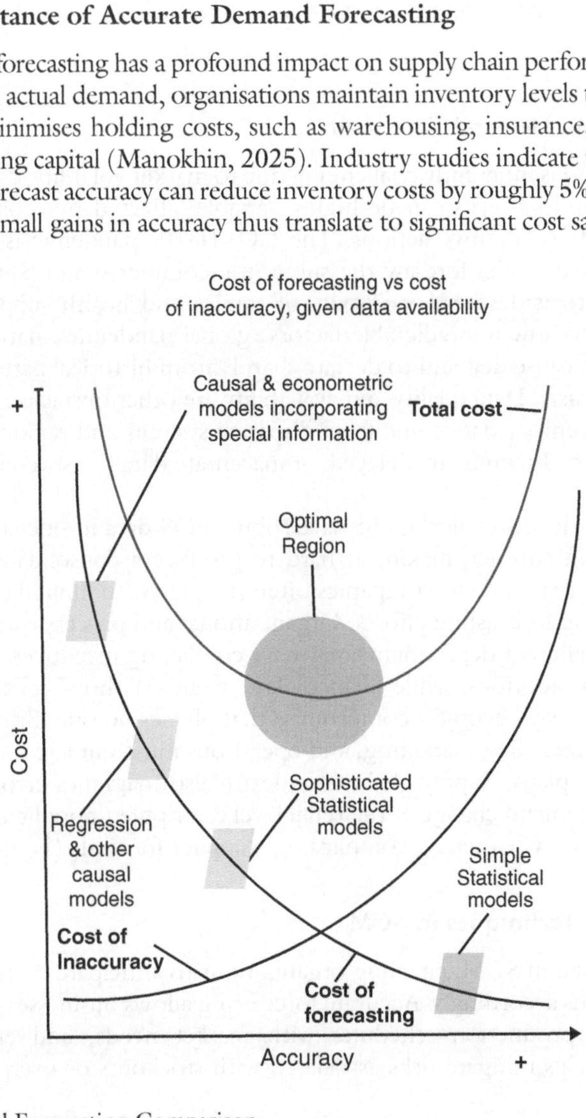

Figure 5.1 Demand Forecasting Comparison.

Better forecasts also protect revenue and customer relationships. Stockouts, when demand exceeds forecasted supply, cause lost sales and unhappy customers. ***Harvard Business Review*** notes that typical stockouts result in about 4% of sales being lost on average (Manokhin, 2025). By contrast, companies with highly accurate forecasts can capture those sales. McKinsey research suggests that using AI-based forecasting can reduce product unavailability (and lost sales) by up to 65% (Manokhin, 2025). In practical terms, this means more products are on shelves when customers want them, boosting service levels and loyalty.

Improved forecasting also reduces the need for expensive last-minute fixes. Expedited shipments or overproduction may result in companies paying premiums. By contrast, a precise forecast allows production and procurement to proceed smoothly. For example, an automotive manufacturer that implemented AI-driven forecasting saw its forecast errors cut by 50%, saving over USD 10 million annually in inventory costs (dotData, 2022). Globally, the scale of forecasting errors is enormous: in 2023, retailers lost an estimated USD 1.77 trillion due to inventory distortions (a combination of overstocks and stockouts) (Manokhin, 2025). Reducing forecast errors is directly linked to financial performance.

5.4 Challenges in Demand Forecasting

Forecasting demand is inherently challenging due to market volatility, data limitations, and complexity. Demand patterns can be highly variable, affected by economic cycles, consumer trends, and competitive actions. The COVID-19 pandemic is a prime example: almost no predictive model foresaw the surge in e-commerce and panic buying in early 2020, which led to widespread stockouts of staples and health supplies. Such sudden shocks demonstrate how unpredictable factors (global pandemics, natural disasters, geopolitical crises) can cause demand to deviate sharply from historical patterns, undermining even the best forecasts. Data quality and availability are other obstacles. In many organisations, sales and inventory data come from disparate systems and regions, sometimes with inconsistent formats. Incomplete, delayed, or inaccurate data can severely degrade forecast accuracy.

For example, a global retailer might have robust POS data in one country but rely on manual estimates in another, making it hard to produce a consolidated global forecast. Especially in emerging markets, companies often struggle with limited data infrastructure, further complicating forecasting efforts. Organisational and process issues further complicate forecasting. Different departments may have conflicting incentives: marketing may be optimistic about promotions, while finance plays it safe. Without effective collaboration, the official forecast may become a compromise that pleases no one. Bridging these gaps is an ongoing challenge; sales, marketing, and operations must validate forecasts before they become actionable plans. Supply chain complexity also magnifies errors: in multi-tiered networks, a small demand change at the retail level can ripple unpredictably upstream (the "Bullwhip Effect" see Chapter 2), complicating supplier forecasts (Figure 5.2).

5.5 Forecasting Techniques in SCM

Forecasting is pivotal in SCM, enabling organisations to anticipate customer demand and plan their operations accordingly. Accurate forecasting allows businesses to optimise inventory levels, align production schedules with market needs, and enhance efficiency. Forecasting also helps mitigate risks associated with stockouts or overproduction, which

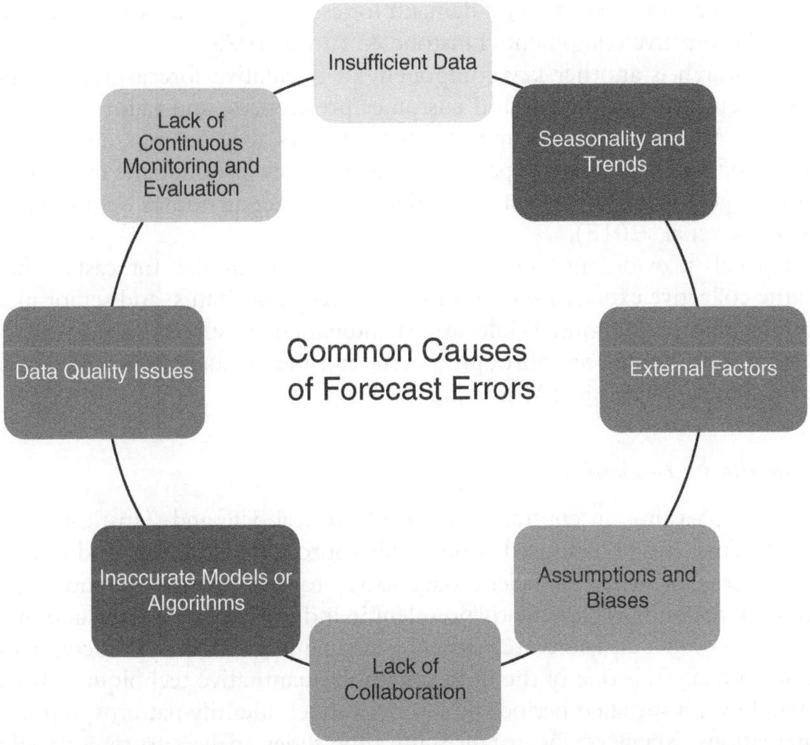

Figure 5.2 Common Causes of Forecast Error.

can erode profitability and damage customer satisfaction. While no forecasting method guarantees complete accuracy, a well-executed approach combines quantitative precision with qualitative insight to create robust and adaptable predictions.

Broadly, forecasting techniques can be categorised into two primary approaches: qualitative and quantitative. Each approach offers unique strengths and is selected based on the availability of data, the nature of the market, and the specific goals of the organisation. Increasingly, companies are adopting hybrid methods integrating qualitative and quantitative approaches to harness the best of both worlds.

5.5.1 *Qualitative Forecasting*

Qualitative forecasting relies on expert judgement, experience, and market insights rather than hard data or statistical models. This approach is particularly valuable when historical data is unavailable or unreliable, such as when launching a new product, entering an emerging market, or navigating a disruptive economic environment. The flexibility of qualitative methods allows organisations to adapt quickly to changing circumstances and incorporate real-time insights.

One widely used qualitative technique is the Delphi method, a structured approach that gathers input from a panel of experts through multiple rounds of surveys. The goal is to achieve a consensus on future demand, especially in uncertain or unfamiliar markets. For example, in the early stages of the COVID-19 pandemic, companies used Delphi panels to estimate the impact of lockdowns on demand for essential goods, such as medical supplies and personal protective equipment (Linstone & Turoff, 1975).

Market research is another key component of qualitative forecasting. Businesses can identify emerging trends, understand customer preferences, and tailor their offerings by gathering data directly from consumers through surveys, focus groups, and interviews. For example, a food and beverage company introducing a new product line may conduct focus groups to gauge consumer interest and refine its product attributes before full-scale production (Kotler et al., 2015).

Expert panels provide another valuable source of qualitative forecasts. These panels leverage the collective experience of industry experts, consultants, and senior managers to develop informed predictions. While expert judgement is subjective and susceptible to biases, structuring the process through diverse and independent perspectives can yield a balanced and reliable forecast (Armstrong, 2001).

5.5.2 Quantitative Forecasting

Quantitative forecasting, in contrast, relies on historical data and statistical techniques to generate objective and precise predictions. This approach is ideal for products with stable demand patterns or when sufficient data exists to identify trends and relationships. Quantitative forecasting is particularly prevalent in industries such as retail and manufacturing, where data-driven decisions are critical to maintaining efficiency and competitiveness.

Time series analysis is one of the most common quantitative techniques. By examining past demand over a specified period, time series models identify patterns, trends, and seasonal fluctuations. Retailers, for instance, use time series analysis to forecast sales during holiday seasons, ensuring adequate stock levels for peak periods (Makridakis et al., 1998).

Regression analysis explores the relationship between demand and influencing variables, such as price, advertising, or economic indicators. For example, an automotive company may use regression models to predict vehicle sales based on changes in fuel prices or consumer income. These models help businesses understand how external factors impact demand, enabling them to adjust pricing strategies or production volumes accordingly (Chopra & Meindl, 2024).

Econometric modelling combines economic theory with statistical techniques to analyse complex demand drivers. For instance, econometric models can assess the impact of inflation or interest rate fluctuations on consumer spending patterns. This approach provides a nuanced understanding of the macroeconomic factors influencing demand, making it valuable for long-term strategic planning (Gujarati & Proter, 2009).

While quantitative forecasting methods offer consistency and accuracy, they are less effective in predicting abrupt shifts in demand or unprecedented events. For example, traditional models struggled to account for the sudden surge in online shopping during the COVID-19 pandemic, highlighting the need for adaptive and flexible forecasting approaches.

5.5.3 Hybrid Forecasting Methods

In today's dynamic business environment, many organisations adopt hybrid forecasting methods that combine qualitative and quantitative approaches. This integration leverages the strengths of both techniques, enabling businesses to create more comprehensive and adaptive forecasts.

Hybrid forecasting often begins with a quantitative baseline, such as a time series analysis or regression model. This data-driven forecast is refined using qualitative insights from market research or expert panels. For instance, a consumer electronics company launching a new product might use historical sales data from similar products to establish an initial forecast, which is adjusted based on market surveys and competitor analysis.

The hybrid approach is particularly effective in industries where demand is influenced by unpredictable factors, such as technological innovation or shifting consumer preferences. By blending statistical accuracy with contextual understanding, hybrid methods help organisations navigate complexity and uncertainty (Chopra & Meindl, 2024).

5.6 The Importance of Accurate Demand Forecasting

Accurate demand forecasting has a profound impact on supply chain performance (see Figure 5.3). When forecasts closely match actual demand, organisations maintain inventory levels that align with market needs. This minimises holding costs, such as warehousing, insurance, and obsolescence, and frees up working capital (Manokhin, 2025). Industry studies indicate that even a 10–20% improvement in forecast accuracy can reduce inventory costs by roughly 5% (Manokhin, 2025). Small gains in accuracy translate to significant cost savings. Better forecasts also protect revenue and customer relationships.

Stockouts, when demand exceeds forecasted supply, cause lost sales and unhappy customers. *Harvard Business Review* notes that typical stockouts result in about 4% of sales being lost on average (Manokhin, 2025). By contrast, companies with highly accurate forecasts can capture those sales. McKinsey research suggests that using AI-based forecasting can reduce product unavailability (and lost sales) by up to 65% (Manokhin, 2025). In practical terms, this means more products are on shelves when customers want them, boosting service levels and loyalty. Improved forecasting also reduces the need for expensive last-minute fixes.

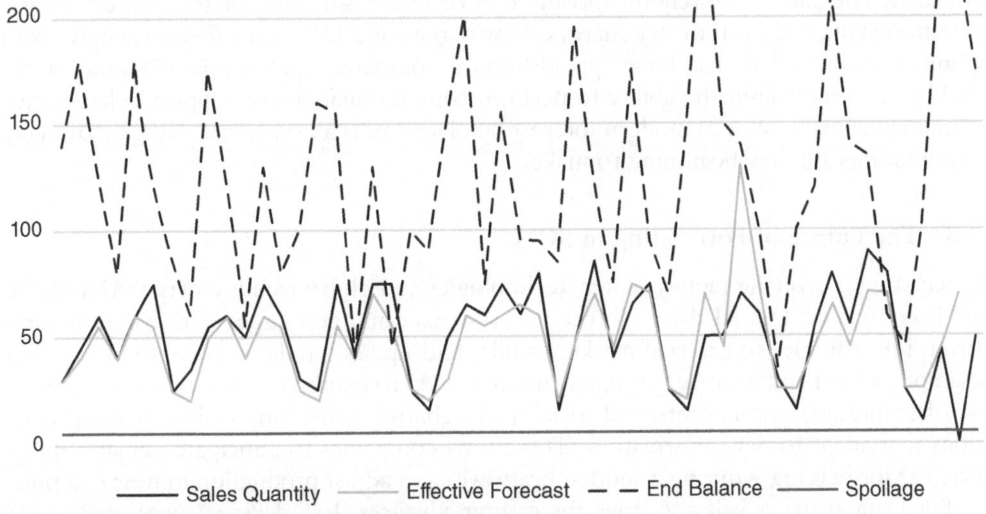

Figure 5.3 Measuring Forecast Accuracy.

Companies with poor forecasts often pay premiums for expedited shipments or overproduction. By contrast, a precise forecast allows production and procurement to proceed smoothly. For example, an automotive manufacturer that implemented AI-driven forecasting saw its forecast errors cut by 50%, saving over USD 10 million annually in inventory costs (dotData, 2022). Globally, the scale of forecasting errors is enormous: in 2023, retailers lost an estimated USD 1.77 trillion due to inventory distortions (a combination of overstocks and stockouts) (Manokhin, 2025). Reducing forecast error is directly linked to financial performance.

5.7 Challenges in Forecasting

Even with robust techniques, forecasting accuracy is never perfect. One major challenge is market uncertainty. Rapidly changing consumer preferences or disruptive innovations can invalidate past trends. For instance, if a competitor unexpectedly releases a substitute product at a lower price, demand can shift abruptly; forecasts based solely on historical sales will miss this. In GSCs, currency fluctuations or trade policy changes can also affect demand. An unexpected tariff might depress sales in an overseas market, rendering previous forecasts obsolete.

Another challenge is aligning forecasts with fast-moving business priorities. If a company changes strategy mid-cycle, such as emphasising a new product line or exiting a market, the current estimates must be revised. In many organisations, multiple forecast versions exist (e.g., one for sales, one for manufacturing) and reconciling these can be difficult. Without clear communication and governance, the final planning forecast may drift from the reality of the market or organisational goals.

Data issues are perennial as well. Accurate forecasting requires clean, timely data. Many organisations find that integrating data across countries or divisions is a recurring obstacle. Missing data, reporting lags, or inconsistent product definitions can introduce errors. Companies often address this by investing in data warehousing and master data management, but these solutions take time and discipline to implement.

Finally, technological and process limitations hamper forecasting. Despite advances in AI, many companies still rely on spreadsheets or legacy software for their core forecasts (Destino et al., 2022). Industry surveys show that as of 2022, nearly 75% of supply chain planners continued to use basic spreadsheets or outdated applications (Destino et al., 2022). Such tools limit the ability to perform complex analytics or support collaborative planning. Transitioning to modern forecasting platforms is a non-trivial change that many organisations are only beginning to make.

5.8 The Future of Forecasting in SCM

Forecasting is evolving rapidly as new technologies and global trends emerge. AI and ML are becoming central. AI-driven forecasting systems can ingest large, diverse data streams (from internal sales to external market trends) and update predictions continuously. For example, a food and beverage company might use AI to combine historical sales data with weather forecasts, local events, and social media chatter, generating daily demand predictions that adapt to new information. This allows companies to anticipate demand spikes (such as for beverages during a sudden heatwave) and adjust production in near real time.

Big Data analytics will also drive forecasting advances. IoT devices, social media, and global market data provide new inputs. For instance, logistics sensors can inform planners about the status of shipments, automatically adjusting forecasts if delays occur. Social media sentiment analysis can detect rising consumer interest in a product before sales data reflect it. Even unstructured data like news articles or economic reports can be integrated. As these data sources grow, forecasting models will become increasingly holistic and accurate.

Sustainability and transparency are shaping future forecasts as well. Consumers increasingly prefer eco-friendly products and transparent supply chains. Demand planners will start to factor these considerations in. For example, if a company sources limited sustainable materials, it will forecast demand for green products separately and adjust production to avoid shortages or overuse of precious resources. Blockchain and other traceability tools will let planners know exactly when materials will be available, further refining forecasts.

Finally, forecasting is moving towards fully integrated, autonomous systems. Leading companies are developing end-to-end planning platforms where AI updates forecasts and plans the supply network automatically, and human planners focus on exceptions. Unilever's experience illustrates this shift: by deploying an integrated planning platform, Unilever achieved centralised demand planning and real-time insights across its global operations (Durak, 2023). In this vision of the future, demand forecasts update dynamically across the supply chain, enabling truly agile and resilient operations.

5.9 Conclusion

Demand forecasting and planning are critical for contemporary supply chains. Accurate forecasts enable organisations to align resources with customer needs, reducing costs and boosting service quality. As shown above, improvements in forecast accuracy yield measurable benefits: lower inventory costs, fewer stockouts, and higher sales capture (Manokhin, 2025). Modern analytics and collaborative tools make achieving these improvements increasingly feasible.

However, technology alone is not enough. Effective forecasting and planning also require high-quality data, cross-functional coordination, and adaptability to global uncertainties. Companies that invest in data analytics, foster collaborative planning processes, and build organisational agility will unlock the full value of demand planning. In an ever-changing world market, those who master demand forecasting and planning will gain a strategic advantage, ensuring their supply chains remain efficient, cost-effective, and resilient.

5.10 Demand Planning in SCM

Demand planning is the cornerstone of effective SCM, bridging the gap between forecasted demand and the operational processes required to meet that demand. Demand planning aligns procurement, production, and distribution activities with anticipated market needs, enabling businesses to optimise their resources while minimising costs. As consumer expectations and market dynamics evolve, demand planning becomes increasingly essential for maintaining operational efficiency and customer satisfaction.

Accurate demand planning balances supply and demand, preventing common pitfalls such as stockouts or overstock situations. Stockouts occur when a product is unavailable to meet customer demand, leading to lost sales, damaged brand reputation, and reduced customer loyalty. Conversely, overstock results in higher holding costs, increased risk of product obsolescence, and, in some cases, forced markdowns or disposals. Striking the right balance requires precise forecasting, cross-functional collaboration, and a commitment to adaptability.

5.10.1 The Importance of Demand Planning

Demand planning is pivotal in achieving operational efficiency, cost control, and customer satisfaction. It ensures businesses maintain adequate inventory levels to meet anticipated demand without incurring unnecessary holding costs. This delicate balance enhances service levels while reducing the financial and operational risks of inventory mismanagement.

For example, retailers preparing for holiday shopping peaks rely on robust demand planning to ensure shelves are well-stocked with in-demand products. Without accurate planning, these businesses risk stockouts during critical sales periods, resulting in lost revenue and dissatisfied customers. Conversely, overestimating demand can lead to excessive inventory, which ties up capital and increases storage costs. Effective demand planning mitigates these risks, helping businesses optimise their operations and respond effectively to market fluctuations (Simchi-Levi et al., 2024).

Demand planning is also integral to long-term strategic planning (see Figure 5.4). By providing insights into future demand patterns, it informs decisions regarding capacity expansion, supplier partnerships, and market entry strategies. For instance, a manufacturer entering a new geographic market may use demand planning to estimate product volumes, allocate resources, and ensure a seamless supply chain operation in the new territory. Demand planning also fosters cross-functional alignment. It compels marketing, sales, finance, and operations to agree on expected demand. For instance, if a marketing team plans a major campaign, they share this information during planning sessions so the demand plan can be increased accordingly. This prevents scenarios where sales inflate orders without procurement preparing raw materials. One manufacturer noted that integrating S&OP across global regions allowed it to respond quickly to demand shifts, avoiding costly emergency sourcing.

5.10.2 Collaborative Demand Planning

Collaboration is a fundamental aspect of successful demand planning. Internally, it involves sales, marketing, finance, supply chain, and often executive leadership. Each group contributes unique insights: sales teams provide real-time customer feedback and order trends; marketing advises on upcoming campaigns and product launches; finance ensures the plan

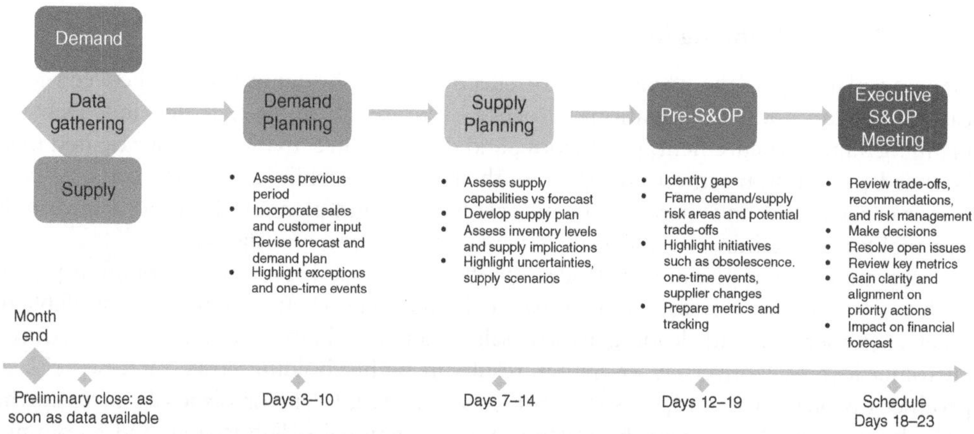

Figure 5.4 Integrated Demand Planning.

fits budget constraints; operations and procurement confirm feasibility with current capacities and supplier lead times. By working together, these teams create a single, consensus demand plan. For example, a consumer electronics company holds monthly S&OP meetings where sales present major deals, marketing outlines promotions, and the demand planning team shows the updated forecast. If sales forecasts suddenly rise, procurement can accelerate parts orders, or production can reallocate capacity. This reduces conflicting objectives (such as overselling a region only to have no stock) and keeps everyone aligned.

Collaboration also extends outside the company. Sharing forecasts with key suppliers and distributors increases transparency and responsiveness. For instance, a global appliance manufacturer uses collaborative planning programmes with its largest component suppliers. By sharing updated demand plans for refrigerators and ovens every month, its suppliers can schedule production and raw material purchases more efficiently, reducing lead times. Similarly, leading retailers often share sales forecasts with their brand suppliers to improve replenishment planning. On a global scale, collaborative demand planning can synchronise entire networks. For example, Unilever shares POS and forecast data with its retail partners worldwide. This near-real-time collaboration enables Unilever to adjust production and distribution seamlessly across regions in Europe, Asia, and the Americas. When demand jumps in one country, factories elsewhere ramp up output accordingly, avoiding stockouts. Such partnerships turn forecasts into coordinated action, making the supply chain more agile and cost-efficient.

5.11 Advanced Technologies in Demand Planning

Advanced technologies have transformed demand planning into a data-rich, highly automated discipline. Modern demand planning software centralises data and automates forecasting and planning functions. These platforms ingest data from ERP systems, POS, e-commerce, and external sources (like weather and economic indicators) to produce unified demand plans. They often include features such as scenario analysis and optimisation engines. For instance, a planning platform can simulate the impact of a 10% price discount or a major promotion, showing how inventory and production plans must adjust under each scenario.

Big data analytics underpins this evolution. By integrating social media sentiment, market trends, and competitor data, companies gain deeper insights into demand drivers. A beverage company might analyse Twitter mentions of a new flavour to boost its forecast or use satellite data on crop health to anticipate raw material availability. ML takes this further: ML algorithms identify complex patterns in vast datasets and improve over time. For example, a large African e-commerce platform serving 800 million consumers used ML models trained on three years of sales history, promotions, and external factors. This system achieved over 95% accuracy in weekly Stock Keeping Unit (SKU)-level forecasting (Prescienceds, 2024). After deployment, the company reduced stockouts dramatically, with over 85% of products in stock year-round versus only 50% before (Prescienceds, 2024). This case shows how advanced analytics can turn raw data into highly reliable plans.

The IoT and real-time tracking also enhance demand planning. Sensors and Radio-Frequency Identification (RFID) devices update inventory and transit statuses instantly. If a shipment of goods is delayed at sea, the planning system can automatically flag this and adjust the demand plan (for example, by expediting alternative shipments). Supply chain control towers, which aggregate live data from across the network, give planners unprecedented visibility. For instance, a consumer electronics company uses a control tower fed by

IoT-connected warehouses and trucks to update demand plans hourly. If inventory falls below the threshold due to high local sales, the system triggers replenishment orders automatically. Collectively, these technologies drive towards autonomous planning. Leading companies are moving to end-to-end platforms where AI updates forecasts and plans continuously, and human planners focus only on exceptions. For example, Unilever's integrated platform generates demand forecasts and production plans automatically; planners now intervene only when alerts indicate an unusual event (e.g., a sudden demand spike or supply disruption) (Durak, 2023). The trend is clear: demand planning is becoming faster, more accurate, and increasingly self-adaptive.

5.12 Challenges in Demand Planning

Despite these advancements, demand planning faces challenges similar to forecasting, with an added operational dimension (see Figure 5.5). Demand uncertainty continues to be the core issue. Events like economic shocks or pandemics can quickly invalidate even the most sophisticated plans. For instance, during COVID-19, many demand planning systems had to be reset as e-commerce demand surged and normal retail plummeted. Companies responded by increasing the frequency of planning cycles and creating contingency plans, but the fundamental unpredictability remains.

Seasonal and promotional variations are another complexity. Many industries (fashion, toys, beverages) experience regular peaks. Forecasting and planning for these require capturing seasonal trends and ramping up supply well before the peak. Missing the lead time means lost sales; overreacting means excess post-season inventory. Successful planners use historical seasonality in their models and also rely on early indicators (pre-orders, marketing signals) to fine-tune the plan. For example, a toy manufacturer finalises production plans for Christmas toys by the second quarter; any delay means either running out of stock or being stuck with unsold inventory after the holidays.

Aligning demand plans with overall business goals is also critical. Large, diversified companies may have multiple product lines and regional units, each with different priorities. A centralised demand plan must balance these. Conflicts can occur, for instance, aggressive

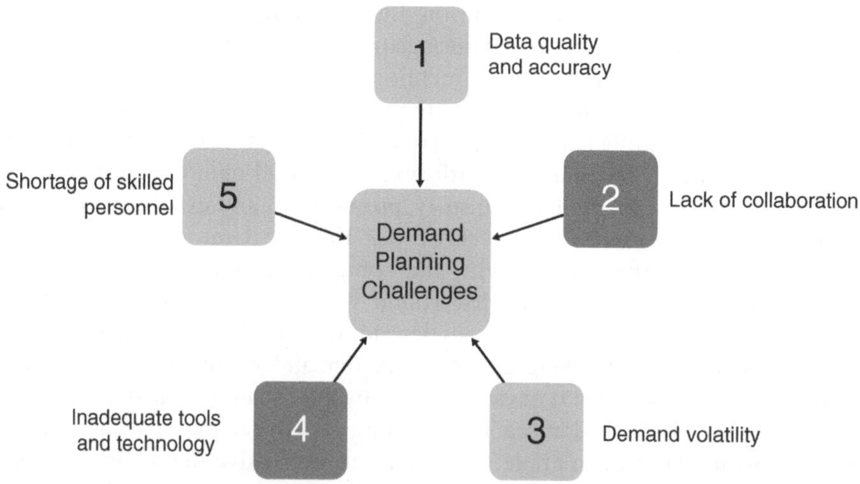

Figure 5.5 Common Demand Planning Challenges.

sales targets might push one division to order extra inventory, while another region hits capacity limits. Regular S&OP governance and executive oversight help keep the plan focused and aligned with strategy. For example, one global manufacturer realigned its planning process by involving finance and strategy teams in its demand reviews, ensuring that the plan supported corporate objectives and financial targets.

Data integration remains a hurdle as well. Even with advanced systems, integrating demand signals from numerous channels (online, physical stores, third-party distributors) across multiple countries is complex. Ensuring consistent definitions and timely data flows requires ongoing effort. Leading companies invest in data harmonisation projects and master data management to support this, recognising that accurate planning hinges on reliable data.

Finally, human and organisational factors persist. Demand planning requires skilled planners who combine analytical ability with market insight. Such talent can be scarce, especially when planning complexity grows. Companies address this by training programmes and building planning centres of excellence. Change management is also key: implementing new planning technologies can face resistance. Organisations must involve stakeholders early, demonstrate quick wins, and show how planning improvements benefit every function. Overcoming these challenges is as much about people and processes as it is about software.

5.13 The Future of Demand Planning

Demand planning will continue to advance as the business landscape and technologies evolve. AI and predictive analytics will play central roles in enabling real-time, adaptive plans. For example, AI agents may soon update demand plans hourly based on live data streams from IoT devices in stores and trucks. Some companies are already piloting such continuous replenishment systems: when a product's stock runs low, the system automatically triggers an order based on the AI forecast.

Sustainability will become an integral part of demand planning. Planners will incorporate environmental objectives, such as minimising waste and emissions, alongside traditional goals. A retail chain committed to green practices might adjust its demand plan to consolidate shipments and prefer slower, lower-carbon transport if forecasts allow. Materials constraints (such as limited supplies of recycled inputs) might also enter planning assumptions, ensuring that plans align with sustainability targets.

Collaboration will expand beyond existing boundaries. Digital supply networks, possibly using blockchain or secure cloud platforms, will enable partners across the globe to work from a common forecast. Imagine a future where a raw material supplier in South America, a manufacturer in Asia, and a retailer in Europe all see the same demand outlook in real time. This would allow truly end-to-end planning, reducing inefficiencies and aligning production with consumer demand worldwide.

Moreover, as cloud and Software as a Service forecasting tools spread, even small and medium enterprises in Oceania or Africa will adopt advanced planning capabilities. This democratisation of demand planning will strengthen GSCs by improving coordination at all levels. For example, an African agricultural exporter could use a cloud-based demand planning platform to align shipments with crop forecasts and European retail demand, reducing waste and improving farmer incomes. In summary, demand planning is set to become more data-driven, collaborative, and sustainability-conscious. Organisations that invest in these capabilities now will be best positioned to thrive in a fast-changing global market.

5.14 Conclusion

Demand forecasting and planning are indispensable for modern supply chains. They enable organisations to anticipate customer needs and proactively align their operations, resulting in smoother flows of goods and higher customer satisfaction. As this chapter has shown, integrating quantitative models with qualitative insights produces the most robust forecasts. Converting these forecasts into coordinated demand plans ensures that procurement, production, and distribution work in harmony with market demand.

The benefits of excellence in demand planning are clear: lower inventory costs, fewer stockouts, and stronger financial performance (Manokhin, 2025). By embracing advanced analytics and fostering collaboration, companies can realise these benefits. At the same time, organisations must remain vigilant to challenges like data quality and demand uncertainty. In the global economy, supply chains that can forecast and plan effectively will outperform competitors, achieving cost efficiency and resilience.

Q&A Section

Here is a short quiz to test your knowledge. The answers are provided in Appendix C.

1. What is the main purpose of demand forecasting in SCM?
2. What is the difference between qualitative and quantitative forecasting?
3. Why is the Delphi method used in qualitative forecasting?
4. What are some common techniques in quantitative forecasting?
5. How can companies improve the accuracy of their forecasts?
6. What role does demand planning play in SCM?
7. Why is collaboration important in demand planning?
8. What advanced technologies are transforming demand planning?
9. What challenges do businesses face in demand planning?
10. How can companies address demand uncertainty in their forecasts?

6 Inventory Management

Learning Outcomes

By the end of this chapter, learners will be able to:

- Define core inventory concepts (EOQ, JIT, SS) and when to apply each.
- Calculate EOQ and a simple SS estimate for a specified service level.
- Analyse the cost vs service trade-off and propose an inventory policy for a SKU.
- Assess the role of technology and KPIs in modern inventory control.
- Design an inventory segmentation (e.g., ABC/XYZ) and justify prioritisation decisions.

6.1 Introduction

Inventory management is a foundational function in contemporary SCM (see Figure 6.1). It governs the planning, control, and optimisation of stock held across the network to satisfy demand while minimising total cost and risk. Effective inventory management

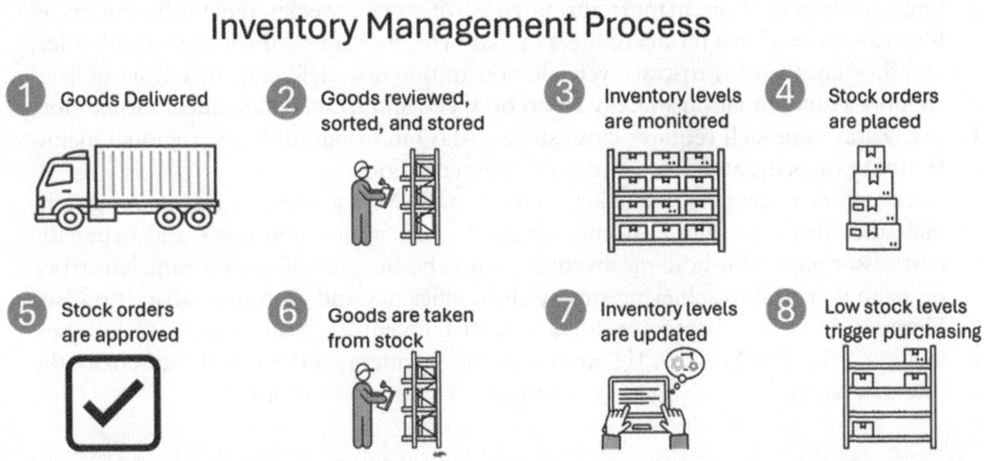

Figure 6.1 Inventory Management at a Glance.

DOI: 10.4324/9781003740568-6

bridges strategic objectives and operational execution; it shapes procurement, production scheduling, warehousing, and distribution decisions. This chapter expands on classical inventory techniques, such as EOQ, JIT, and SS design, while integrating contemporary developments in analytics, automation, and collaborative models. It emphasises global perspectives, highlighting how multinational organisations coordinate inventory across time zones, regulatory regimes, and consumer markets.

6.2 The Importance of Inventory Management in SCM

Effective inventory management is essential for ensuring the smooth functioning of supply chain operations. It plays a crucial role in customer satisfaction. By maintaining adequate stock levels, businesses can fulfil customer orders promptly and accurately, leading to higher levels of customer satisfaction and loyalty. Efficient inventory management helps to streamline operations, reduce lead times, and improve overall productivity. By minimising stockouts and excess inventory, businesses can optimise resource utilisation and reduce costs.

Inventory decisions determine working capital intensity, service levels, and operational resilience, and thus materially affect profitability and competitiveness. Poor inventory choices manifest as either excess holdings, with high carrying costs and obsolescence risk, or shortages, with lost sales and reputational damage. Contemporary organisations must therefore balance cost minimisation with responsiveness and risk mitigation across distributed networks. This balance is particularly complex for companies operating globally, where lead times, customs delays, and demand seasonality vary markedly between regions.

Case Study – Zara/Inditex (Global Fast Fashion)

Inditex's Zara operates one of the most responsive inventory systems in retail, combining localised, short manufacturing runs with twice-weekly replenishment cycles for many stores. That model reduces markdowns, increases sell-through at full price, and shortens the cash-to-cash cycle, demonstrating how deliberate inventory policies support a differentiation strategy based on speed and freshness. Readers should note that Zara's approach requires close store-to-HQ information flows, regional manufacturing capacity, and deliberate SKU rationalisation.

Inventory management is a key element of SCM, focusing on maintaining optimal stock levels to fulfil customer demand while minimising costs. Balancing the costs associated with holding inventory with the benefits of having sufficient stock on hand is critical to achieving supply chain efficiency and customer satisfaction (see Figure 6.2). This chapter explores essential inventory management techniques, including the EOQ model, JIT inventory management, and SS. It also discusses the role of advanced technologies in optimising inventory decisions.

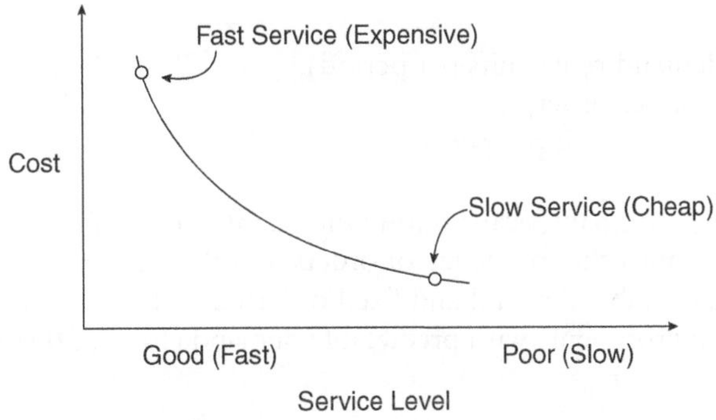

Figure 6.2 Service Level vs Cost Trade-off.

6.3 The Importance of Inventory Management in SCM Operations

Effective inventory management is essential for effectively managing supply and demand. It allows businesses to meet customer needs promptly, avoid stockouts, and control costs associated with storage and ordering. Poor inventory management can result in overstocking, leading to increased holding costs, or understocking, which can cause missed sales opportunities and customer dissatisfaction.

The primary objectives of inventory management are to:

1 Minimise the total costs associated with ordering, holding, and stockouts.
2 Ensure sufficient stock levels to meet anticipated demand.
3 Maximise service levels by having the right products available at the right time.

Balancing these objectives requires a range of strategies and techniques, which are discussed in the following sections (Muller, 2019).

6.4 Economic Order Quantity

The EOQ model is one of the most widely used inventory management techniques. EOQ calculates the optimal order size that minimises total inventory costs, including ordering and holding costs. This model provides companies with a straightforward method to determine how much to order and when to order, helping to reduce excess inventory and lower associated costs.

6.4.1 EOQ Model Explained

The EOQ model balances ordering and holding costs to determine the ideal order quantity. The formula for EOQ is:

$$EOQ = \sqrt{\frac{2DS}{H}}$$

Where:

D represents the demand rate (units per period),
S is the ordering cost per order,
H is the holding cost per unit per period.

By calculating EOQ, companies can identify the quantity that minimises total costs, allowing them to reduce both the frequency of orders and the amount of inventory held. The EOQ model assumes stable demand and fixed ordering and holding costs, which makes it most suitable for environments with predictable demand (Rossi, 2021).

6.4.2 *Benefits of Using EOQ*

EOQ's strengths are simplicity and clarity; it quantifies the trade-off between frequency and inventory investment, making it an effective teaching tool and a starting point for policy design. However, its assumptions (stable D, constant S and H, single SKU) make it less suitable for seasonal products, multi-location networks, or items with variable lead times. In practice, organisations often use EOQ as a diagnostic input to more sophisticated replenishment engines embedded in ERP/WMS platforms.

Case Study – Automotive Supplier Adaptation of EOQ

A global Tier-1 components supplier used EOQ to establish baseline order sizes for stable commodity parts, while layering dynamic SS and demand-driven replenishment for bespoke kits. The approach reduced ordering overheads without endangering line availability in multiple plants across Asia and Europe, illustrating hybridised use of EOQ within complex production systems.

6.5 JIT Inventory Management

JIT aims to minimise inventory through synchronised production and supply, delivering materials to the production point precisely when required. JIT depends on reliable suppliers, stable production processes, and tight information flows; its benefits include reduced holding costs, lower obsolescence, and improved cash position. However, JIT is sensitive to disruptions, which has led many organisations to combine JIT with contingency buffers in recent years.

6.5.1 *Principles of JIT*

The JIT approach originated in the manufacturing industry and focuses on reducing waste by ensuring that materials are available precisely when they are required. JIT is focused on purchasing, or producing, what you need as opposed to using guess-work and purchasing/producing stock just in case (see Figure 6.3). JIT requires:

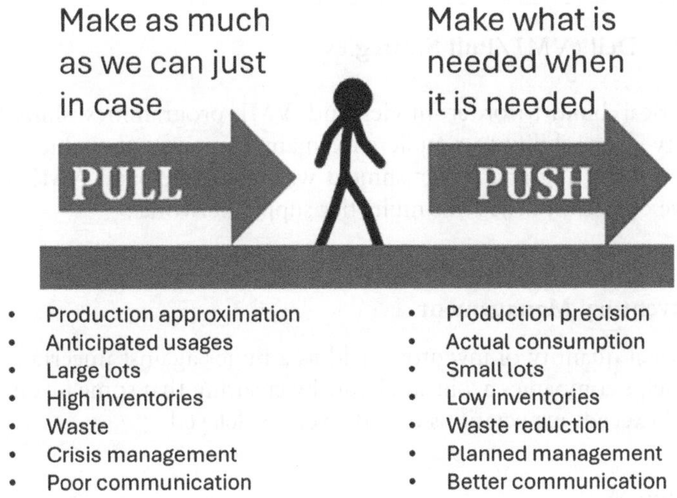

Figure 6.3 JIT vs JIC.

1 **Accurate Demand Forecasting:** Since inventory levels are kept low, companies must accurately forecast demand to avoid stockouts.
2 **Supplier Coordination:** JIT relies on strong relationships and efficient communication with suppliers to ensure timely deliveries.
3 **Efficient Production Processes:** JIT works best when production processes are optimised for quick response times.

By minimising the amount of inventory held at any given time, JIT reduces holding costs and the risk of obsolescence. However, it requires high levels of coordination with suppliers and can be challenging to implement in volatile markets (Cohen & Roussel, 2013).

6.5.2 Advantages and Challenges of JIT

Advantages include lower inventory carrying costs and stronger incentives for supply quality and timeliness. Challenges include supplier dependence, exposure to transport disruption, and the requirement for exceptionally accurate demand signals. Following global disruptions since 2020, many organisations have adopted a "JIT plus resilience" approach, retaining JIT's efficiency while adding targeted SS or dual sourcing for critical components:

Case Study – Toyota (JIT and Resilience)

Toyota pioneered JIT in the TPS, yet Toyota's recent performance during supply shocks demonstrates how JIT and resilience can coexist. Toyota's deeper supplier integration, transparent part-level visibility, and selective buffering of critical parts enabled it to outperform many competitors during semiconductor and logistics disruptions of the GFC and COVID-19, showing that JIT organisations can improve resilience via supplier collaboration and targeted buffers.

Case Study – Dell (VMI/Pull Strategies)

Dell's historical build-to-order model and VMI programmes shifted inventory responsibility and visibility to suppliers for many components, reducing Dell's own holding costs while aligning replenishment with actual demand. VMI is, in effect, a collaborative extension of JIT for multi-tier supply networks.

6.6 SS in Inventory Management

SS is an additional quantity of inventory held as a buffer against uncertainties in demand and supply. It helps companies avoid stockouts by ensuring that some inventory is available even if demand exceeds expectations or if delivery is delayed.

6.6.1 *Calculating SS*

SS protects against uncertainty in demand and lead time, with formulas ranging from simple fixed buffers to statistically derived levels based on service-level targets. A common statistical method is:

$$Safety\ Stock = z \times \sigma_{LT}$$

where z = z-score corresponding to the desired service level, and σ_{LT} = standard deviation of demand during the lead time. Time-based and probabilistic calculations are used depending on data availability and SKU criticality. Practical frameworks distinguish between critical and non-critical SKUs, applying more conservative buffers to high-value or mission-critical items.

The amount of SS required depends on factors such as lead time, demand variability, and the level of service the company wants to maintain. Holding SS allows companies to manage uncertainties in the supply chain, but this also increases holding costs (Muller, 2019).

6.6.2 *Balancing SS and Costs*

Effective SS management involves finding a balance between the level of inventory and the associated costs. While SS helps prevent stockouts and improve service levels, excessive SS can lead to higher holding costs and reduced profitability. Companies must carefully calculate SS levels to achieve the desired service level without incurring unnecessary expenses.

6.6.3 *SS Trade-offs and Global Application*

Service targets vary by market; premium urban retail channels may require very high fill rates, while remote or low-value channels tolerate lower service levels. Multinational organisations must therefore tailor SS by region, channel, and SKU lifecycle stage, recognising that currency fluctuations, customs delays, and seasonal events change the underlying demand and lead-time distributions.

Case Study – Walmart and AI-Enabled SS Optimisation

Walmart's investments in advanced forecasting and inventory optimisation reduced stockouts and optimised SS at scale across thousands of SKUs, demonstrating how modern analytics can lower working capital while preserving service levels. It is important to note that algorithmic SS tuning requires high-quality, consistent data across channels.

6.7 Technology and Data Analytics in Inventory Management

Modern inventory management is increasingly data-driven, combining ERP, WMS, demand planners, and external data streams. Key technologies include:

1. RFID and barcode scanning for item-level visibility, enabling near-real-time inventory accuracy.
2. Warehouse automation and robotics, improving throughput and reducing human error as seen in high-volume fulfilment centres.
3. Advanced analytics and ML, producing probabilistic forecasts, dynamic SS, and automated reorder recommendations.
4. VMI and collaborative replenishment platforms, aligning supplier production with end-market demand.

Case Study – Amazon (Automation and Item-Level Throughput)

Amazon's continual investment in robotics (acquired from Kiva Systems and subsequently developed in-house) and warehouse automation has significantly increased throughput and improved inventory visibility at scale, enabling fast fulfilment across diverse geographies. Australian and international logistics operations increasingly mirror parts of Amazon's automation playbook, while adapting to local labour markets and regulations.

Case Study – Woolworths (RFID Trials in Australia)

Woolworths trialled RFID to track fresh produce and temperature across its supply chain, highlighting how item-level tracking improves inventory accuracy and cold-chain integrity in perishable categories. Such initiatives show the practical value of visibility technologies in markets with large distances and perishable supply chains, like Australia.

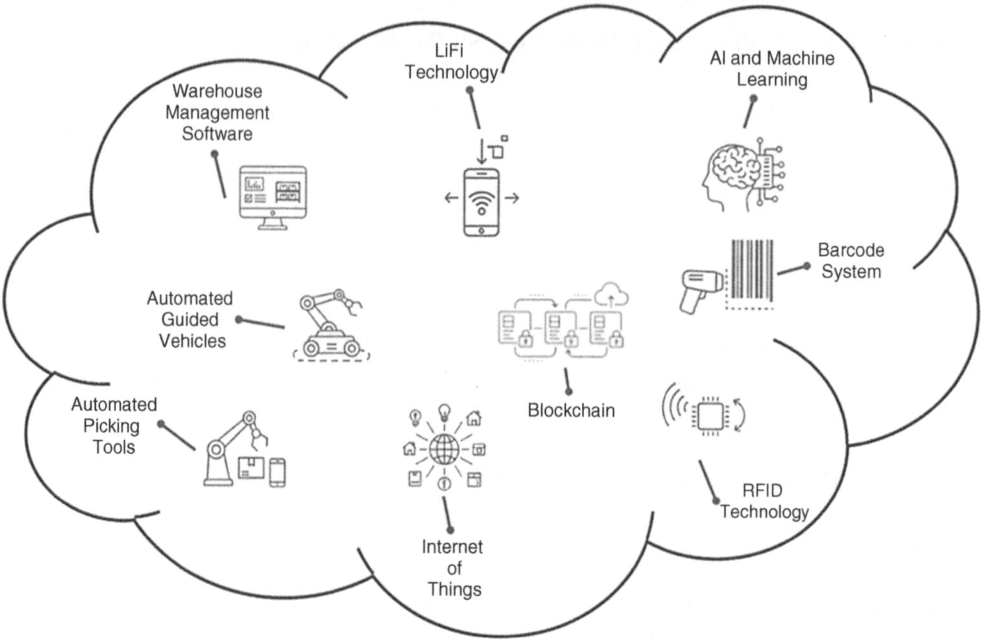

Figure 6.4 Inventory Management Technology Stack.

6.7.1 Inventory Management Software

Inventory management software provides a centralised platform for tracking inventory levels, managing orders, and monitoring stock movements in real time (see Figure 6.4). Key features of this software include:

1. **Automated Reorder Points:** The software can automatically generate purchase orders (POs) when inventory levels reach predefined reorder points, streamlining the replenishment process.
2. **Low-Stock Alerts:** The system can send alerts to relevant personnel when stock levels are low, enabling timely action to avoid stockouts.
3. **Real-Time Inventory Tracking:** Real-time tracking of inventory allows businesses to monitor stock levels across multiple locations and identify discrepancies or anomalies promptly.
4. **Integration with Other Systems:** Inventory management software can integrate with other systems, such as ERP systems, POS systems, and WMS, to facilitate data exchange and synchronisation.

6.7.2 Big Data and ML

Big data and ML have the potential to transform inventory management by enabling organisations to analyse vast amounts of data to uncover valuable insights. By leveraging these technologies, businesses can:

1. **Improve Forecast Accuracy:** ML algorithms can analyse historical sales data, seasonal trends, and other relevant factors to generate highly accurate demand forecasts. This helps organisations to avoid stockouts and excess inventory.

2 **Optimise Inventory Levels:** By analysing real-time data on sales, inventory levels, and customer behaviour, businesses can optimise inventory levels to meet demand while minimising costs.
3 **Identify Trends and Patterns:** ML algorithms can identify hidden patterns and trends in data that may not be apparent to human analysts. This can help businesses to make more informed decisions about inventory management.
4 **Personalise Inventory Strategies:** By analysing customer data, businesses can personalise inventory strategies for different customer segments. This can help to improve customer satisfaction and loyalty.

6.7.3 The Role of Predictive Analytics

Predictive analytics, a subset of data analytics, uses statistical techniques and ML algorithms to forecast future events. In the context of inventory management, predictive analytics can be used to:

1 **Predict Demand Fluctuations:** By analysing historical data and external factors, predictive analytics can help businesses to anticipate changes in demand, allowing them to adjust inventory levels accordingly.
2 **Identify Potential Supply Chain Disruptions:** Predictive analytics can help to identify potential disruptions in the supply chain, such as supplier shortages or transportation delays, enabling businesses to take proactive measures to mitigate their impact.
3 **Optimise Inventory Allocation:** By analysing historical sales data and customer behaviour, predictive analytics can help businesses to optimise the allocation of inventory across different locations and channels.

6.7.4 Challenges and Considerations

While technology and data analytics offer significant benefits for inventory management, there are also challenges to consider:

1 **Data Quality and Integrity:** The quality and integrity of data are crucial for accurate analysis and decision-making. Organisations must ensure that data is clean, accurate, and up-to-date.
2 **Implementation Costs:** Implementing advanced inventory management systems and data analytics tools can be costly, particularly for small and medium-sized businesses.
3 **Resistance to Change:** Change management is essential to ensure the successful adoption of new technologies and processes. Organisations must address employee concerns and provide adequate training to facilitate a smooth transition.

By addressing these challenges and leveraging the power of technology and data analytics, organisations can significantly improve their inventory management practices, reduce costs, and enhance customer satisfaction.

Advancements in technology and data analytics have transformed inventory management practices. Modern inventory management systems use big data, ML, and predictive analytics to improve decision-making, forecast demand more accurately, and optimise stock levels.

6.8 KPIs and CI

Inventory KPIs quantify performance and guide improvement. Essential KPIs include inventory turnover, days of inventory, carrying cost of inventory, perfect order rate, fill rate, stockout rate, and obsolete inventory percentage. Regularly tracking these metrics enables organisations to detect drift, prioritise improvement projects, and measure the impact of policy changes. (Appendix A lists common Inventory KPIs and formulas).

6.9 Global and Regional Considerations

Inventory policies cannot be transposed unchanged across borders. Key drivers that differ by region include lead-time variability, import regulations, transportation reliability, seasonality, and customer tolerance for stockouts. For example:

1 Latin American routes sometimes face higher lead-time variability due to port congestion, implying higher SS.
2 Europe's short transit times may support leaner regional inventories when coupled with flexible cross-docking.
3 Australia's geographic dispersal increases distribution costs and complicates last-mile replenishment for remote communities, strengthening the case for regional DCs and demand-driven replenishment for rural SKUs.

Case Study – Multi-regional Grocery Supply Chains

Large grocery chains operating in Europe, Asia, and Oceania segment SKUs by perishability and channel, placing higher buffers for perishable goods in regions with uncertain transport and tighter buffers for non-perishables in urban hubs where replenishment lead times are short. This regional segmentation reduces waste and aligns service levels to local customer expectations. (See Woolworths RFID trials for perishables governance).

6.10 Best Practices and Governance

1 Segment inventory by value, variability, and criticality; use ABC/XYZ segmentation to focus resources where they matter most.
2 Adopt collaborative replenishment; share forecasts and inventory positions with key suppliers to enable VMI or CPFR.
3 Invest in master data management; consistent SKU definitions and timely sales data are prerequisites for any advanced optimisation.
4 Use scenario planning and SS tiers; maintain different buffers for routine and critical SKUs to balance cost and resilience.
5 Measure and iterate; implement a quarterly review cadence that links KPI changes to root-cause actions and CI initiatives.

6.11 Conclusion

Inventory management remains central to supply chain performance, influencing cost, service, and resilience. Classical techniques such as EOQ and JIT remain valuable conceptual tools, but modern practice combines those principles with data analytics, automation, and collaborative models to manage complexity across global networks. Case studies from Zara, Toyota, Dell, Walmart, Amazon, and Woolworths show that no single technique is universally superior, organisations achieve superior outcomes by aligning inventory policy to strategy, investing in visibility and analytics, and continuously adapting policies to regional realities.

Q&A Section

Here is a short quiz to test your knowledge. The answers are provided in Appendix C.

1. What is the main purpose of inventory management in supply chain operations?
2. What are the primary objectives of inventory management?
3. What does the EOQ model calculate?
4. What is the formula for EOQ based on?
5. What is JIT inventory management?
6. What are the key requirements for JIT to work effectively?
7. What is SS and why is it held?
8. How is SS typically calculated?
9. What role does technology play in modern inventory management?
10. Name one best practice for effective inventory management.

7 Procurement and Supplier Management

Learning Outcomes

By the end of this chapter, learners will be able to:

- Outline the procurement lifecycle and key SRM activities.
- Apply supplier selection criteria (TCO, quality, traceability) to evaluate bids.
- Construct a supplier scorecard and interpret its implications for sourcing strategy.
- Assess supplier risks and propose resilience measures (diversification, contracts).
- Evaluate ethical and sustainability considerations in procurement decisions.

7.1 Introduction

Procurement and supplier management are strategic functions within contemporary SCM; they enable an organisation to secure the goods, services, and capabilities required to deliver value to customers (Monczka et al., 2016). Procurement is no longer a purely transactional activity; it is an orchestrated process that aligns sourcing strategy with corporate objectives, risk appetite, and sustainability commitments (Christopher, 2016). Supplier management extends procurement into the post-contractual domain, encompassing performance management, innovation, collaboration, and joint risk mitigation.

As supply chains grow more complex and globalised, procurement and supplier management have become increasingly strategic. Effective procurement practices help organisations achieve cost savings, ensure quality, and mitigate risks. Similarly, robust supplier management enhances supply chain resilience and fosters innovation through collaborative relationships. This chapter explores the procurement process, criteria for supplier selection, and the role of SRM in achieving these objectives (Figure 7.1).

7.1.1 The Strategic Role of Procurement and Supplier Management

Procurement and supplier management are no longer seen as purely operational functions but as strategic enablers of organisational success. Organisations can achieve significant competitive advantages by aligning procurement practices with business objectives.

DOI: 10.4324/9781003740568-7

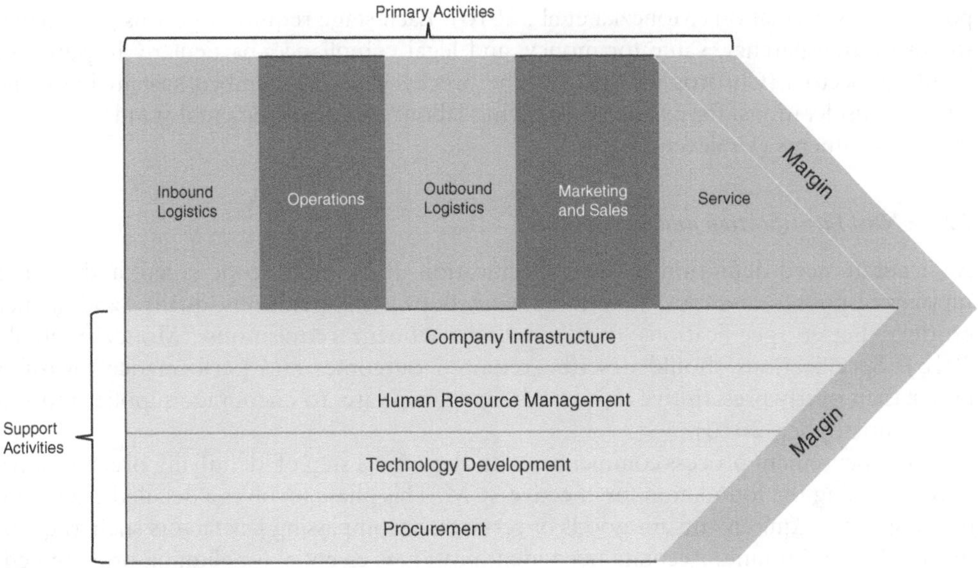

Figure 7.1 Procurement Value Chain.

One of procurement's key strategic roles is cost management. Effective procurement practices enable organisations to negotiate favourable terms, optimise spending, and achieve economies of scale. This improves profitability and frees up resources for investment in other strategic initiatives.

Procurement also plays a critical role in supporting sustainability goals. Organisations are turning to procurement to drive change as stakeholders increasingly demand environmentally and socially responsible practices. Sustainable procurement practices, such as sourcing from ethical suppliers and prioritising eco-friendly materials, contribute to the organisation's reputation and long-term viability.

Supplier management enhances supply chain agility and resilience, enabling organisations to respond effectively to disruptions and changing market conditions. By fostering strong supplier relationships, organisations can secure reliable access to critical inputs and adapt to challenges more efficiently.

Procurement and supplier management are integral to the success of modern supply chains, offering a strategic advantage in cost management, sustainability, resilience, and innovation. Organisations can optimise their operations and achieve their strategic objectives by adopting a structured procurement process, selecting the right suppliers, and prioritising SRM. As supply chains continue to evolve, the importance of procurement and supplier management will only grow, making these functions indispensable for organisational success in a competitive global landscape.

7.2 The Procurement Process

7.2.1 Overview and Stages

Procurement is a staged process, typically described as: need identification, market analysis and supplier shortlisting, solicitation (RFI/RFQ/Request for Proposal (RFP)), bid evaluation and selection, contracting and negotiation, order placement and delivery, and post-delivery evaluation (Monczka et al., 2016). Each stage requires rigorous governance to ensure transparency, value for money, and legal compliance, particularly in public or regulated sectors (Christopher, 2016). The process must also embed sustainability and ethical considerations, for example, specifying labour and environmental standards within tender documents (Unilever, 2023).

7.2.2 Need Identification and Specification

An accurate need definition reduces specification drift, limits scope creep, and focuses supplier responses, and cross-functional workshops with operations, quality, and finance produce better specifications than single-department requisitions (Monczka et al., 2016). Specifications should describe required outcomes and performance measures rather than overly prescriptive inputs, where appropriate, to encourage supplier innovation (Christopher, 2016).

The procurement process commences with the critical step of identifying organisational needs, forming the foundation for effective SCM. This phase involves a detailed evaluation of the specific requirements for goods or services, encompassing key factors such as quantity, quality, and timing. Accurate need identification is essential for aligning procurement activities with broader organisational objectives while avoiding excess inventory or resource shortages.

A comprehensive analysis of operational requirements is fundamental to this process. By assessing the current and projected demands of the organisation, procurement teams can ensure that their purchasing decisions are both strategic and efficient. Demand forecasting plays a pivotal role, using historical data, market trends, and predictive analytics to anticipate future needs. This proactive approach enables organisations to plan for fluctuating demands while maintaining optimal stock levels, thereby reducing the risks associated with overstocking or under-supply (Bailey et al., 2015).

Identifying needs also requires close collaboration across departments to align procurement strategies with operational goals. For instance, manufacturing teams may specify precise quality standards for raw materials, while logistics departments provide insights into timing and delivery requirements. This interdisciplinary approach ensures that procurement decisions are informed by the practical realities of the organisation's operations, ultimately enhancing supply chain efficiency.

Incorporating these practices into the procurement process not only supports operational objectives but also contributes to cost efficiency and customer satisfaction. By ensuring that procurement activities are guided by accurate and well-informed need identification, organisations can strengthen their supply chains and position themselves for long-term success in a competitive market.

Case Study – Siemens Amberg

At Siemens' Amberg electronics plant, procurement works closely with R&D and manufacturing to translate performance requirements into detailed supplier specifications for control software and component tolerances. This collaborative front-end reduces redesign cycles and shortens time to market, demonstrating that early supplier involvement improves technical fit and reduces total cost.

7.2.3 Market Analysis and Strategic Sourcing

Market analysis assesses supplier capability, concentration, and geopolitical exposure, and strategic sourcing segments spend and defines supply strategies by category (Monczka et al., 2016). Strategic sourcing frequently uses TCO rather than purchase price alone by incorporating freight, inventory, quality failure, and carbon costs (Chopra & Meindl, 2024) (Monczka et al., 2016). This critical step ensures that potential suppliers are not only capable of meeting the organisation's specific requirements but also align with its operational and strategic objectives. Through this process, procurement teams can establish a reliable and competitive supply base.

Market analysis entails comprehensive research and evaluation of potential suppliers, focusing on their capacity to fulfil the organisation's needs effectively. Key considerations in this evaluation include the supplier's reputation, financial stability, and track record of performance. A supplier's reputation often reflects their reliability and commitment to quality, while financial stability ensures their ability to sustain long-term operations. Similarly, performance history provides valuable insights into the supplier's ability to deliver on time and meet quality standards. These factors collectively minimise the risks associated with supplier selection and contribute to a robust procurement strategy (Sollish & Semanik, 2012).

The insights gained from market analysis allow organisations to create a shortlist of qualified suppliers. This refined list serves as a foundation for further negotiations and contract discussions, ensuring that the selected suppliers can provide the required goods or services at competitive prices. Additionally, this process promotes transparency and accountability, fostering trust between the organisation and its supply chain partners.

By investing time and resources in market analysis and supplier identification, organisations can optimise their procurement processes and build resilient supply chains. This approach not only supports operational efficiency but also enhances the organisation's ability to adapt to market changes and maintain a competitive edge in an increasingly dynamic business environment.

Case Study – Unilever Sustainable Sourcing

Unilever's Sustainable Agriculture Programme integrates smallholder farmers into its raw material supply base, procurement teams evaluate social and environmental risk alongside price, and long-term contracts improve traceability and price stability across regions in India, Brazil, and Nigeria, exemplifying strategic sourcing that combines TCO and social value (Unilever, 2023).

7.2.4 Solicitation, Evaluation, and Contracting

Once potential suppliers have been identified, the procurement process moves into soliciting bids or proposals. This is typically achieved by issuing a RFP or RFQ. These formal documents outline the organisation's specific requirements and invite suppliers to submit detailed offers. This step serves as the foundation for evaluating supplier capabilities and selecting the best partner for the organisation's needs.

The RFP process is generally used when procurement involves complex requirements or services, necessitating suppliers to provide detailed technical and commercial proposals.

Conversely, an RFQ is more appropriate for standardised products or services, focusing primarily on price and delivery terms. Both methods aim to ensure that suppliers are fully informed about the organisation's needs, including quality standards, delivery timelines, and contract terms. This structured approach fosters clarity and alignment between the buyer and potential suppliers (Bailey et al., 2015).

One of the key benefits of the RFP/RFQ process is its emphasis on transparency. By providing a standardised framework for evaluating bids, organisations can compare offers objectively, assessing factors such as cost, quality, reliability, and value-added services. This process also encourages healthy competition among suppliers, which can drive down costs and improve quality. Suppliers, in turn, are motivated to present their most competitive offers, showcasing their ability to meet or exceed the organisation's expectations.

Moreover, the solicitation process strengthens accountability by documenting the procurement requirements and the evaluation criteria. This ensures that decisions are fair, well documented, and aligned with the organisation's goals. By adopting a rigorous and transparent approach to soliciting bids or proposals, organisations can secure quality goods and services at competitive prices, ultimately enhancing supply chain performance.

7.2.4.1 Designing Effective RFPs and Evaluation Frameworks

Well-designed RFPs communicate objectives, evaluation criteria, and contractual expectations, and public sector procurement commonly uses weighted evaluation matrices to balance price, quality, sustainability, and local content. For complex purchases, procurement may use two-stage bidding or a RFP plus demonstration to reduce vendor risk and improve fit (Monczka et al., 2016).

Case Study – Public Procurement (Best Practice Evaluation)

Several Australian state procurement frameworks use weighted criteria with separate pass/fail compliance gates for workplace safety and financial probity; this reduces the risk of awarding to the lowest price supplier who cannot meet service obligations and aligns procurement with public policy objectives.

7.2.4.2 Contract Negotiation and Risk Allocation

Contracts allocate risk, set KPIs, define remedies, and create governance mechanisms such as escalation paths and joint review committees. Negotiation should aim for clarity on performance metrics, data sharing, intellectual property, and termination conditions (Monczka et al., 2016). Where supply is critical, contracts may include dual-sourcing clauses, minimum capacity guarantees, and supplier business continuity plans.

Case Study – Automotive Tier-1 (Risk Allocation)

A Tier-1 automotive supplier negotiated contracts with semiconductor vendors that included capacity reservation clauses and shared investment in buffer inventory. This contractual architecture reduced production stoppages during component shortages, illustrating how targeted contractual clauses can reduce operational risk.

7.2.5 Supplier Selection Criteria and Multi-dimensional Scoring

The evaluation of bids represents a pivotal stage in the procurement process, as organisations carefully assess supplier proposals to identify the best partner for their needs. This process involves a structured review of the submissions against predefined criteria such as price, quality, delivery timelines, and terms of service. By adhering to these criteria, organisations ensure that the assessment is both objective and aligned with their strategic goals.

The selection of suitable suppliers is a cornerstone of effective procurement and SCM. A carefully executed supplier selection process enables organisations to establish partnerships with suppliers who can consistently meet their operational requirements and strategic objectives. This process involves evaluating potential suppliers against a range of criteria to ensure that they are capable of delivering the required goods or services to the desired standard.

Supplier selection begins with an assessment of the supplier's ability to meet the organisation's specific needs. This involves examining their production capabilities, financial stability, and track record in delivering quality products or services. A supplier's operational capacity, including their ability to handle fluctuations in demand, is critical to ensuring reliability and reducing the risk of disruptions within the supply chain. Financial stability, on the other hand, reflects the supplier's capacity to sustain long-term operations and maintain investment in quality and innovation (Sollish & Semanik, 2012).

Price is often a significant factor, as organisations seek to manage costs effectively. However, selecting a supplier based solely on the lowest bid can be detrimental if other critical factors, such as quality or reliability, are compromised. Therefore, quality assurance is paramount, as it directly impacts the organisation's ability to meet its operational and customer requirements. Delivery timelines are also carefully scrutinised to ensure suppliers can meet the organisation's schedules without delays that could disrupt production or service delivery. Additionally, the evaluation considers terms of service, including warranties, after-sales support, and flexibility in accommodating changes to requirements (Sollish & Semanik, 2012).

Negotiation is a key aspect of the evaluation process. Organisations may engage with shortlisted suppliers to clarify aspects of their proposals, address ambiguities, and refine terms to better align with organisational needs. This collaborative approach ensures mutual understanding between the buyer and supplier, fostering a partnership built on shared expectations.

The ultimate objective of evaluating bids is to select the supplier that offers the best value for money. This involves balancing cost considerations with factors such as quality, reliability, and the supplier's ability to adapt to the organisation's long-term needs. A thorough and transparent evaluation process not only secures optimal procurement outcomes but also establishes a foundation for strong supplier relationships, supporting the organisation's broader supply chain objectives.

7.2.6 Quality of Goods or Services

The quality of goods or services provided by suppliers is a vital consideration in the supplier selection process, as it directly influences the organisation's output and customer satisfaction. High-quality inputs are essential for maintaining operational efficiency, meeting customer expectations, and upholding the organisation's reputation in the marketplace. Therefore, organisations place significant emphasis on evaluating the quality standards of potential suppliers to ensure reliability and consistency.

Assessing a supplier's quality management systems is a fundamental step in this process. Organisations examine whether suppliers adhere to recognised quality certifications, such as ISO 9001, which demonstrate a commitment to maintaining rigorous quality standards. Additionally, a review of the supplier's track record, including their history of defect rates, on-time delivery (OTD) of quality products, and responsiveness to quality issues, provides valuable insights into their ability to meet expectations. This evaluation helps organisations identify suppliers who are not only capable of delivering high-quality products but also committed to CI (Monczka et al., 2016).

Focusing on quality in supplier selection offers numerous advantages. Consistently high-quality goods or services reduce the risk of defects, which can lead to costly returns, rework, or production delays. Moreover, reliable quality minimises the potential for customer complaints, fostering customer satisfaction and loyalty. These benefits collectively contribute to improved operational efficiency, cost savings, and enhanced market competitiveness.

Ensuring quality extends beyond the initial selection process, as it forms the foundation of a successful long-term supplier relationship. By prioritising quality during supplier selection, organisations establish partnerships with suppliers who share their commitment to excellence. This alignment creates a resilient supply chain capable of consistently delivering value to customers while supporting the organisation's strategic objectives.

7.2.7 Cost and TCO

Cost plays a central role in supplier selection, but focusing solely on the initial purchase price often provides an incomplete picture of a supplier's financial impact. To make informed and sustainable procurement decisions, organisations consider the concept of TCO. This approach involves evaluating not only the upfront cost but also additional expenses such as transportation, handling, storage, and maintenance over the lifespan of the product or service. By adopting a comprehensive view of costs, organisations ensure their procurement strategies are both cost-effective and aligned with long-term operational objectives.

The TCO framework provides a more accurate representation of the financial implications associated with a supplier. For instance, while a supplier offering a lower purchase price may initially seem advantageous, their products might incur higher transportation or storage costs due to bulkier packaging or distant shipping origins. Additionally, suppliers with inconsistent quality may lead to increased expenses in terms of repairs, returns, or lost customer satisfaction. Assessing TCO helps organisations identify these hidden costs and evaluate the overall value offered by a supplier (Sollish & Semanik, 2012).

Balancing cost considerations with quality is crucial in this analysis. Procurement decisions based solely on cost can compromise product quality, which can have cascading effects on operational efficiency and customer relationships. Conversely, suppliers who deliver consistent quality at a higher purchase price may represent better long-term value when the reduced likelihood of defects or delays is considered.

By integrating TCO into their supplier evaluation process, organisations enhance their ability to make strategic and financially sound decisions. This approach not only supports cost optimisation but also ensures that procurement aligns with broader supply chain objectives, such as quality, reliability, and sustainability. In a competitive market, understanding and applying TCO enables organisations to build resilient supply chains that deliver both short-term savings and long-term value.

7.2.8 Reliability and Delivery Performance

Reliability and timely delivery are critical factors in supplier selection, as they directly impact an organisation's ability to maintain smooth operations and adhere to production schedules. A supplier's ability to consistently meet delivery deadlines ensures that production lines remain operational, minimising the risk of costly disruptions and delays. For this reason, evaluating a supplier's reliability is an integral part of the procurement process.

Organisations assess suppliers' reliability by examining their logistics capabilities, lead times, and historical performance. Logistics capabilities encompass the supplier's infrastructure, transportation networks, and ability to manage supply chain complexities. Efficient and well-managed logistics systems enable suppliers to deliver goods consistently and in a timely manner. Lead times, or the duration between placing an order and receiving the goods, are scrutinised to ensure they align with the organisation's operational requirements. Suppliers with shorter, predictable lead times offer greater flexibility and responsiveness, which are crucial in dynamic market conditions (Bailey et al., 2015).

Historical performance data is another valuable tool for assessing reliability. By reviewing past records of on-time deliveries, organisations can gauge a supplier's track record and predict future performance. Consistently reliable suppliers reduce the risk of disruptions, enabling organisations to maintain production schedules, meet customer demand, and uphold service quality.

Beyond meeting deadlines, reliable suppliers contribute to the stability and efficiency of the broader supply chain. Their dependability fosters trust and strengthens the partnership, enabling organisations to focus on strategic objectives without concerns about supply interruptions. Selecting suppliers with proven delivery performance enhances the organisation's ability to optimise inventory management and avoid the costly consequences of delays, such as production downtime or expedited shipping fees.

By prioritising reliability and delivery performance in supplier selection, organisations build resilient supply chains capable of supporting their operational and strategic goals. This focus ensures that procurement activities contribute to overall efficiency, customer satisfaction, and competitive advantage.

7.2.9 Financial Stability

Assessing the financial stability of potential suppliers is a critical component of the supplier selection process, as it provides insights into their capacity to sustain operations and meet long-term organisational demands. A financially stable supplier is more likely to maintain uninterrupted service, invest in the necessary resources, and adapt to changing market conditions, ensuring reliable support for the organisation's supply chain.

Organisations evaluate financial stability by reviewing a range of indicators, such as financial statements, credit ratings, and past performance trends. Financial statements, including balance sheets, income statements, and cash flow reports, offer a clear picture of a supplier's profitability, liquidity, and overall financial health. Credit ratings, often provided by independent agencies, reflect the supplier's ability to meet financial obligations, further reinforcing their reliability. By analysing these metrics, organisations can identify suppliers who demonstrate financial resilience and the capacity to invest in infrastructure, technology, or personnel required to meet future demands (Monczka et al., 2016).

The significance of financial stability extends beyond operational reliability. Suppliers experiencing financial difficulties are more likely to face disruptions, such as delays in production, workforce reductions, or even insolvency, which could jeopardise their ability to deliver. These risks can have cascading effects on the organisation's supply chain, leading to production halts, increased costs, and diminished customer satisfaction. Therefore, selecting a supplier with strong financial health mitigates these risks and supports the organisation's overall stability.

Financial stability also plays a role in fostering trust and collaboration between organisations and their suppliers. A supplier with a robust financial foundation is better positioned to commit to long-term partnerships, share risks, and invest in initiatives that drive mutual growth and innovation. By prioritising financial stability in supplier evaluation, organisations enhance the resilience and sustainability of their supply chains, ensuring consistent support for their operational and strategic objectives.

7.2.10 Reputation and Past Performance

The reputation and past performance of a supplier are essential factors in the supplier selection process, as they offer valuable insights into the supplier's reliability, trustworthiness, and overall capability. By examining a supplier's history and standing within the industry, organisations can make informed decisions that minimise risks associated with engaging new suppliers. A strong reputation and proven track record serve as indicators of a supplier's ability to meet commitments and deliver consistent quality.

Organisations typically gather information about a supplier's reputation through various sources, including industry reports, customer reviews, and references from previous clients. Industry reports provide an objective assessment of the supplier's market standing and operational practices, while customer reviews offer real-world insights into the supplier's ability to meet deadlines, deliver quality goods or services, and maintain effective communication. References from other organisations that have worked with the supplier help validate their claims and provide additional assurance regarding their performance (Sollish & Semanik, 2012).

Evaluating past performance is equally critical. Reviewing metrics such as OTD rates, defect rates, and responsiveness to customer concerns provides a detailed understanding of how the supplier has performed in similar engagements. This analysis not only highlights a supplier's strengths but also identifies potential risks or areas for improvement, enabling the organisation to make a balanced and well-informed decision.

The importance of a supplier's reputation and past performance extends beyond operational considerations. A reputable supplier enhances the organisation's own credibility by association, particularly in industries where consumers and regulators closely scrutinise quality and reliability. Additionally, working with a supplier known for ethical practices and sustainability can support the organisation's CSR goals.

By prioritising reputation and past performance during the supplier selection process, organisations reduce uncertainty and establish partnerships built on trust and mutual reliability. This approach supports the creation of a resilient supply chain capable of meeting operational demands and adapting to market challenges.

7.2.11 Alignment with Ethical and Sustainability Standards

The alignment of suppliers with an organisation's ethical and sustainability standards has become a critical aspect of modern procurement and SCM. As consumers, stakeholders, and regulatory bodies increasingly emphasise CSR, organisations are prioritising suppliers who demonstrate a commitment to ethical practices, environmental sustainability, and social responsibility. This approach ensures that procurement decisions not only fulfil operational needs but also support the organisation's broader values and long-term objectives.

Evaluating suppliers based on their ethical practices involves assessing their adherence to labour laws, fair trade principles, and transparency in business operations. Organisations must ensure that suppliers maintain fair wages, safe working conditions, and the absence of exploitative practices within their operations and supply chains. This commitment helps protect the organisation's reputation and fosters trust among stakeholders (Moncza et al., 2015).

Sustainability considerations are equally important. Suppliers are assessed on their environmental impact, including their resource usage, waste management, and efforts to reduce carbon emissions. Organisations increasingly favour suppliers who prioritise renewable energy, sustainable sourcing, and eco-friendly production processes. Such practices not only contribute to environmental preservation but also align with global sustainability initiatives, positioning the organisation as a responsible market leader.

The integration of ethical and sustainability standards into supplier selection has significant long-term benefits. Suppliers who align with these values help organisations mitigate risks associated with non-compliance, such as reputational damage or regulatory penalties. Moreover, these partnerships enhance the organisation's ability to meet the expectations of environmentally conscious consumers and investors, fostering competitive advantage.

By embedding ethical and sustainability criteria into procurement decisions, organisations build a responsible and resilient supply chain. This approach ensures that operational efficiency is achieved without compromising on social or environmental accountability, reflecting the organisation's commitment to positive change and sustainable development.

Case Study – Nestlé (Supplier Scoring, Innovation)

Nestlé applies supplier scorecards across regions, blending performance metrics with supplier innovation capability assessments, enabling the company to prioritise partners who can co-develop products and address traceability requirements across Latin America and Europe.

Case Study – Mining Procurement

In extractive industries, companies such as BHP and Rio Tinto run extended due diligence on local subcontractors, assessing capability to deliver under remote conditions and ensuring community engagement and regulatory compliance. This reduces reputational and operational risk in distant jurisdictions.

7.3 Supplier Relationship Management

SRM converts selected suppliers into value-creating partners through governance, joint planning, and performance review, and SRM tiers suppliers by strategic importance, dedicating more resources to key suppliers that supply critical components or services (Monczka et al., 2016). Effective SRM includes governance forums, joint innovation programmes, and

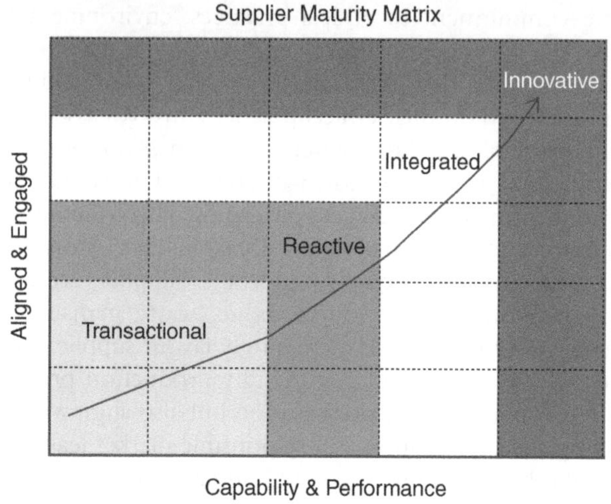

Figure 7.2 Supplier Maturity Model.

transparent performance dashboards (Christopher, 2016). The Supplier Maturity Model (see Figure 7.2) shows the pathway to supplier alignment, capability, and performance.

SRM involves monitoring the supplier's performance to confirm compliance with the agreed terms and conditions. This includes evaluating factors such as quality, timeliness of delivery, and adherence to service standards. A systematic approach to performance management helps organisations identify and address any issues promptly, safeguarding operational efficiency and continuity.

Effective supplier management is built on a foundation of ongoing communication and collaboration. Maintaining open lines of communication fosters transparency and trust, enabling both parties to discuss challenges and identify opportunities for improvement. Collaboration further strengthens the relationship by aligning supplier activities with the organisation's strategic goals. When challenges arise, a problem-solving approach that emphasises mutual understanding and cooperation helps maintain the integrity of the partnership (Sollish & Semanik, 2012).

Building robust supplier relationships offers long-term benefits that extend beyond immediate transactions. Strong partnerships enable organisations to secure better quality products or services, achieve cost savings through negotiated terms, and enhance service levels through improved responsiveness. Suppliers who feel valued and engaged are more likely to prioritise the organisation's needs, invest in innovation, and share valuable market insights, further enhancing the partnership's value.

SRM is not only about performance monitoring but also about fostering a culture of mutual benefit and CI. By investing in these relationships, organisations create a resilient supply chain capable of adapting to market changes and disruptions. This proactive approach contributes to sustained competitive advantage and supports the achievement of long-term organisational objectives.

7.3.1 Performance Management and CI

KPIs for SRM include OTD, quality defects per million, lead-time variability, and innovation impact metrics, and regular business reviews, root cause analysis, and CI initiatives ensure value is sustained and improved over time (Monczka et al., 2016).

Case Study – Siemens and Supplier Co-innovation

Siemens' Amberg plant runs structured supplier development programmes, including joint problem solving and capability investment, which reduced defect rates and increased throughput, showing how SRM converts suppliers into contributors to operational excellence.

7.3.2 Collaborative Models – VMI, CPFR, and Co-development

Collaborative replenishment models such as VMI and CPFR share data and planning responsibility to reduce inventory and improve service, and co-development agreements allow suppliers to participate in product design, shortening development cycles (Christopher, 2016; Monczka et al., 2016).

Case Study – Dell and VMI, and DHL and E-commerce Hubs

Dell's historic VMI arrangements shifted inventory and replenishment responsibility to suppliers, lowering Dell's working capital. At the same time, DHL's Pan-African e-commerce hubs show collaborative logistics partnerships that accelerate market access for SMEs in Africa, illustrating the benefits and executional requirements of collaborative supply models across regions.

7.4 Supplier Risk Management and Resilience

7.4.1 Identifying and Categorising Supplier Risk

Supplier risks include operational, financial, geopolitical, compliance, and ESG risks, and organisations should map suppliers across a risk matrix, prioritising monitoring resources on suppliers whose failure would have the greatest impact (Ivanov & Das, 2020).

Case Study – COVID-19 Response (Pharmaceutical and FMCG)

During the COVID-19 pandemic, companies such as major pharmaceutical and FMCG organisations diversified suppliers, invoked alternative logistics routes, and implemented near-shoring for critical items, reducing exposure to single-country disruptions. These measures illustrate practical resilience when supplier networks are stressed (Ivanov & Das, 2020; Sheffi, 2020).

7.4.2 Mitigation Strategies and Contractual Levers

Mitigation includes dual sourcing, SS, near-shoring, insurance, contractual remedies, and advanced organisations layer real-time monitoring and supplier scorecards with scenario planning and supplier continuity testing (Monczka et al., 2016). Importantly, mitigation choices must consider cost, lead time, and strategic fit (Chopra & Meindl, 2024).

Case Study – Automotive Semiconductor Shortages

Several automotive companies negotiated priority allocations with semiconductor suppliers, entered consortia for supply visibility, and invested in buffer inventories, showing pragmatic contract and portfolio strategies to preserve production continuity.

7.5 Procurement Ethics, Sustainability, and Social Value

7.5.1 Embedding ESG in Procurement Decisions

Procurement is a powerful lever for sustainability, from specifying low-carbon materials to requiring supplier labour standards, and organisations that integrate ESG into procurement create upstream incentives for suppliers to decarbonise and improve labour practices, adding resilience and reputational value (Monczka et al., 2016; Unilever, 2023).

Case study – Unilever and Smallholder Inclusion

Unilever's programme shows how procurement that factors social value can stabilise supply, improve farmer incomes, and align with corporate sustainability claims across continents (Unilever, 2023).

7.5.2 Anti-corruption, Transparency, and Modern Slavery Compliance

Modern procurement must address corruption and modern slavery risks, particularly in GSCs, and due diligence, clause inclusion, audits, and supplier training are practical mechanisms for compliance, with public disclosure increasing accountability (Monczka et al., 2016). Legislative and regulatory compliance carries with it a level of complexity that is generally beyond the skills of many organisations and requires the services of specialist law firms to ensure compliance.

Case Study – Apparel Industry and Modern Slavery Remediation

Several global apparel companies established supplier audits, remediation plans, and capacity building in Southeast Asia, combining auditing with supplier development to reduce risk and improve conditions, showing the need to move beyond audits to capability building.

7.5.3 Best Practices in Procurement and Supplier Management

Implementing best practices in procurement and supplier management is essential for organisations seeking to achieve their strategic objectives and optimise supplier relationships. These practices promote transparency, consistency, and collaboration while enhancing decision-making processes and ensuring alignment with organisational goals. By adopting these approaches, organisations can strengthen their procurement strategies and build more resilient and effective supply chains.

Establishing clear procurement policies is fundamental to maintaining consistency and fairness in supplier selection and contract management. Well-defined policies provide a framework for making objective decisions, ensuring that all suppliers are evaluated against transparent criteria. This approach reduces the risk of bias, fosters trust among suppliers, and reinforces accountability within the procurement process. Clear policies also streamline contract negotiations, minimising misunderstandings and protecting the interests of both parties (Monczka et al., 2016).

Leveraging data-driven decision-making is another best practice that enables organisations to make informed and proactive procurement choices. By utilising advanced data analytics tools, organisations can access real-time information about supplier performance, market trends, and potential risks. This insight supports accurate supplier evaluations, improves forecasting, and enhances risk management by identifying vulnerabilities before they escalate.

Regular supplier audits are vital for maintaining high standards and ensuring compliance with contractual obligations. Audits provide a structured mechanism for evaluating supplier performance; identifying areas for improvement; and addressing gaps in quality, delivery, or adherence to ethical and sustainability standards. This ongoing evaluation fosters CI and strengthens supplier relationships, contributing to long-term success.

Promoting cross-functional collaboration in procurement is equally critical. Involving different departments, such as operations, finance, and sustainability, ensures that supplier management strategies align with the organisation's overarching objectives. Collaborative decision-making enhances information sharing and integrates diverse perspectives, resulting in more holistic and effective procurement strategies.

By embedding these best practices into procurement and supplier management, organisations can enhance operational efficiency, mitigate risks, and achieve strategic alignment. These approaches not only optimise supplier relationships but also support the development of resilient and sustainable supply chains capable of meeting the demands of a dynamic business environment.

7.6 Technology, Data, and the Future of Procurement

7.6.1 Digital Procurement Platforms and Analytics

E-procurement platforms, supplier portals, and analytics transform sourcing by increasing transparency, shortening cycle times, and enabling category analytics, and ML can identify anomalous pricing, supplier risk signals, and optimisation opportunities across large portfolios (Christopher, 2016). The Procurement Technology Map (see Figure 7.3) illustrates Procurement 4.0 and its supporting technologies.

Case Study – Walmart/AI Use in Procurement and Logistics

Walmart's investments in analytics and procurement systems have improved SS decisions and supplier collaboration, reducing stockouts and streamlining replenishment, and these technological investments scale across global operations and show the benefits of analytics-driven procurement (Chopra & Meindl, 2024).

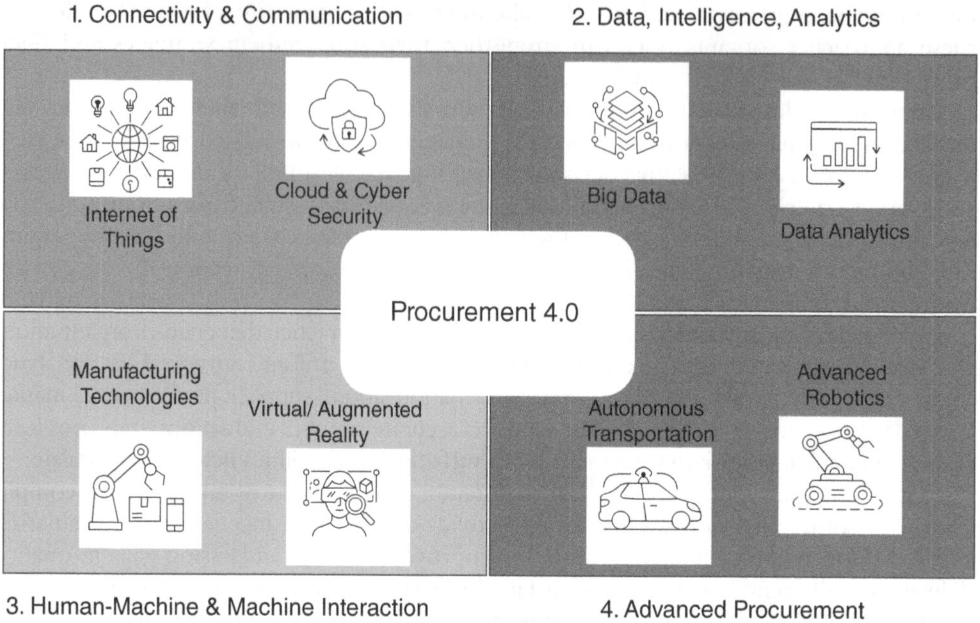

Figure 7.3 Procurement Technology Map.

7.6.2 Blockchain, Traceability, and Supplier Collaboration

Blockchain and distributed ledger technologies offer potential for provenance and immutable records, especially in food and high-value goods supply chains, and pilot programmes in agri-food and luxury goods show promise for traceability and consumer trust (Christopher, 2016).

7.7 Best Practices and Governance

1 Segment spend and apply the right strategy per category; use TCO and strategic importance, not price alone (Monczka et al., 2016).
2 Embed cross-functional need definition; include operations, quality, legal and sustainability early in specification development.
3 Tier suppliers and allocate SRM resources accordingly; invest in key suppliers for joint value creation (Monczka et al., 2016).
4 Build supplier resilience via portfolio design; include dual sourcing and near-shoring where strategic (Ivanov & Das, 2020) (Chopra & Meindl, 2024).
5 Integrate ESG criteria into procurement and contracts; measure and report supplier sustainability performance (Unilever, 2023).

7.8 Conclusion

Procurement and supplier management are strategic, multifaceted disciplines that extend beyond cost control; they create opportunities for innovation, resilience, and social value when executed with rigour (Christopher, 2016; Monczka et al., 2016). By integrating robust sourcing processes, contractual risk allocation, SRM, and technology, organisations can convert suppliers into partners who contribute to competitive advantage. The integrated case studies in this chapter illustrate how companies across sectors and geographies operationalise these principles.

SRM adds significant value to the procurement process. It goes beyond mere transactional relationships by fostering collaboration and cooperation between organisations and their suppliers. SRM encourages continuous communication, helping to align objectives, mitigate risks, and address challenges in a timely manner. This collaborative approach also provides the opportunity to explore innovation and improve operational efficiencies, benefiting both parties involved. Moreover, SRM supports the integration of ethical and sustainable practices within the supply chain, ensuring that organisations can meet their social responsibility goals while maintaining their business objectives.

The development of strong supplier partnerships is essential for building a resilient supply chain. Effective supplier management practices enable organisations to quickly respond to disruptions and adapt to changes in market conditions, ensuring continuity of supply and minimising operational downtime. These strategic partnerships not only support immediate supply chain needs but also contribute to the long-term growth and sustainability of the business. By prioritising supplier relationships, organisations create a solid foundation for growth, characterised by increased trust, innovation, and mutual benefit.

Overall, a well-managed procurement and supplier management strategy enhances supply chain resilience, reduces risk, and contributes to sustainable organisational growth, making it a cornerstone of successful SCM (Christopher, 2016; Monczka et al., 2016).

Q&A Section

Here is a short quiz to test your knowledge. The answers are provided in Appendix C.

1. What is the main goal of procurement in SCM?
2. Why is need identification important in the procurement process?
3. What is the purpose of conducting a market analysis in procurement?
4. What is a RFP used for?
5. How are bids evaluated during supplier selection?
6. Why is contract finalisation crucial in procurement?
7. What is SRM?
8. Why is a supplier's reputation important in the selection process?
9. How does SRM contribute to risk management?
10. What is a key benefit of aligning suppliers with ethical and sustainability standards?

8 Production and Operations Management

Learning Outcomes

By the end of this chapter, learners will be able to:

- Explain production planning concepts and the S&OP/Integrated Business Planning (IBP) cycle.
- Apply lean manufacturing principles and identify waste in a production process.
- Use basic quality management tools (TQM/DMAIC/SPC) to analyse a defect case.
- Design a production control response to a capacity or quality shock.
- Critique the trade-offs between lean efficiency and resilience in a manufacturing context.

Production and operations management constitutes the operational backbone of supply chains, encompassing the planning, coordination, control, and CI of resources required to produce goods and services efficiently. Effective production and operations systems align capacity with demand, ensure consistent quality, and create the conditions for sustainable competitiveness across domestic and international markets (Slack et al., 2019; Stevenson, 2021).

This chapter delves into three core aspects of production and operations management: production planning, lean manufacturing, and quality management. Together, these principles and methodologies form the foundation of operational excellence in modern supply chains.

8.1 Production Planning

Production planning organises the conversion of inputs into finished goods that satisfy customers, while balancing cost, lead time, and flexibility. Core instruments include the Master Production Schedule (MPS), Material Requirements Planning (MRP), S&OP, or IBP, and capacity planning. Effective planning requires a combination of deterministic modelling, stochastic analysis, and human judgement, particularly where demand exhibits seasonality or volatility (Heizer et al., 2020; Stevenson, 2021).

DOI: 10.4324/9781003740568-8

8.1.1 MPS, MRP, and S&OP

The MPS provides a detailed time-phased plan for finished goods, while MRP translates the MPS into component requirements, accounting for lead times and bill of materials structures (Stevenson, 2021). S&OP or IBP integrates commercial, supply, and financial plans, and thereby aligns the organisation's strategic priorities with operational constraints. Recent global practice emphasises an IBP cycle that is monthly, scenario-driven, and supported by analytics, to reconcile short-term fulfilment with long-term strategy (Simchi-Levi & Timmermans, 2021).

Case Study – Woolworths Group, Australia

Woolworths Group uses an integrated S&OP process (see Figure 8.1) to manage grocery seasonality across Australia, combining POS data, promotions planning, and supplier collaboration to avoid stockouts during peak holiday periods, while controlling wastage for perishable categories (Woolworths Group, 2023). This example demonstrates how retail S&OP must connect promotional calendars with logistics and supplier capacity to align supply with short, sharp demand spikes (Christopher, 2016; Woolworths Group, 2023).

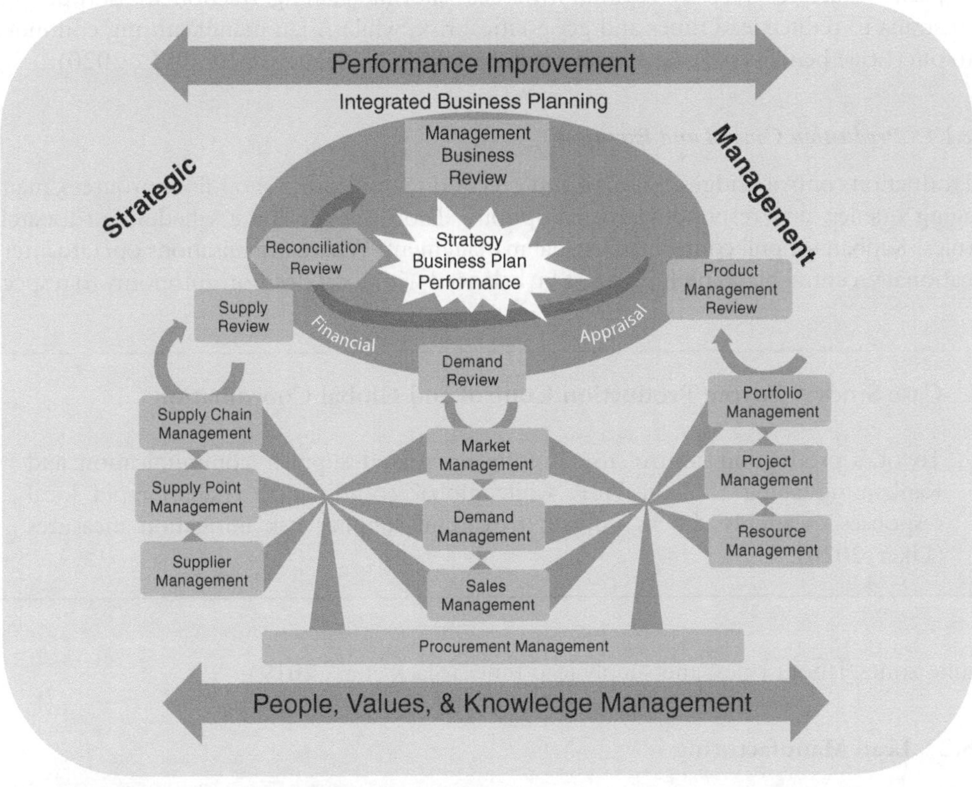

Figure 8.1 Integrated S&OP/IBP Cycle.

8.1.2 Capacity Planning and Flexibility

Capacity planning assesses workforce, equipment, and facility capabilities to meet forecasted demand. Strategic choices include long-term capacity additions, medium-term subcontracting or overtime, and short-term use of temporary labour or outsourcing. Contemporary practice increasingly combines capacity modelling with digital twins and scenario analysis, which allows organisations to simulate demand shocks and test contingency options (Ivanov et al., 2019).

Case Study – Siemens, Amberg Electronics Plant, Germany

Siemens' Amberg plant combines flexible capacity layouts with digital monitoring to reallocate production rapidly across lines, thereby increasing throughput and reducing changeover times. The plant's use of sensors and local automated cells exemplifies how capacity and flexibility planning are now embedded in smart factories (Liker, 2020; Siemens, 2024).

8.1.3 Global Perspective

Capacity strategies vary by region, with near-shoring gaining traction in Europe and Australia to reduce lead times and geopolitical risk, while Asian manufacturing continues to offer scale benefits for cost-sensitive segments (He & Zhang, 2020; PWC, 2020).

8.1.4 Production Control and Execution

Production control bridges planning and execution, monitoring shop-floor progress, managing queues, and responding to disruptions. Tools include finite scheduling, dispatch rules, Kanban for pull control, and visual management. Where organisations operate internationally, central planning hubs must be balanced with local decision autonomy to respect time zones, labour rules, and supply lead times (Slack et al., 2019).

Case Study – Toyota Production Control and Global Coordination

Toyota's production control uses tightly integrated supplier communication and Kanban signalling to limit WIP, while global coordination enables rapid local responses to supply shocks, subject to careful supplier risk mitigation measures (Liker, 2020).

8.2 Lean Manufacturing

Lean manufacturing prioritises value creation for the customer by systematically identifying and eliminating waste from processes (see Figure 8.2). Lean is not a set of isolated tools, but a managerial philosophy underpinned by CI, respect for people, and flow orientation (Imai, 1986; Womack & Jones, 1996).

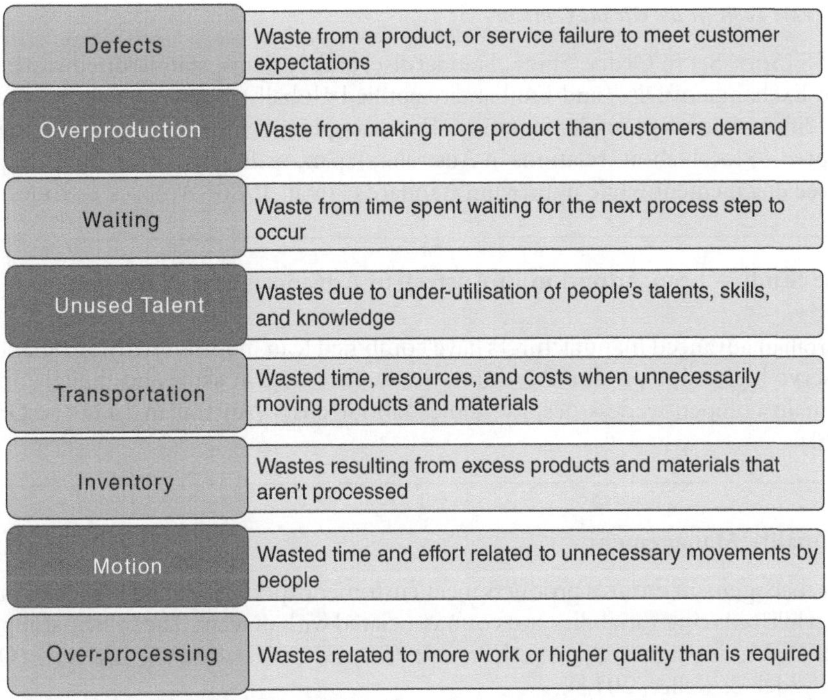

Figure 8.2 The Eight Wastes of Lean.

8.2.1 Principles and Waste Elimination

Lean principles emphasise value, VSM, flow, pull systems, and CI or kaizen. The commonly cited eight types of waste provide a diagnostic framework for prioritising improvement opportunities (Engineering with Management, 2025; Womack & Jones, 1996).

Case Study – Toyota and Supplier Integration for Waste Reduction

Toyota's approach, encapsulated in the TPS, focuses on jidoka, also known as autonomation or "automation with a human touch", a principle within the TPS, is focused on stopping production when an abnormality is detected. Together with JIT, it aids in reducing inventory, shortening lead times, and improving quality via empowered problem-solving at the line. Toyota's supplier development programmes illustrate how lean extends beyond the factory gate, embedding capability in upstream suppliers (Liker, 2020).

Additional Case Study – Zara, Inditex, Spain, Fast Fashion

Zara's vertical model combines near-market manufacturing, rapid design-to-store cycles, and tight inventory control to implement a lean/agile hybrid. The company reduces markdowns and overproduction by using frequent replenishment rather than long production runs, demonstrating lean thinking adapted to fast consumer markets (Blanchard, 2022).

8.2.2 Lean Tools in the Global Context

VSM, 5S (Sort, Set in Order, Shine, Standardise, and Sustain), standardised work, "Single Minute Exchange of Die", and Kanban are applied globally; however, cultural and labour system differences affect implementation. For example, 5S and suggestion schemes might be adapted to local labour relations in Australia, Japan, or European countries to preserve employee engagement while improving standards (Imai, 1986; Womack & Jones, 1996).

Case Study – Lean Adoption in Australian Advanced Manufacturing

Australian advanced manufacturers have combined lean methods with automation to preserve high-value production domestically, investing in skills and digital tools to maintain competitiveness despite higher labour costs (Australian Industry Group, 2020).

8.3 Quality Management

Quality management ensures products meet customer expectations and regulatory requirements, while reducing variability and costs associated with defects. The principal approaches include TQM, Six Sigma, Statistical Process Control (SPC), and CI (Kaizen) (Oakland, 2014; Pyzdek & Keller, 2014).

8.3.1 TQM, Six Sigma, and SPC

TQM creates an organisational culture oriented to quality across functions, emphasising leadership, employee involvement, and customer focus (Oakland, 2014). Six Sigma complements TQM by applying a rigorous statistical methodology, DMAIC, pronounced "du-may-ik" (Define, Measure, Analyse, Improve, and Control) (see Figure 8.3) to reduce

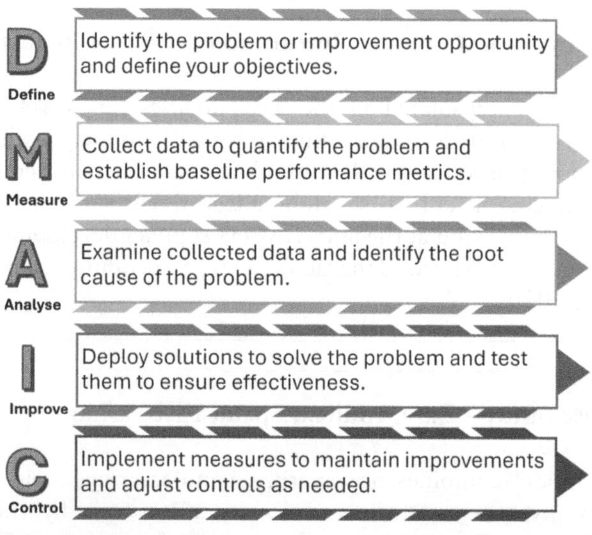

Figure 8.3 DMAIC in Practice.

process variation and defects (Pyzdek & Keller, 2014). SPC and control charts provide online monitoring that enables early detection of process shifts (Montgomery, 2013).

Case Study – Motorola and the Foundations of Six Sigma

While Motorola originally developed Six Sigma, later adopters such as General Electric scaled it as a strategic programme. Six Sigma projects targeting high-value defects delivered measurable cost savings and reliability improvements in electronics and aerospace sectors, illustrating the technique's capacity to produce quantifiable quality gains (Pyzdek & Keller, 2014).

Case Study – Pharmaceutical Quality and Regulatory Compliance

In highly regulated sectors such as pharmaceuticals, TQM and SPC are essential. Cross-functional quality teams and robust control plans prevent non-conformances that could lead to regulatory action, supply interruptions, and reputational damage (Oakland, 2014).

8.3.2 Quality, Culture, and People

Quality management is inseparable from people management. Kaizen programmes, suggestion schemes, and structured problem-solving empower the workforce to address root causes. Evidence suggests that organisations with embedded quality cultures achieve superior long-term performance because CI becomes part of daily work rather than periodic projects (Imai, 1986; Oakland, 2014).

Case Study – Nestlé, Latin America, AI for Quality Forecasting

Nestlé's AI-driven analytics for seasonal categories links quality monitoring to demand forecasting, reducing product variability at peak production times and enabling pre-emptive corrective actions, thus blending statistical quality control with modern data science (Nestlé, 2024; Waller & Fawcett, 2013).

8.4 Conclusion

Production and operations management remain central to supply chain performance. Effective production planning aligns capacity and demand through tools such as MPS, MRP, and IBP, and requires scenario capability and cross-functional governance (Stevenson, 2021). Lean manufacturing provides a robust philosophy for waste elimination and flow improvement, adaptable to both high-volume manufacturing and agile retail environments (Liker, 2020; Womack & Jones, 1996). Quality management, anchored in TQM, Six Sigma, and SPC, safeguards customer trust and regulatory compliance and is increasingly augmented by analytics and Industry 4.0 technologies (Montgomery, 2013; Oakland,

2014; Siemens, 2024). Across all topics, globalisation, sustainability, and digital transformation modify traditional practices, and organisations that integrate people, process, and technology with an international mindset will sustain operational advantage.

Q&A Section

Here is a short quiz to test your knowledge. The answers are provided in Appendix C.

1. What is the main goal of production and operations management?
2. What is production planning?
3. What does a MPS outline?
4. What is the purpose of capacity planning in production?
5. What is lean manufacturing focused on?
6. Name two types of waste that lean manufacturing seeks to eliminate.
7. What is TQM?
8. What is the goal of Six Sigma?
9. How does SPC support quality management? SPC uses statistical techniques to monitor process performance and control quality.
10. What is Kaizen, and why is it important?

9 Logistics and Distribution

Learning Outcomes

By the end of this chapter, learners will be able to:

- Describe the major logistics functions and transport mode considerations.
- Evaluate network topologies and recommend distribution strategies for given constraints.
- Apply basic routing or hub-and-spoke logic to a distribution problem.
- Identify warehouse KPIs and interpret dashboard metrics for performance improvement.
- Propose last-mile solutions that balance cost, speed, and sustainability.

9.1 Introduction to Logistics and Distribution

Logistics and distribution constitute the operational bridge between production and the point of consumption; they determine whether customer promises are delivered in full, on time, and in good condition (Christopher, 2016). In an era of globalised trade, rapid e-commerce growth, and heightened sustainability expectations, logistics is simultaneously a cost centre and a source of competitive differentiation (Rushton et al., 2017).

At its core, logistics encompasses the planning, implementation, and control of the movement and storage of goods, services, and information throughout the supply chain (see Figure 9.1). This process spans transportation, warehousing, inventory management, and order fulfilment. Distribution, as a subset of logistics, focuses on the strategic and operational activities involved in moving goods from the manufacturer to the end consumer. By integrating these functions, organisations create a cohesive system that maximises resource utilisation, minimises costs, and ensures timely product delivery.

This chapter delves into the critical elements of logistics and distribution, including transportation management, warehouse operations, and distribution network design. It explores the strategic decisions companies must make to optimise these processes and highlights their importance in achieving a resilient and customer-focused supply chain.

DOI: 10.4324/9781003740568-9

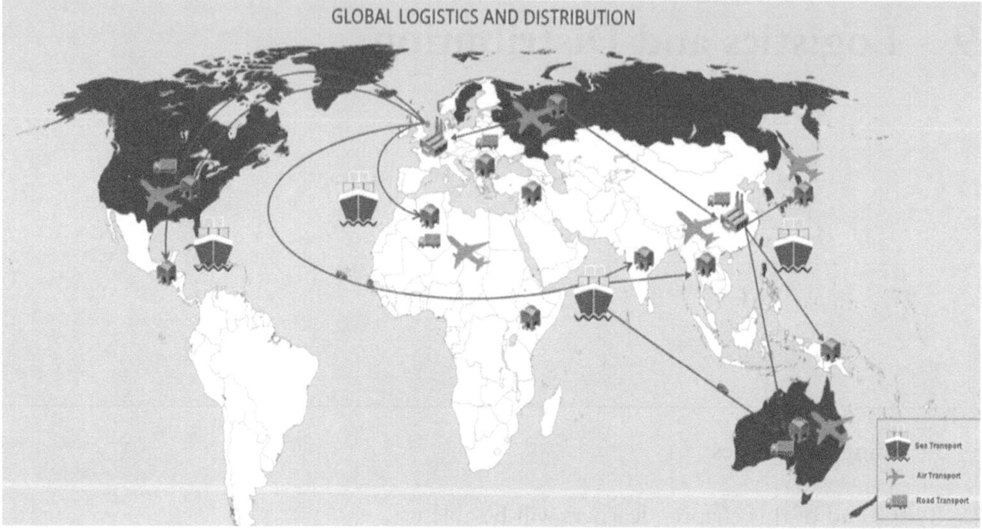

Figure 9.1 Logistics and Distribution.

9.1.1 The Logistic Value Proposition and Strategic Trade-offs

Logistics decisions balance three interdependent objectives, namely cost, service, and speed, with sustainability increasingly treated as a fourth constraining objective (Christopher, 2016; Grant et al., 2017). For example, faster transport modes raise costs and carbon intensity, while inventory buffers reduce stockout risk at the expense of working capital. Effective network design, therefore, requires explicit articulation of trade-offs, supported by quantitative models and scenario testing (Rushton et al., 2017).

Case Study – Woolworths Group, Australia, Seasonal Fulfilment Trade-offs

Woolworths' grocery network uses scenario-based S&OP inputs to adjust DC activations and transport lanes during holiday peaks, balancing service levels for perishable goods against the elevated costs and spoilage risk associated with increased throughput (Woolworths Group, 2023). This practical example illustrates how retailers operationalise trade-offs between speed, freshness, and cost (see also Christopher, 2016; Hubner et al., 2013).

9.1.2 Strategic Considerations in Logistics and Distribution

Developing an effective logistics and distribution strategy requires a holistic approach that considers cost efficiency, customer satisfaction, and adaptability to changing market conditions. Businesses must weigh the trade-offs between speed and cost, balancing the need for rapid deliveries with budget constraints. Additionally, companies must remain agile to respond to disruptions such as supply chain bottlenecks, natural disasters, or geopolitical events.

Sustainability is increasingly shaping strategic decisions in logistics and distribution. Customers and stakeholders demand greater transparency and environmental accountability, prompting organisations to adopt greener practices. For instance, companies demonstrate their commitment to sustainability by investing in renewable energy-powered warehouses, optimising delivery routes to reduce fuel consumption, and collaborating with eco-friendly transport providers.

Technological advancements continue to redefine the possibilities in logistics and distribution. AI and ML enable predictive analytics to forecast demand and optimise supply chain operations. IoT devices provide real-time visibility into inventory levels and shipment statuses, enhancing decision-making and reducing inefficiencies. Blockchain technology is also gaining traction, offering secure and transparent systems for tracking goods throughout the supply chain (Christopher, 2016).

9.2 Transportation Management

Transportation management is the single most significant non-inventory logistical cost for most organisations; therefore, mode choice (see Figure 9.2), consolidation strategies, and routing optimisation materially affect total landed cost and service reliability (Bowersox et al., 2013).

Transportation management is a cornerstone of logistics and distribution, encompassing the planning, execution, and optimisation of goods movement across supply chain networks. It plays a pivotal role in determining the efficiency, cost-effectiveness, and reliability of supply chain operations. The transportation process involves selecting appropriate modes, planning optimal routes, scheduling deliveries, and optimising load. As GSCs grow increasingly complex, effective transportation management has become indispensable for businesses aiming to maintain competitiveness and meet customer expectations.

The choice of transportation modes directly influences overall supply chain performance. Each mode – road, rail, air, and maritime – has unique advantages and limitations, and their effective integration often determines the success of logistics operations. Technological advancements and sustainability initiatives are also reshaping transportation management, making it a dynamic and rapidly evolving field.

9.2.1 Road Transport

Road transport provides door-to-door flexibility and is indispensable for last-mile fulfilment; however, it is vulnerable to congestion, driver shortages, and regulatory fragmentation

Mode of Transport	Typical usage	Advantages	Disadvantages
Road	• Door-to-door. • Ideal for mixed cargo. • Typically used for first and final leg.	• Most flexible for door-to-door. • Relatively inexpensive.	• Limited to continental transport. • Urban congestion. • Damage to roads.
Rail	• For domestic, continental, and inter-continental transport.	• Ideal for heavy goods and long distances. • Environmentally friendly.	• Connection to rail systems required. • Complete trains require large volumes (thus low frequency). • Otherwise handling in yards (low transport speed).
Air	• To ensure fast transport.	• Fast and safe.	• Expensive. • Limits on size and weight. • Typically as part of multimodal transport.
Sea	• Bulk shipments, where long lead time is acceptable.	• Ideal for bulky and heavy goods. • Highly standardised sea containers worldwide. • Less costly than air for inter-continental transport.	• Inflexible routes. • Long lead time. • Inflexible timetables (ship will not wait for a missing container).

Figure 9.2 Mode Choice Matrix.

across borders (Coyle et al., 2017). In large, sparsely populated countries such as Australia, fuel, distances, and intermodal transfer times must be built into lead-time calculations.

Road transport is among the most versatile and widely used modes of transportation due to its flexibility and adaptability. It enables direct-to-door delivery, making it particularly effective for short to medium distances and last-mile logistics. Road transport is essential for connecting suppliers, warehouses, and customers, especially in local and regional markets. Trucks and vans are the primary vehicles used in this mode, capable of accommodating a wide range of cargo types and volumes.

However, road transport is not without its challenges. Traffic congestion, fluctuating fuel prices, and weather conditions can disrupt delivery schedules and increase costs. Regulatory variations across regions further complicate operations, requiring businesses to navigate differing standards for vehicle emissions, safety, and driver qualifications. Despite these obstacles, road transport remains integral to supply chains, as other modes cannot match its flexibility (Coyle et al., 2017).

Technological innovations are significantly enhancing road transport efficiency. Global Positioning System (GPS) tracking and route optimisation software enable companies to minimise travel distances, reduce fuel consumption, and improve delivery accuracy. For example, logistics providers such as Linfox and Toll have adopted dynamic routing technologies to streamline operations and enhance customer service. These advancements improve operational efficiency and contribute to sustainability by reducing greenhouse gas emissions.

Case Study – Linfox, Toll, and Dynamic Routing in Australia

Major Australian carriers have implemented dynamic routing and telematics to compress empty-running kilometres and improve utilisation, reducing per-unit transport cost while lowering emissions intensity (Coyle et al., 2017). These operational investments translate into improved OTIF (On Time In Full) performance for retail and grocery customers.

9.2.2 Rail Transport

Rail is effective for high-volume, long-distance flows, particularly bulk commodities and containerised freight between gateways and regional hubs, offering superior energy efficiency per tonne-kilometre (Bowersox et al., 2013). Limitations include fixed infrastructure and first/last-mile transfer costs.

Rail transport offers cost advantages compared to road transport, as trains can carry larger volumes at a lower cost per tonne-kilometre. Additionally, rail transport is considered environmentally friendly due to its reduced fuel consumption and lower emissions relative to other modes.

Despite its advantages, rail transport is constrained by infrastructure requirements. Rail networks are fixed, limiting accessibility to locations without established connections. This dependency on infrastructure reduces its flexibility, making it less suitable for last-mile delivery. Consequently, rail is often used with road transport to bridge the gap between rail terminals and final destinations (Bowersox et al., 2013).

Rail transport plays a vital role in intermodal logistics, where multiple modes are combined to optimise efficiency and cost-effectiveness. For instance, goods transported by rail from manufacturing hubs to regional DCs can then be transferred to trucks for local delivery. This integration between rail and road ensures that businesses can leverage the cost benefits of rail while addressing its limitations in accessibility.

> **Case Study – Intermodal Rail in Europe and Australia**
>
> Retailers and manufacturers increasingly use rail for long domestic hauls, combining rail legs with short truck movements; the economic and carbon benefits of rail are maximised when paired with appropriately located DCs (Rushton et al., 2017).

9.2.3 Air Transport

Air freight supports high-value, time-sensitive goods and is often used for inventory rebalancing during stockouts, new product launches, and perishables requiring speed (Chopra & Meindl, 2024). Air transport's high cost and carbon intensity make it a tactical option, not a baseline channel.

Air transport is the fastest mode of transportation, offering unmatched speed for delivering high-value and time-sensitive goods. Industries such as electronics, pharmaceuticals, and luxury goods rely heavily on air freight to meet stringent delivery timelines and maintain product quality. For instance, perishable items like fresh produce and seafood benefit from the rapid transit offered by air transport, ensuring they reach consumers in peak condition.

However, air transport's speed comes at a premium. High operational costs, including fuel expenses and airport fees, make it the most expensive transportation mode. Cargo capacity is also limited, restricting its use to smaller, high-value shipments. Additionally, air transport has a significant environmental impact, with higher carbon emissions per unit transported than road, rail, or maritime options (Drake, 2012).

Despite these limitations, air transport remains indispensable for GSCs that prioritise speed and reliability. Advances in aviation technology, such as fuel-efficient aircraft and optimised flight paths, are helping to mitigate environmental concerns while reducing costs. Moreover, integrating air transport with other modes, such as maritime or road, creates flexible and efficient intermodal solutions.

> **Case Study – Electronics Product Launch Logistics**
>
> Global consumer electronics companies use air charter capacity for launch windows to ensure in-market synchronisation across regions, accepting higher transport spend to capture market share and preserve brand momentum (Chopra & Meindl, 2024).

9.2.4 Maritime Transport and Containerisation

Maritime shipping remains the backbone of international trade, offering the most cost-efficient transport for bulk and containerised goods over long distances (Rushton et al., 2017). Port congestion, container imbalances, and geopolitical frictions, however, introduce lead-time volatility.

Maritime transport facilitates the movement of goods across global markets. It is the most cost-effective mode for shipping large volumes of cargo over long distances, particularly bulk items like oil, metals, and containerised goods. The economies of scale achieved in maritime transport make it an essential component of supply chains connecting diverse economies.

Despite its cost advantages, maritime transport has notable limitations. It is considerably slower than air or road transport, making it less suitable for time-sensitive shipments. Weather-related disruptions, port congestion, and geopolitical issues can complicate maritime logistics. Additionally, the need for extensive port infrastructure restricts its accessibility to coastal areas, necessitating complementary modes such as road or rail for inland distribution (Rushton et al., 2022).

Sustainability is an increasing focus in maritime transport, driven by regulatory pressures and stakeholder expectations. Innovations such as energy-efficient ship designs, alternative fuels, and optimised shipping routes are helping reduce the environmental impact of maritime logistics. For example, the International Maritime Organisation's regulations on sulphur emissions are prompting shipping companies to adopt cleaner fuels and technologies.

Case Study – Container Imbalances during COVID-19

The pandemic highlighted systemic imbalances, causing sailing cancellations and port congestion that cascaded into longer dwell times and higher demurrage, demonstrating the vulnerability of global liner networks to demand shocks (Ivanov & Das, 2020; Sheffi, 2020).

9.2.5 Multimodal and Intermodal Solutions

Best practice combines modes to optimise cost, lead time, and carbon footprint, supported by integrated documentation (e.g., multimodal bills of lading) and visibility systems that span carriers. Intermodal solutions require coordinated transhipment capacity and contractual clarity between providers (Rushton et al., 2017).

Multimodal transportation combines multiple modes, such as sea and rail or air and road, allowing for an optimised balance between efficiency and cost-effectiveness. For instance, maritime transport can be used for the bulk of an international journey, followed by road transport for final delivery. By combining modes, companies can take advantage of each mode's strengths while mitigating its limitations.

Optimising transportation management reduces operational costs, enhances delivery times, and improves customer satisfaction. An effective transportation management system (TMS) requires real-time monitoring, predictive analytics, and decision-making capabilities to respond to variables such as traffic, fuel prices, and customer demand fluctuations. Advanced digital systems that integrate data from various sources offer significant advantages in forecasting demand, planning routes, and optimising load capacities, further improving logistics performance (Coyle et al., 2017).

Case Study – DHL Pan-Regional Multimodal Corridors

DHL's regional express and freight corridors combine air, sea, and road legs with centralised control towers to reduce transit times and increase visibility for cross-border e-commerce flows, enabling SMEs to reach new markets with managed risk (DHL, 2023).

9.2.6 Technology, Optimisation, and Fleet Electrification

Route optimisation, telematics, and AI-driven expected time of arrival prediction reduce cost and improve customer experience, while electrification of last-mile fleets and modal shift programmes support decarbonisation targets (Chopra & Meindl, 2024; Grant et al., 2017).

GPS tracking systems provide real-time data on shipment locations, enabling companies to monitor progress and address potential delays proactively. Route optimisation software identifies the most efficient paths for transportation, reducing fuel consumption and improving delivery times.

The IoT is another transformative force in transportation management. IoT-enabled sensors on vehicles and cargo provide valuable data on temperature, humidity, and other conditions, ensuring the integrity of sensitive goods. For example, pharmaceutical companies use IoT technology to monitor the cold chain for vaccines and other temperature-sensitive products, ensuring compliance with stringent quality standards.

AI and predictive analytics are further enhancing decision-making in transportation management. These technologies analyse historical and real-time data to forecast demand, optimise fleet utilisation, and anticipate disruptions. For instance, AI-powered platforms can predict weather patterns that may affect transportation routes, allowing companies to adjust schedules and avoid delays.

Case Study – Electric Last-Mile Pilots

Several large retailers and 3PL providers are piloting electric vans and urban consolidation centres to reduce urban emissions and congestion, supported by municipal charging infrastructure investment (Grant et al., 2017; Woolworths Group, 2023).

9.2.7 Sustainability in Transportation Management

Sustainability is a growing priority in transportation management, as businesses and consumers demand environmentally responsible practices. Companies are adopting initiatives such as electric vehicles, alternative fuels, and carbon offset programmes to reduce their environmental impact. Additionally, optimising load capacities and streamlining routes help minimise emissions and improve fuel efficiency.

Collaboration between businesses, governments, and technology providers is critical for advancing sustainability in transportation. Public investments in infrastructure, such as electrified rail networks and charging stations for electric trucks, support the adoption of greener transport solutions. Similarly, partnerships between logistics companies and renewable energy providers enable the transition to cleaner transportation systems.

Transportation management is a critical part of logistics and distribution, involving the planning, execution, and optimisation of moving goods. It includes the selection of appropriate transportation modes, route planning, scheduling, and load optimisation. Transportation has a substantial impact on overall supply chain costs and plays a significant role in the reliability and efficiency of the entire supply chain network.

9.3 Warehouse Management

Warehouses are dynamic fulfilment nodes where inventory, information, and value-added services meet, and modern warehousing emphasises agility, accuracy, and sustainability (Bowersox et al., 2013). Digital Dashboards (see Figure 9.3) extract data from WMS to provide a real-time picture of performance against KPIs. Logistics performance is managed through a balanced set of KPIs, including OTIF, cost per order, inventory days of supply, order cycle time (OCT), and carbon per shipment. Dashboards should enable drill-down to SKU, lane, and customer level to drive CI (Bowersox et al., 2013).

Warehouse management is a critical component of logistics and distribution, serving as the hub where goods are received, stored, and dispatched to meet customer demand. The efficiency of warehouse operations directly impacts the supply chain's overall performance, influencing delivery times, inventory accuracy, and cost management. Effective warehouse

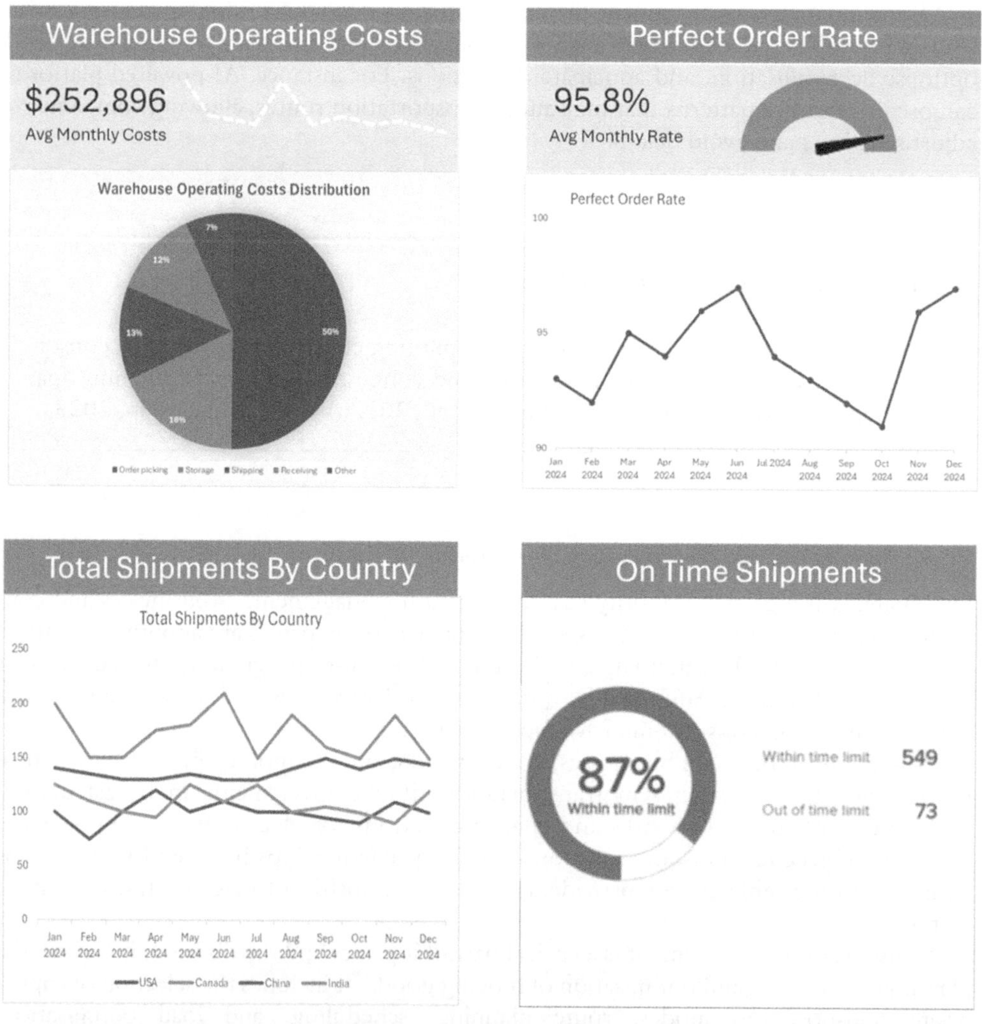

Figure 9.3 Warehouse KPI Dashboard.

management ensures the smooth flow of goods through the supply chain and provides a competitive advantage by enabling organisations to respond quickly to market changes and customer needs.

The primary objectives of warehouse management are to optimise space utilisation, minimise handling costs, and reduce order processing times. Achieving these goals requires advanced technology, strategic planning, and operational excellence. Modern warehouses have evolved from static storage facilities to dynamic hubs, integrating automation, data analytics, and real-time inventory tracking to support complex supply chain operations. This chapter explores the key elements of warehouse management, including inventory control, layout design, handling equipment, and innovative strategies that enhance operational efficiency and agility.

9.3.1 Inventory Control and Replenishment Strategies

Inventory policies (re-order point, periodic review, min/max, QR/kanban, VMI) must be aligned with demand variability, lead times, and service targets. Advanced WMS integrates real-time telemetry and links replenishment to POS data in retail omnichannel contexts (Chopra & Meindl, 2024).

Inventory control is at the heart of effective warehouse management, ensuring that stock levels are aligned with customer demand without incurring the costs associated with overstocking or stockouts. Advanced WMS are vital in maintaining real-time inventory visibility, enabling organisations to track stock levels, turnover rates, and the precise location of goods within the warehouse. These systems support decision-making and streamline inventory replenishment processes by providing accurate and up-to-date information.

Real-time inventory tracking helps businesses address common challenges such as misplaced goods, delayed shipments, and inaccurate stock counts. For example, a retailer relying on outdated inventory records may inadvertently overpromise stock availability, resulting in customer dissatisfaction and lost sales. In contrast, businesses that leverage advanced WMS can provide accurate stock information to customers and ensure timely order fulfilment (Bowersox et al., 2013).

Inventory control also plays a crucial role in reducing holding costs, including storage, insurance, and obsolescence expenses. Maintaining optimal stock levels minimises these costs while ensuring sufficient inventory to meet demand fluctuations. For example, FMCG companies benefit from agile inventory control practices that prevent overstocking perishable items while maintaining availability for high-demand products. By integrating predictive analytics with inventory management, organisations can proactively anticipate demand patterns and adjust stock levels (Chopra & Meindl, 2024).

Case Study – Amazon Fulfilment Automation

Amazon's fulfilment centres use sophisticated WMS, robotics, and predictive replenishment driven by extensive POS and browsing data, lowering cycle times and enabling rapid fulfilment for Prime customers (Chopra & Meindl, 2024). This model is instructive for students studying how data drives operational design.

9.3.2 Layout, Material Handling, and Process Design

Slotting optimisation, pick-face design, and flow-through versus two-block configurations materially affect labour and equipment productivity. Processes should be designed to minimise touches and to support cross-dock flows where appropriate.

The layout and design of a warehouse significantly influence its operational efficiency, affecting everything from order processing times to labour productivity. A well-designed warehouse maximises space utilisation, minimises travel distances within the facility, and ensures the smooth flow of goods from receiving to shipping.

Strategically placing storage racks, aisles, and workstations creates a logical and efficient workflow. For instance, high-demand items should be stored in easily accessible locations near shipping docks, while low-turnover products can be placed in less prominent areas. This approach reduces the time and effort required for picking and packing, which are among the most labour-intensive tasks in warehouse operations (Rushton et al., 2022).

In addition to optimising layout, businesses increasingly adopt advanced picking systems to enhance efficiency. Technologies such as pick-to-light and voice-directed picking guide workers to the exact location of items, reducing errors and improving productivity. For example, an e-commerce fulfilment centre that employs a pick-to-light system can streamline order processing during peak shopping seasons, ensuring timely deliveries and customer satisfaction.

Automation is also transforming warehouse layout and design. Automated storage and retrieval systems (AS/RS) maximise vertical space by efficiently retrieving items from high-density storage areas. These systems are particularly beneficial for warehouses with limited floor space, enabling them to accommodate growing inventory levels without expanding their physical footprint. For instance, a pharmaceutical distributor using AS/RS can store and retrieve medical supplies with precision, ensuring compliance with stringent handling requirements while optimising space utilisation.

Case Study – Cross-Dock Optimisation in Grocery

Grocery DCs often use cross-dock schemes for high-turn SKUs during promotional windows, reducing storage time and preserving freshness while complicating labour scheduling and staging areas (Hubner et al., 2013).

9.3.3 Automation, Robotics, and Human Factors

Automation technologies, from conveyor systems and automated guided vehicles (AGVs) to goods-to-person robotics, must be evaluated by total cost, scalability, and labour market realities. Importantly, technology adoption must be accompanied by workforce reskilling programmes and ergonomic design to preserve safety and retention (Grant et al., 2017).

Handling equipment and technology is pivotal in modern warehouse management, enhancing safety, productivity, and cost efficiency. Equipment such as forklifts, conveyor belts, and pallet jacks facilitates the movement of goods within the warehouse, reducing the physical strain on workers and speeding up operations. However, the integration of advanced technologies, such as robotics and automation, redefines warehouse handling systems' capabilities.

Robotic systems are increasingly deployed to perform repetitive tasks such as picking, sorting, and packing. For example, Amazon's fulfilment centres utilise robotic arms to pick items from shelves and place them into bins for shipping. These systems not only improve accuracy but also allow warehouses to handle larger order volumes with fewer errors. Similarly, AGVs navigate warehouses independently, transporting goods between storage areas and workstations, reducing reliance on manual labour (Drake, 2012).

IoT technology further enhances warehouse operations by providing real-time data on equipment performance and inventory conditions. Sensors embedded in handling equipment monitor parameters such as load weight, temperature, and humidity, ensuring the safe handling of sensitive goods. For instance, cold storage warehouses use IoT-enabled sensors to maintain optimal conditions for perishable items, preventing spoilage and ensuring compliance with quality standards.

Investing in advanced handling equipment and technology requires careful planning and cost-benefit analysis. While these systems offer significant productivity gains, their implementation involves upfront costs and ongoing maintenance. Businesses must evaluate their specific needs, operational scale, and return on investment (ROI) to determine the most suitable solutions.

Case Study – Siemens Amberg and Smart Warehousing

Siemens' factory logistics demonstrate how automated material flow integrated with production schedules reduces internal lead times and synchronises inventory at point-of-use, improving overall throughput (Siemens, 2024).

9.3.4 Warehouse Strategies

Energy-efficient lighting, HVAC optimisation, solar roofing, and packaging reduction programmes reduce operational carbon, and corporate sustainability policies increasingly require green building certifications (Grant et al., 2017).

Innovative warehouse strategies are essential for optimising inventory flow, reducing operational costs, and enhancing responsiveness to customer demand. Techniques such as cross-docking, JIT inventory management, and micro-fulfilment are reshaping warehouse operations to meet the demands of a dynamic market.

Cross-docking minimises storage time by transferring incoming goods directly to outbound shipments. This strategy reduces handling costs, improves inventory turnover, and accelerates delivery. For example, retailers managing seasonal products use cross-docking to move high-demand items quickly through the supply chain, ensuring timely availability in stores.

JIT inventory management focuses on receiving goods only as they are needed, reducing the need for extensive storage and lowering holding costs. While JIT improves efficiency, it requires precise coordination with suppliers to prevent disruptions. For instance, an automotive manufacturer implementing JIT must ensure that parts arrive exactly when needed for assembly, avoiding delays in production schedules (Coyle et al., 2017).

Micro-fulfilment centres are emerging as a response to the growing demand for fast and localised order fulfilment. These compact facilities are strategically located near urban areas, enabling businesses to offer same-day or next-day delivery services. By integrating automation and data analytics, micro-fulfilment centres optimise order processing and inventory management, meeting customer expectations for speed and convenience.

CI is critical in warehouse management, requiring organisations to assess and refine their processes regularly. By embracing innovative strategies and adopting advanced technologies, businesses can enhance efficiency, reduce costs, and maintain a competitive edge in the marketplace. For example, conducting regular audits of warehouse operations and leveraging analytics to identify inefficiencies can drive ongoing improvements and support long-term growth (Richards, 2021).

Case Study – IKEA's Sustainable DCs

IKEA's investment in renewable energy and energy-efficient warehouses, combined with packaging redesign to increase cube utilisation, illustrates how warehouse design supports corporate sustainability targets while improving logistics economics (IKEA, 2023).

9.4 Distribution Network Design

Distribution network design determines where inventory is held, which transport lanes are used, and how service zones are defined, with centralised, decentralised, or hybrid architectures available depending on strategic priorities (Rushton et al., 2017). How an organisation designs its distribution network is driven by four basic topologies (see Figure 9.4): Mesh, Hub and Spoke, Linear, and Tree topologies. These four basic topologies can be merged to create a hybrid topology.

Distribution networks form the critical pathways through which products move from manufacturers to end consumers, serving as the connective tissue of the supply chain. The design and management of these networks are essential for ensuring that goods reach the right place at the right time, in good condition, and at the optimal cost. In today's global and highly competitive markets, effective distribution networks are vital for maintaining customer satisfaction, reducing operational inefficiencies, and supporting business growth.

The core components of distribution networks include channel design, channel relationships, conflict resolution, and adaptability to changing market dynamics. Each of these elements must be carefully managed to align with organisational goals and meet the needs of diverse stakeholders. As distribution systems evolve in response to technological advancements and shifting consumer expectations, businesses must continuously refine their strategies to ensure long-term success.

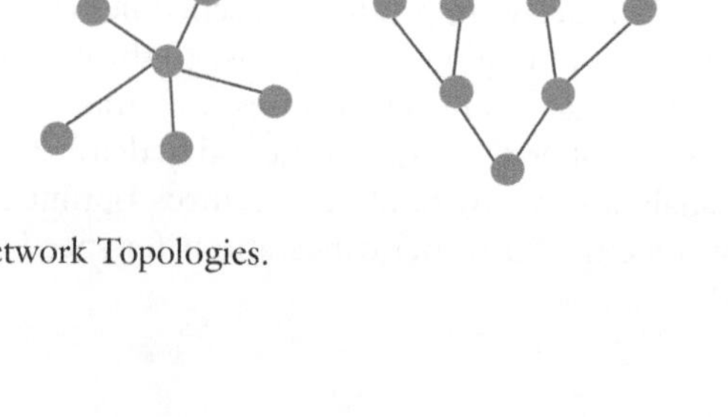

Figure 9.4 Transport Network Topologies.

9.4.1 Centralised, Decentralised, and Hybrid Networks

Centralisation yields inventory economies of scale but increases last-mile lead times, while decentralisation improves responsiveness at higher inventory and infrastructure cost. Hybrid designs allocate fast-moving SKUs to local nodes and slower SKUs to central hubs, balancing inventory and service objectives (Christopher, 2016).

The design of distribution channels determines how products move from manufacturers to end consumers, influencing cost efficiency, market reach, and customer experience. Channels can range from simple direct models, where manufacturers sell directly to customers, to complex multi-level systems involving wholesalers, distributors, and retailers. The choice of channel design depends on factors such as product type, target market, cost considerations, and the desired level of control over the distribution process.

Direct distribution channels offer manufacturers greater control over their brand, pricing, and customer interactions. These channels are particularly advantageous for companies selling high-value or specialised products that require a personalised approach. For instance, premium electronics brands like Apple often use direct channels through their physical and online stores to maintain a consistent brand image and deliver a superior customer experience. Direct channels also allow manufacturers to capture higher profit margins by eliminating intermediaries, though they require significant investment in logistics and customer service infrastructure (Rushton et al., 2022).

Indirect distribution channels, on the other hand, leverage intermediaries such as wholesalers and retailers to reach a broader customer base. This approach is often employed by companies producing commodities or mass-market goods, enabling efficient distribution across multiple regions. For example, a beverage company might use an indirect channel to distribute its products through supermarkets and convenience stores. While indirect channels reduce the manufacturer's operational burden, they require effective coordination and oversight to ensure consistent product quality and availability (Coyle et al., 2017).

Hybrid models combine elements of both direct and indirect channels, providing flexibility and scalability. In this approach, manufacturers may sell directly to customers through e-commerce platforms while partnering with retailers for physical distribution. This strategy allows companies to cater to diverse customer preferences and adapt to changing market conditions. For instance, a clothing brand might operate its online store while distributing products through third-party retail outlets, ensuring convenience and accessibility for customers.

Case Study – Retailer Hybrid Network Design

Large omnichannel retailers locate regional fulfilment centres close to dense population centres for rapid e-commerce fulfilment, while using central import hubs for less time-sensitive replenishment, thereby blending cost efficiency with customer expectations (Rushton et al., 2017).

9.4.2 Cross-Border Distribution, Customs, and Trade Facilitation

International distribution introduces customs, duties, and rules of origin, requiring careful selection of International Commercial Terms, bonded warehouses, and customs brokers to reduce delay risk. Trade facilitation initiatives, such as pre-lodgement of manifests and authorised economic operator schemes, materially reduce clearance times (Rushton et al., 2017).

The effectiveness of a distribution network depends heavily on the quality of relationships among channel members. Collaboration and alignment between manufacturers, intermediaries, and retailers are essential for achieving operational efficiency, minimising conflicts, and delivering customer value. Strong channel relationships are built on trust, transparency, and shared objectives, fostering a cohesive and responsive distribution system.

Effective communication is the foundation of successful channel management. Manufacturers must maintain open lines of communication with their partners to share information on inventory levels, sales performance, and market trends. This exchange of data enables better decision-making and reduces the risk of disruptions. For example, a supplier that provides real-time inventory updates to its retail partners can help prevent stockouts and ensure timely replenishment, enhancing customer satisfaction (Bowersox et al., 2013).

Technology is pivotal in managing channel relationships, with Distribution Management Systems (DMS) offering tools for inventory tracking, order processing, and performance monitoring. By providing real-time visibility across the distribution network, DMS enables channel members to coordinate activities and respond quickly to demand fluctuations. For instance, a distributor using DMS can optimise delivery schedules and reduce lead times, ensuring that retailers receive products exactly when needed.

Training and support are also critical for building strong channel relationships. Manufacturers should invest in training programmes to equip their partners with the knowledge and skills to handle products effectively and provide excellent customer service. For example, a pharmaceutical company may conduct workshops for its distributors to ensure compliance with handling and storage regulations, safeguarding product quality and patient safety.

Case Study – DHL and Customs Pre-clearance Corridors

DHL's customs facilitation services that pre-clear freight in transit regions reduce dwell time at borders and accelerate B2B and B2C deliveries across Africa and Asia, showing how distribution performance is improved by logistics service integration with customs processes (DHL, 2023).

9.4.3 Handling Channel Conflicts

E-commerce growth requires flexible fulfilment, including store fulfilment, dark stores, locker networks, and crowd-sourced delivery. Last-mile efficiency is now a central design variable for consumer satisfaction and profitability.

Conflicts within distribution channels are inevitable, often arising from misaligned objectives, competition among channel members, or misunderstandings about roles and responsibilities. Left unaddressed, these conflicts can undermine the efficiency of the distribution network and erode trust among stakeholders.

One common source of conflict is goal divergence, where different channel members prioritise competing objectives. For example, a manufacturer may focus on maximising market coverage, while a retailer prioritises profitability and inventory turnover. These differing priorities can lead to disputes in pricing, promotions, and order volume. To mitigate such conflicts, it is essential to establish clear roles and responsibilities, set shared goals, and create mechanisms for resolving disagreements (Coyle et al., 2017).

Building trust among channel members is a powerful strategy for reducing conflicts and fostering cooperation. Trust is cultivated through consistent communication, fair treatment, and mutual respect. Manufacturers can strengthen trust by honouring their commitments, such as delivering products on time and providing competitive pricing. Similarly, retailers and distributors can demonstrate reliability by adhering to agreed-upon terms and maintaining transparent business practices.

Conflict resolution strategies like mediation and arbitration provide structured approaches for resolving disputes. These methods involve neutral third parties who facilitate negotiations and help channel members reach mutually beneficial solutions. For example, a mediation process between a manufacturer and a distributor might result in revised pricing agreements that satisfy both parties while preserving the overall integrity of the distribution network.

Case Study – Click and Collect and Store-as-Fulfilment

Many brick-and-mortar retailers convert stores into micro-fulfilment hubs to shorten delivery times and reduce last-mile costs, while balancing in-store service and inventory visibility challenges (Hubner et al., 2013).

9.4.4 Resilience and Adaptation to Market Change

Distribution networks must be stress-tested for natural disasters, port closures, and geopolitical shocks. Techniques include dual sourcing of inbound lanes, alternative transhipment hubs, and rapid DC rerouting plans.

The rapidly changing landscape of consumer preferences, technological advancements, and globalisation has placed new demands on distribution networks. To remain competitive, companies must design networks that are adaptable, agile, and responsive to market changes.

The growth of e-commerce and omnichannel retailing has significantly impacted distribution network design. Modern consumers expect seamless integration of online and offline channels, allowing them to easily shop across multiple platforms. Companies must adapt their networks to support flexible delivery options, such as home delivery, click-and-collect services, and locker pick-up points. For instance, a retailer integrating its brick-and-mortar stores with an e-commerce platform can offer customers the convenience of choosing their preferred fulfilment method, enhancing the overall shopping experience (Richards, 2021).

Data analytics is increasingly used to gain insights into customer behaviour, enabling businesses to optimise inventory levels, forecast demand, and adjust their distribution strategies. Predictive analytics, for example, can identify emerging trends and help companies allocate resources effectively to meet anticipated demand spikes. For instance, a consumer electronics manufacturer may use analytics to ensure sufficient stock availability during product launches, minimising the risk of stockouts.

Agility in distribution networks is critical for responding to disruptions such as supply chain bottlenecks, natural disasters, or geopolitical events. Companies that prioritise flexibility, such as by maintaining diversified supplier bases and leveraging local DCs, are better equipped to navigate these challenges. For example, a food and beverage company with a decentralised distribution network can continue serving regional markets even if one facility experiences disruptions, ensuring business continuity and customer satisfaction.

> **Case Study – COVID-19 and Network Reconfiguration**
>
> During the COVID-19 crisis, organisations with flexible networks and multiple cross-dock options were able to reallocate inventory and reroute shipments more rapidly than those reliant on single gateways, underscoring the value of adaptive network architecture (Ivanov & Das, 2020; Sheffi, 2020).

9.5 Conclusion

Logistics and distribution are indispensable functions of a successful supply chain. Effective transportation management, warehouse optimisation, and well-designed distribution networks allow organisations to minimise costs, enhance service quality, and maintain a competitive edge in the marketplace. In today's rapidly evolving business landscape, CI, technological innovation, and adaptability are essential for logistics and distribution systems to meet the increasing demands of customers and the complexities of global markets. By strategically managing these functions, businesses can achieve operational excellence and enhance customer satisfaction, contributing to long-term success.

Q&A Section

Here is a short quiz to test your knowledge. The answers are provided in Appendix C.

1. What is the role of logistics and distribution in SCM?
2. Why is transportation management important?
3. What are the main modes of transportation in logistics?
4. What advantages does road transport offer?
5. Why is rail transport cost-effective for long distances?
6. How does air transport benefit high-value, time-sensitive goods?
7. What makes maritime transport indispensable for global trade?
8. What is warehouse management's primary focus?
9. How does inventory control improve logistics operations?
10. Why is adaptability crucial in distribution networks?

10 Introduction to Information Technology in SCM

Learning Outcomes

By the end of this chapter, learners will be able to:

- Explain the role of ERP, WMS, and TMS in integrated SCM systems.
- Differentiate descriptive, diagnostic, predictive, and prescriptive analytics in SCA.
- Assess the potential benefits and limitations of emerging technologies (IoT, AI, blockchain, digital twins).
- Design a basic data governance checklist addressing master data, security, and ethics.
- Recommend a phased change management plan for implementing a new SCM IT capability.

IT is no longer an enabling adjunct to SCM; it is a core strategic capability that underpins visibility, responsiveness, and resilience in global supply networks (Christopher, 2016; Monk & Wagner, 2013). The accelerating volume of data, the ubiquity of sensors, and the maturation of analytics mean that organisations can now sense, decide, and act across multiple tiers of the supply chain in near real time (Waller & Fawcett, 2013).

IT is pivotal in optimising SCM in today's interconnected global economy (see Figure 10.1). Modern supply chains are complex, involving multiple stakeholders, intricate processes, and vast networks spread across the globe. Effective IT systems enable organisations to manage these complexities by streamlining operations, enhancing collaboration, and supporting data-driven decision-making. By integrating advanced IT tools and systems, businesses can reduce costs, improve transparency, and gain a competitive advantage.

The increasing reliance on IT in SCM is driven by the growing volume of data generated across the supply chain, the need for real-time visibility, and the demand for resilience in an unpredictable market environment. Key technological advancements, such as ERP systems; SCA; and emerging innovations like the IoT, AI, and blockchain, are transforming how supply chains operate. This chapter explores the capabilities and applications of these technologies, highlighting their impact on efficiency, collaboration, and adaptability.

DOI: 10.4324/9781003740568-10

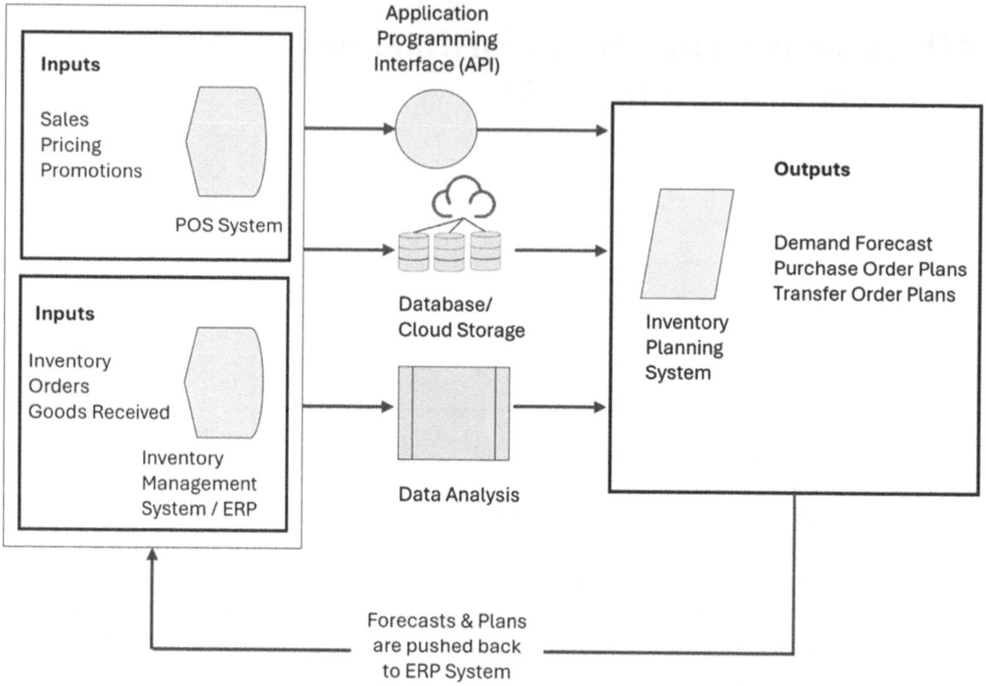

Figure 10.1 Technology Stack in SCM.

10.1 ERP Systems in SCM

ERP systems are the backbone of modern SCM, integrating various business processes and supporting the seamless flow of information across an organisation. ERP systems consolidate functions such as procurement, inventory management, production, and distribution into a unified platform. By providing real-time visibility and control, ERP systems help optimise supply chain performance and support informed decision-making.

10.1.1 Role and Architecture

ERP systems provide the transactional backbone for SCM, integrating procurement, inventory, production planning, finance, and order fulfilment into a single data model (Monk & Wagner, 2013; Olson, 2011). Modern ERP architectures are modular and increasingly cloud-native (see Figure 10.2), enabling organisations to adopt core modules first and add advanced planning or analytics later, while supporting multi-country ledgers, multi-currency transactions, and local tax/regulatory compliance. ERP, therefore, provides the "single source of truth" that facilitates coordinated decision-making across geographies (Caserio & Trucco, 2018).

For example, an ERP system can synchronise inventory data with production schedules, ensuring that raw materials are available when needed and reducing the risk of production delays. Similarly, ERP systems enable organisations to monitor order statuses and delivery timelines, improving customer service and satisfaction. By providing a single source of truth, ERP systems enhance operational coherence and reduce errors associated with manual data entry and fragmented information systems (Monk & Wagner, 2013).

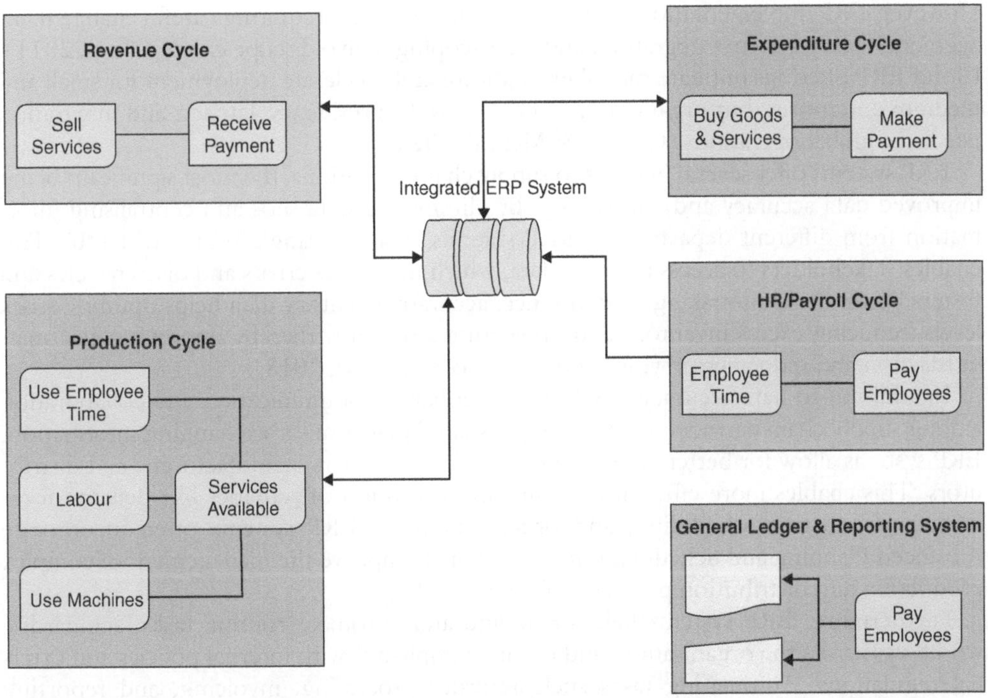

Figure 10.2 Integrated ERP System.

One of ERP systems' primary benefits is its scalability and adaptability to different industries and business sizes. For instance, large multinational corporations can use ERP systems to coordinate operations across multiple geographies. At the same time, SMEs can implement modular ERP solutions tailored to their specific needs. Cloud-based ERP systems have further democratised access to these tools, enabling organisations of all sizes to benefit from advanced IT capabilities without significant upfront investments in infrastructure (Chopra & Meindl, 2024).

Case Study – Nestlé and Global ERP Harmonisation

Nestlé's phased ERP harmonisation across regions was designed to standardise master data, improve order-to-cash and procurement processes, and enable consolidated reporting while preserving country-level customisation for regulatory compliance. The programme emphasised data governance, staged roll-outs, and local training to limit disruption, showing how multinational organisations balance global standards with local variance (Monk & Wagner, 2013; Nestlé, 2024).

10.1.2 Benefits and Limitations

ERP delivers benefits in data accuracy, process standardisation, and auditability, improving the reliability of inventory records and financial reconciliation (Monk & Wagner, 2013).

However, ERP implementations can be costly and complex, requiring careful change management, legacy-system integration, and clear scoping to avoid scope creep (Olson, 2011). Cloud ERP offerings mitigate capital expenditure and accelerate deployment for small and medium enterprises, but organisations must assess data residency, latency, and integration needs for global operations (Chopra & Meindl, 2024).

ERP systems offer several benefits to supply chain operations, the most significant being improved data accuracy and consistency. By eliminating data silos and centralising information from different departments, ERP systems create a "single source of truth". This enables stakeholders to access uniform data, which minimises errors and discrepancies and fosters better decision-making. For instance, accurate inventory data helps optimise stock levels, reducing excess inventory and preventing stockouts, thereby improving customer satisfaction and reducing carrying costs (Caserio & Trucco, 2018).

In addition to data accuracy, ERP systems enhance communication and collaboration among supply chain partners. By providing a shared platform for exchanging information, ERP systems allow for better coordination between suppliers, manufacturers, and distributors. This enables more efficient planning and execution of activities like demand forecasting, production scheduling, and order fulfilment. ERP systems often incorporate Advanced Planning and Scheduling modules, which improve the management of complex production and distribution processes (Olson, 2011).

Furthermore, ERP systems help streamline and automate routine tasks, standardise workflows across the organisation, and ensure compliance with internal policies and external regulations. Automating tasks such as order processing, invoicing, and reporting reduces human error and allows supply chain professionals to focus on strategic objectives. Increased efficiency, therefore, translates into cost savings and operational improvements (Simchi-Levi & Timmermans, 2021).

Case Study – A Large Retailer's ERP Modernisation (Regional Perspective)

A major supermarket group replaced its ageing on-premises ERP with a cloud solution to enable faster store roll-outs across Southeast Asia. This reduced time-to-value for new markets but required a rigorous data cleansing and local regulatory mapping phase to ensure compliance with GST/VAT rules in each country.

10.1.3 Enhancing Visibility and Transparency with ERP

A critical advantage of ERP systems is their ability to provide real-time supply chain visibility, allowing organisations to track goods and monitor processes from procurement to delivery. This visibility enables early identification of potential disruptions, facilitating proactive interventions to minimise risks. Additionally, ERP systems offer valuable insights through data analytics, supporting activities such as demand forecasting and risk management. By enabling comprehensive oversight, ERP systems empower organisations to make informed decisions and improve supply chain resilience (Caserio & Trucco, 2018).

ERP systems play a transformative role in SCM by consolidating business functions, improving data accuracy, enhancing collaboration, and increasing transparency. With these capabilities, organisations can achieve higher efficiency, agility, and competitiveness in their supply chain operations.

10.2 SCA – From Descriptive to Prescriptive

SCA leverages data and analytical tools to enhance supply chain efficiency and effectiveness. By analysing large datasets from various stages of the supply chain, SCA offers insights into demand forecasting, inventory management, and transportation logistics, enabling organisations to make data-driven decisions and optimise processes (Chopra & Meindl, 2024).

10.2.1 Analytics Typology and Capability Ladder

SCA ranges from descriptive dashboards, through diagnostic and predictive analytics, to prescriptive optimisation that recommends or executes actions (Waller & Fawcett, 2013). Organisations progress along an analytics maturity curve (see Figure 10.3), as they institutionalise data pipelines, invest in statistical and ML capabilities, and embed decision automation into operational systems. A pragmatic taxonomy is useful for teaching: descriptive (what happened), diagnostic (why it happened), predictive (what may happen), and prescriptive (what should we do) analytics (Waller & Fawcett, 2013).

SCA leverages advanced data analysis techniques to extract actionable insights from the vast amounts of data generated within the supply chain. Businesses can optimise operations, forecast demand, and mitigate risks using predictive, prescriptive, and descriptive analytics. These capabilities are particularly valuable in today's dynamic market environment, where agility and responsiveness are critical for success.

Predictive analytics uses historical data and statistical models to anticipate future demand patterns, enabling organisations to plan proactively. For example, a retailer might use predictive analytics to forecast seasonal demand fluctuations, ensuring adequate stock levels during peak periods. Prescriptive analytics goes a step further by recommending optimal actions based on data analysis, such as identifying the most cost-effective transportation routes or inventory replenishment strategies (Waller & Fawcett, 2013).

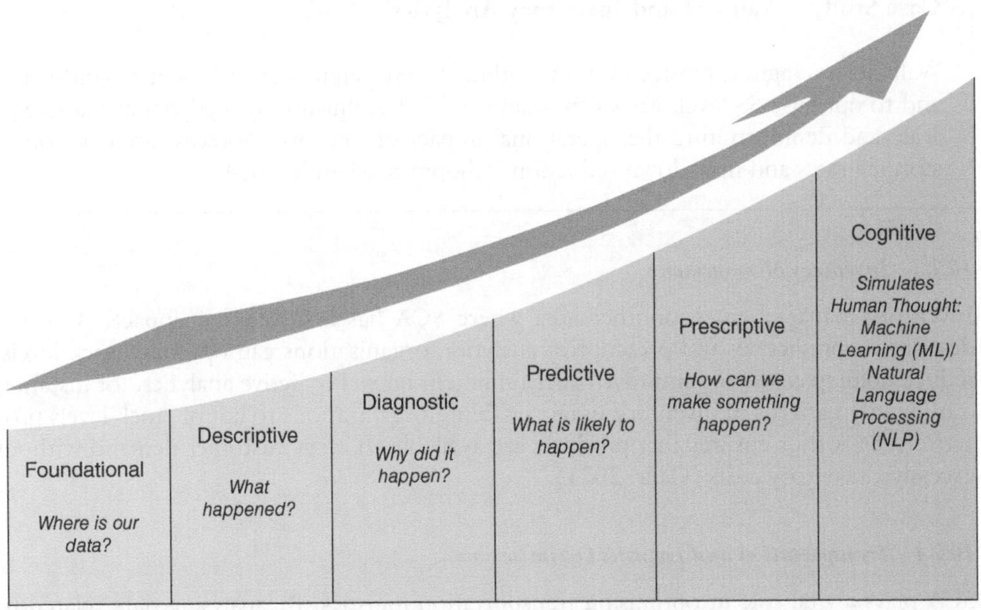

Figure 10.3 Analytics Maturity Curve.

Real-time analytics is another transformative capability of SCA, enabling organisations to monitor supply chain performance and address issues as they arise. For instance, a logistics provider can use real-time data to track shipment locations and predict delivery delays, allowing for proactive interventions to minimise customer impact. Integrating analytics with IT systems such as ERP and IoT enhances visibility and fosters a more agile supply chain (Chopra & Meindl, 2024).

10.2.2 Demand Forecasting

Demand forecasting is one of the most significant applications of SCA. Accurate demand forecasts allow organisations to align production, inventory, and distribution strategies with expected customer needs. By analysing historical data, market trends, and economic indicators, supply chain analysts can generate precise forecasts that reduce the risk of overstocking or stockouts. For example, predictive models can highlight seasonal variations in demand, allowing companies to prepare accordingly, minimise excess inventory, and improve customer service (Chopra & Meindl, 2024).

Case Study – Nestlé's AI Forecasting in Latin America

Nestlé deployed ML models to improve forecast accuracy for seasonal SKUs across multiple Latin American markets, integrating POS data with promotional plans and weather indicators, and reduced forecast error during peak seasons by a measurable margin, thereby lowering both stockouts and obsolescence risk (Nestlé, 2024).

Case Study – Walmart and Inventory Analytics

Walmart leverages extensive POS and online data to refine replenishment algorithms and to optimise SS levels across thousands of SKUs, illustrating analytics at massive scale and demonstrating the operational impact of improved forecast accuracy on store fill rates and markdown reduction (Chopra & Meindl, 2024).

10.2.3 Inventory Management

Inventory management is another area where SCA has a substantial impact. By using descriptive, predictive, and prescriptive analytics, organisations can optimise stock levels, reduce holding costs, and improve order fulfilment rates. Predictive analytics, for instance, can identify patterns in inventory usage, enabling organisations to adjust stock levels proactively. SCA thus ensures that products are available to meet customer demand without excessive inventory costs (Gaur, 2021).

10.2.4 Transportation and Logistics Optimisation

SCA plays a vital role in optimising transportation logistics. By analysing data related to delivery times, shipping routes, and transportation costs, companies can determine the most efficient ways to move goods, leading to cost savings and improved delivery performance. Real-time tracking of shipments enhances visibility, enabling timely interventions to prevent disruptions. Furthermore, by utilising optimisation algorithms, companies can streamline route planning and to improve delivery efficiency (Colehower, 2023).

10.2.5 Enhancing Resilience through Analytics

SCA contributes to supply chain resilience, particularly in the face of unexpected disruptions such as natural disasters or pandemics. Analytics allows organisations to simulate various scenarios, assess potential impacts, and develop contingency plans. By preparing for potential risks, companies can mitigate disruptions and ensure continuity in supply chain operations. Analytics thus plays a critical role in building resilient and adaptive supply chains (Gaur, 2021).

In summary, SCA is a powerful tool that allows organisations to use data-driven insights to enhance demand forecasting, inventory management, transportation logistics, and supply chain resilience. As technologies like AI and ML evolve, the capabilities of SCA will continue to grow, further enhancing supply chain efficiency and resilience (Chopra & Meindl, 2024).

10.3 Emerging Technologies in SCM

Emerging technologies, including the IoT, AI, and blockchain, are revolutionising SCM by introducing new levels of connectivity, automation, and transparency.

10.3.1 IoT – Visibility and Condition Monitoring

The IoT connects physical devices and sensors across the supply chain, enabling real-time data collection and communication (see Figure 10.4). IoT applications include tracking inventory levels, monitoring transportation conditions, and ensuring compliance with quality standards. For example, IoT-enabled temperature sensors can track the conditions of perishable goods during transit, ensuring that they remain within specified ranges and preventing spoilage. The IoT enhances supply chain visibility by providing real-time insights and supports proactive decision-making (Ashton, 2009).

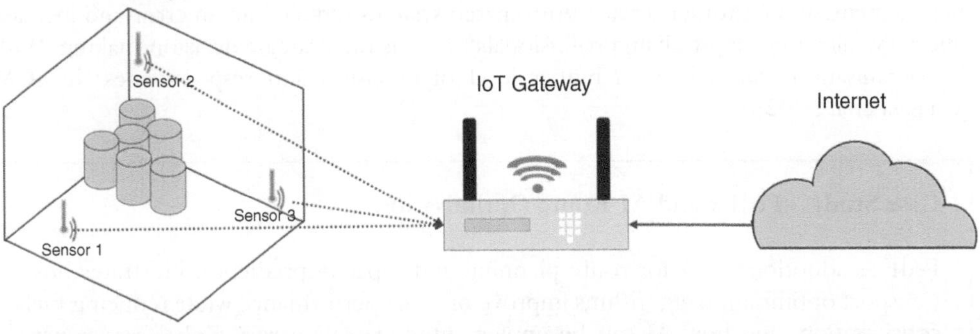

Figure 10.4 IoT Data Pipeline.

AI brings advanced computational capabilities to SCM, automating complex tasks and improving decision-making. ML algorithms analyse large datasets to identify patterns and optimise processes like demand forecasting and inventory management. AI-powered chatbots are also transforming customer service by providing instant responses to inquiries and tracking order statuses. Additionally, AI applications in warehouse automation, such as robotic picking systems, improve efficiency and reduce labour costs (Ivanov & Dolgui, 2020).

Blockchain technology addresses the growing demand for transparency and traceability in supply chains. By creating an immutable and decentralised ledger, blockchain ensures that every transaction and movement within the supply chain is securely recorded and verifiable. This capability is particularly valuable for industries with stringent regulatory requirements, such as pharmaceuticals and food production. For example, a blockchain-based system can track the origin of raw materials, ensuring compliance with sustainability and ethical sourcing standards (Min, 2019).

Case Study – Siemens Amberg and Sensor-Driven Quality Control

At the Amberg plant, Siemens uses thousands of sensors to detect process deviations in near real time, integrating IoT streams with MES and ERP to stop lines automatically and initiate root-cause workflows, demonstrating the operational value of tightly coupled sensor-to-action loops (Siemens AG, 2024).

10.3.2 AI and ML

AI and ML accelerate pattern recognition, anomaly detection, and optimisation. Typical SCM applications include demand forecasting, yield optimisation, predictive maintenance, and automated decision agents in procurement and warehousing (Ivanov, 2021; Min, 2010). Importantly, models must be explainable and validated across markets, since data distributions often vary by region.

AI is transforming SCM by enabling advanced data analysis and automation. AI algorithms can analyse large datasets to identify patterns, trends, and correlations, improving demand forecasting and inventory optimisation. For instance, ML models can predict supply chain disruptions and suggest corrective actions, helping organisations minimise downtime and maintain continuity in operations (Min, 2010).

AI-powered automation also streamlines processes such as order processing, warehouse management, and customer service. Automated systems reduce human error and increase efficiency, allowing supply chain professionals to focus on strategic decision-making. With AI, organisations can achieve a higher level of precision and responsiveness in SCM (Chawla et al., 2023).

Case Study – FedEx and AI Route Optimisation

FedEx's adoption of AI for route planning and capacity prediction illustrates how transport optimisation algorithms improve on-time performance while reducing fuel consumption, and how AI can be implemented at scale across global carrier networks (AI Expert Network, 2024).

10.3.3 Blockchain for Provenance and Trust

Blockchain offers immutable event recording and shared ledgers, which aid provenance, traceability, and smart contract execution. Use cases are strongest where multiple parties require a single authoritative record, for example, in pharmaceuticals, high-value goods, and certified-origin agricultural supply chains (Colehower, 2023; Min, 2019).

Blockchain, known for its decentralised and immutable ledger, offers significant benefits for SCM. Blockchain provides a secure, transparent record of transactions, enhancing trust and accountability among supply chain partners. This is particularly valuable in industries requiring stringent authentication, such as pharmaceuticals and food, where blockchain can verify the provenance and authenticity of goods (Gaur, 2021).

Blockchain can also improve efficiency by automating contract execution through smart contracts, reducing the need for intermediaries and lowering transaction costs. Moreover, blockchain's transparency ensures that all stakeholders have access to the same information, facilitating faster and more coordinated responses to disruptions (Colehower, 2023).

Case Study – Agri-Food Pilots and Traceability

Several multinational food companies have piloted blockchain to record farm-to-fork provenance, enabling rapid identification of contaminated lots and supporting claims of ethical sourcing across supplier networks in Africa, Europe, and Asia (Colehower, 2023; Min, 2019).

10.3.4 Digital Twins and Simulation

Digital twins are virtual models of physical supply chain assets and processes that support scenario analysis, capacity planning, and disruption modelling. They enable organisations to test "what-if" interventions without operational risk, which is especially valuable for global networks facing complex interdependencies (Ivanov et al., 2019).

Case Study – Port Operations Digital Twin

A major global port operator deployed a digital twin to simulate berth allocations, crane moves, and hinterland capacity under contingency scenarios, reducing average vessel turnaround times and improving berth utilisation in a congested regional context (DHL, 2023).

10.3.5 Enhancing Sustainability with Emerging Technologies

These emerging technologies contribute to sustainability in SCM. IoT can optimise route planning, reducing fuel consumption and emissions in transportation. AI can identify inefficiencies in production processes and suggest improvements, lowering energy use and waste generation. Blockchain can verify suppliers' sustainability claims, ensuring that materials are sourced responsibly. By improving transparency, efficiency, and accountability, these technologies help companies meet regulatory requirements and consumer expectations for sustainable practices (Battacharya & Battacharyya, 2024a).

The integration of IoT, AI, and blockchain technology into SCM not only improves efficiency and resilience but also contributes to sustainable supply chain practices. As these technologies evolve, they will become increasingly vital for companies seeking a competitive edge in a dynamic market environment.

10.4 IT for Collaboration, Platforms, and Standards

10.4.1 Supplier Portals, Electronic Data Interchange (EDI) and APIs

One of the most significant benefits of IT in SCM is its ability to enhance collaboration among supply chain stakeholders. Cloud-based platforms enable seamless communication and data sharing between suppliers, manufacturers, distributors, and retailers, fostering a more integrated and efficient supply chain. For instance, collaborative planning and forecasting tools allow partners to align their strategies and improve demand accuracy, reducing the risk of overstocking or stockouts (Christopher, 2016).

Effective collaboration depends on standardised data exchange, through EDI, APIs, and supplier portals that support POs, advance shipping notices, and invoice reconciliation. Cloud supplier portals democratise access for SMEs in emerging markets, improving onboarding and compliance (Christopher, 2016).

IT also plays a critical role in enhancing supply chain resilience, enabling organisations to anticipate and respond to disruptions. Advanced analytics and AI-powered systems can identify vulnerabilities and model potential scenarios, allowing businesses to develop contingency plans. For example, during the COVID-19 pandemic, many organisations relied on IT systems to monitor supplier performance and reconfigure distribution networks in response to changing conditions (Ivanov, 2021).

Case Study – DHL's Supplier Portal for SMEs in Africa

DHL's regional platform enabled small exporters to upload customs documentation and track consignments, reducing cross-border friction and improving access to international marketplaces for SMEs (DHL, 2023).

10.4.2 Platform Business Models and Marketplaces

Platform models, such as freight marketplaces and logistics-as-a-service, increase capacity availability and enable dynamic pricing, which is particularly useful across heterogeneous regional logistics markets (Chopra & Meindl, 2024). Platforms also surface rich data that can be monetised for benchmarking and capacity planning.

10.5 Data Governance, Cybersecurity, and Ethical Considerations

10.5.1 Data Governance and Master Data Management

Analytics and operational reliability depend on consistent master data for items, suppliers, and customers. Organisations that neglect data governance encounter analytic bias, inventory mis-reconciliation, and poor decision-making. A centralised master data governance function, supported by local stewards and clear data-quality Service Level Agreements, is essential for multi-country operations (Caserio & Trucco, 2018; Monk & Wagner, 2013).

10.5.2 Cybersecurity and Resilience

Increased connectivity raises cybersecurity risk. Supply chains are now frequent targets of ransomware and supply chain attacks; therefore, security must be designed into IT architectures, with network segmentation, identity and access management, and incident response playbooks. Cyber risk also carries operational implications, for example, the need to isolate critical systems and run manual fallbacks for ERP/TMS in extreme scenarios (Ivanov, 2021).

10.6 Implementation, Change Management, and Capability Building

10.6.1 Staged Implementations and Benefits Realisation

Successful IT roll-outs follow staged implementations, with MVP pilots, data cleansing sprints, and post-go-live hypercare. Rapid pilot learning in one geography, followed by controlled regional roll-outs, reduces risk and improves local buy-in. Benefits realisation plans with clear KPIs and baseline metrics are essential to demonstrate value and to secure further investment (Olson, 2011).

10.6.2 Skills, Organisational Change, and Supplier Readiness

IT is as much about people as technology, and organisations must invest in analytics skills, change management capability, and supplier enablement to secure returns. SMEs in developing regions often need supplier onboarding support, training, and access to lightweight portals to participate effectively in GSCs (Monczka et al., 2016).

10.7 Sustainability, Regulation, and Global Perspectives

10.7.1 Enabling Sustainability with IT

IT enables measurement and optimisation of carbon by lane, facility, and SKU, and supports circular economy processes through traceability and product-life reporting. Combining IoT telemetry with lifecycle analytics allows organisations to quantify emissions and to prioritise interventions that deliver the best carbon reduction per dollar (Battacharya & Battacharyya, 2024a).

10.7.2 Regulatory and Cross-border Data Considerations

Global deployments must consider data residency, privacy laws, and cross-border transfer restrictions. Architectures that support regional data zones while enabling aggregated analytics via secure federated queries offer a compromise between regulatory compliance and global insight (Caserio & Trucco, 2018).

10.8 Challenges and Future Directions

While the benefits of IT in SCM are significant, implementing these technologies is not without challenges. High upfront costs, data security concerns, and the need for skilled personnel are common barriers to adoption. Additionally, integrating new technologies with legacy systems can be complex and time-consuming, requiring careful planning and execution.

Looking ahead, the role of IT in SCM is expected to grow, driven by continued technological advancements and increasing demands for efficiency and sustainability. Integrating 5G networks will enable faster and more reliable data transmission, supporting real-time decision-making across the supply chain. Similarly, quantum computing advancements can potentially revolutionise complex optimisation problems, such as route planning and inventory allocation.

Sustainability will also shape the future of IT in SCM, with technologies like AI and blockchain enabling more transparent and accountable supply chains. For instance, AI can optimise transportation routes to reduce carbon emissions, while blockchain can verify suppliers' environmental credentials.

IoT also facilitates predictive maintenance by monitoring equipment and identifying potential issues before they result in breakdowns. For example, IoT sensors in manufacturing equipment can alert maintenance teams when performance deviates from normal, allowing for proactive repairs that minimise downtime and enhance operational efficiency (Colehower, 2023).

10.9 Conclusion

IT is transforming SCM by enhancing efficiency, transparency, and resilience. ERP systems streamline business functions; SCA enables data-driven decision-making; and emerging technologies like IoT, AI, and blockchain offer new opportunities for innovation. Together, these technologies enable organisations to build agile, responsive, and sustainable supply chains that meet the demands of a rapidly changing market.

Future developments, including 5G, edge analytics, and quantum optimisation, will expand the frontier of what is possible, increasing the premium on organisations that can integrate technology, people, and process across global networks (Battacharya & Battacharyya, 2024a; Ivanov, 2021).

The adoption of these technologies requires ongoing investment, employee training, and strategic alignment with business goals. However, the benefits – enhanced efficiency, improved decision-making, and greater adaptability – make these efforts worthwhile. As SCM continues to evolve, integrating IT will be essential for companies looking to maintain a competitive advantage and achieve long-term success.

Q&A Section

Here is a short quiz to test your knowledge. The answers are provided in Appendix C.

1 How does IT enhance SCM?
2 What role do ERP systems play in SCM?
3 How do ERP systems benefit data accuracy in SCM?
4 Why is supply chain visibility important, and how do ERP systems support it?
5 What is SCA, and why is it valuable?
6 How does demand forecasting benefit from SCA?
7 How does the IoT enhance supply chain visibility?
8 What advantages does AI bring to SCM?
9 How does blockchain technology improve transparency in SCM?
10 In what ways do emerging technologies support sustainability in SCM?

11 Risk Management in Supply Chains

Learning Outcomes

By the end of this chapter, learners will be able to:

- Identify the typology of supply chain risks (demand, supply, operational, financial, environmental, reputational).
- Apply qualitative and quantitative tools to assess and prioritise risk exposures.
- Develop mitigation options (portfolio sourcing, buffers, control towers) for a specified risk.
- Construct an incident response outline and recovery metric set for a major disruption.
- Evaluate the interplay between resilience and sustainability in risk strategy.

11.1 Introduction

Supply chain risk management (SCRM) encompasses the identification, assessment, mitigation, and governance of events that can interrupt the flow of goods, services, information, and cash across an organisation's network. In a globalised economy, supply chains face a broad spectrum of hazards, including pandemics, natural disasters, cyber-attacks, geopolitical shocks, and supplier insolvency, and these events interact in ways that amplify impact, for example by creating cascading disruptions across tiers and geographies (Ivanov & Das, 2020; Sheffi, 2020).

Risk management is an essential aspect of modern SCM (see Figure 11.1), given the complex and interconnected nature of global supply networks. In today's volatile business environment, risks can emerge from various sources, including demand fluctuations, supply disruptions, operational failures, financial uncertainties, environmental factors, and reputational concerns. For businesses to maintain resilience and long-term sustainability, effectively identifying and managing these risks is critical. This chapter explores the different types of risks that affect supply chains and offers strategies for mitigating these risks to ensure supply chain continuity and stability.

DOI: 10.4324/9781003740568-11

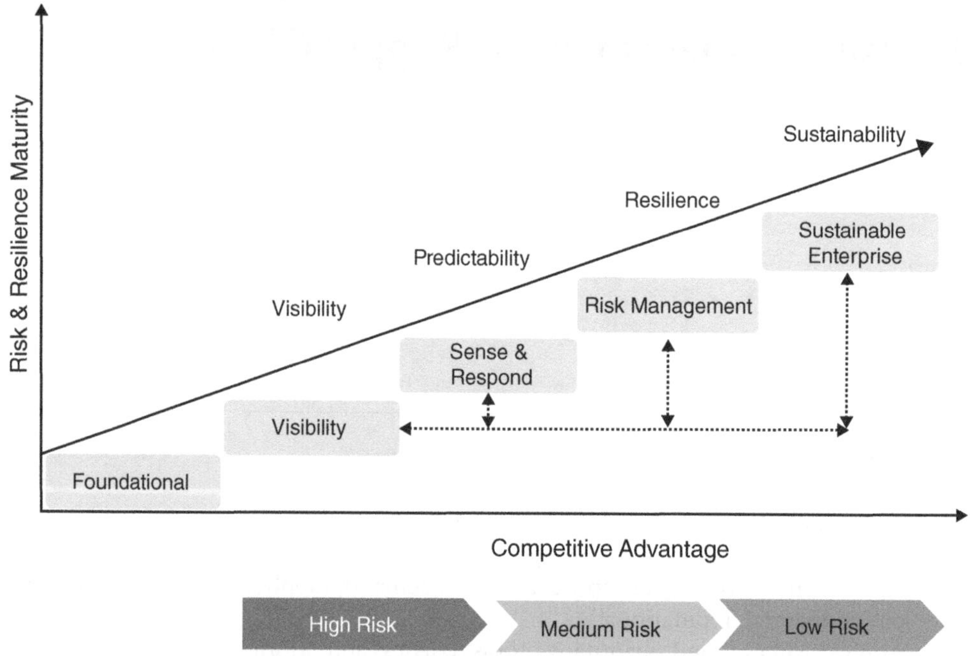

Figure 11.1 SCM Risk Management.

11.2 Identifying Risks in Supply Chains

Risk management begins with identifying the various threats that can disrupt the smooth flow of goods and services across supply chains. Some risks are predictable, while others are unexpected or external in nature. Identifying and assessing these risks is a crucial step in building a robust risk management framework. The following sections explore the most common types of risks encountered in supply chains.

11.2.1 Typology of Supply Chain Risks

A pragmatic taxonomy distinguishes: operational risks (process failures, quality issues), supplier risks (single-sourcing, capacity loss), logistics risks (port closure, transport capacity), financial risks (currency volatility, credit), strategic risks (loss of market access), environmental risks (extreme weather, climate change), health risks (pandemics), and cyber risks (ransomware, data breaches) (Ivanov & Das, 2020; Monczka et al., 2016). Each risk type manifests differently across regions, and a robust risk register records the location, likelihood, impact, and velocity (time to effect) of each exposure.

Case Study – Maersk and Systemic Cyber Risk

In June 2017, Maersk was one of the largest casualties of the NotPetya malware, with operations at multiple terminals and IT systems paralysed for days, and the company subsequently reported direct NotPetya-related costs in the hundreds of millions of US dollars (Maersk's estimate and reporting vary by source). The Maersk experience exposes how a cyber incident, although digital in origin, can have immediate and severe operational and financial impacts across international logistics networks, and it highlights the need for network segmentation, robust backups, and incident playbooks (Steinberg et al., 2021; Swinhoe, 2019).

11.2.2 Risk Drivers in a Global Context

Global supply networks increase exposure to cross-border regulations, customs delays, tariffs, and geopolitical tensions, as well as to geographically correlated climate events. Organisations sourcing from concentrated regions or from politically sensitive countries face a compounded risk of simultaneous disruption. Multi-tier mapping and geopolitical exposure analysis are therefore essential inputs into credible risk identification (Chopra & Meindl, 2024; Ivanov & Das, 2020).

Case Study – Suez Canal Blockage (*Ever Given*)

The six-day grounding of the merchant vessel *Ever Given* in the Suez Canal in March 2021 blocked a major global artery, delaying hundreds of container ships and temporarily constraining the movement of roughly 10–15% of seaborne trade, thereby revealing the vulnerability of chokepoints in global logistics. The incident is a vivid teaching example of how a single physical disruption can propagate through inventories, production schedules, and demand fulfilment across regions (Leonard & Kapadia, 2021; Tran et al., 2025).

11.2.3 Demand Risk

Demand risk arises from fluctuations in customer demand, which various factors, such as economic conditions, changes in consumer preferences, market trends, and competitive actions, can influence. When demand is unpredictable, businesses face the dilemma of either holding excessive inventory, leading to higher storage costs, or facing stockouts, which may result in lost sales and customer dissatisfaction (Christopher, 2022). Demand forecasting, while helpful, cannot entirely eliminate this risk, especially in industries subject to seasonal or cyclical shifts.

The COVID-19 pandemic underscored the importance of managing demand risk, as businesses struggled to predict shifts in demand for essential and non-essential goods. For instance, supply chains in the retail and manufacturing sectors were severely disrupted due to changes in consumer purchasing behaviour during lockdowns (Sheffi, 2020). As a result, companies must be equipped to deal with demand variability through flexible supply chain strategies.

11.2.4 Supply Risk

Supply risk is a critical concern for businesses that rely on a global supply network. It involves potential disruptions in the supply of materials or components essential for production. These disruptions can occur due to several factors, such as geopolitical instability, natural disasters, changes in regulations, and supplier insolvency. The recent supply chain crisis during the pandemic demonstrated the vulnerability of GSCs to disruptions, as factories were shut down, transportation networks were blocked, and workers were unavailable.

In particular, the automotive and electronics industries faced significant disruptions due to shortages of semiconductors, which severely affected production timelines and delivery commitments. To reduce supply risk, businesses are increasingly looking to diversify their supply sources, engage in strategic supplier relationships, and develop contingency plans (Waters, 2023).

11.2.5 Operational Risk

Operational risks are internal risks that arise from within a company's operations and systems. These risks are associated with the processes, equipment, personnel, and technology that support the flow of goods and services. Examples of operational risks include equipment breakdowns, human error, poor quality control, and cybersecurity breaches. In a supply chain context, these failures can lead to production delays, increased operational costs, and compromised product quality.

Cybersecurity threats have become increasingly important as more businesses digitalise their operations. Cyberattacks can disrupt supply chains by targeting key systems such as ERP software, resulting in data breaches, ransomware attacks, or system shutdowns. Implementing robust cybersecurity measures and regularly updating systems are critical to mitigate such risks.

11.2.6 Financial Risk

Financial risk arises from fluctuations in exchange rates, interest rates, commodity prices, and other financial variables that can impact the cost of goods and the profitability of supply chain operations. Globalisation has increased exposure to financial risks, as companies engage in international trade and source goods from multiple countries. The volatility of financial markets, as seen during the global financial crisis and the COVID-19 pandemic, can affect supply chain costs, especially for businesses that deal with international suppliers (Maarmoun, 2015).

A common strategy to mitigate financial risk is the use of hedging instruments such as forward contracts, futures contracts, and options, which allow companies to lock in prices and minimise exposure to currency fluctuations and commodity price volatility.

11.2.7 Environmental Risk

Environmental risks refer to the potential disruptions caused by natural events or long-term environmental changes. Extreme weather conditions, such as hurricanes, floods, and droughts, can damage infrastructure, disrupt transportation routes, and delay shipments. As climate change continues to exacerbate the frequency and severity of such events, companies must prepare for the potential impacts on their supply chains (Kleindorfer & Saad, 2022).

In addition to disruptions caused by extreme weather, companies also face the risks associated with compliance with environmental regulations, such as emissions reduction targets and waste management laws. These regulations may impose additional costs or force companies to adjust their sourcing or manufacturing practices.

11.2.8 Reputational Risk

Reputational risk involves the potential harm to a company's public image and brand equity due to negative publicity or unethical practices within the supply chain. Issues such as labour rights violations, environmental damage, and poor working conditions can lead to consumer backlash, legal penalties, and loss of business. In an era of increased transparency and social media influence, reputational risks can escalate quickly, leading to long-term damage to a brand's reputation and customer loyalty.

Reputation management is particularly critical for companies operating in GSCs where supply practices may come under scrutiny by activists, non-governmental organisations, and the media (Sodhi & Tang, 2012).

11.3 Assessing and Measuring Risk

11.3.1 Qualitative and Quantitative Assessment Tools

Risk assessment combines qualitative approaches, such as heat maps and bow-tie diagrams, with quantitative methods, including Monte Carlo simulation, probabilistic lead-time modelling, and stress testing. A useful progression begins with qualitative mapping, and then layers probabilistic analysis for high-impact exposures (Ivanov et al., 2019; Sheffi, 2020).

An effective Risk Assessment Toolbox will employ a Risk Assessment Matrix, a variety of Risk Assessment Methods, a fully documented Risk Assessment Process, and robust Risk Management Strategies (see Figure 11.2).

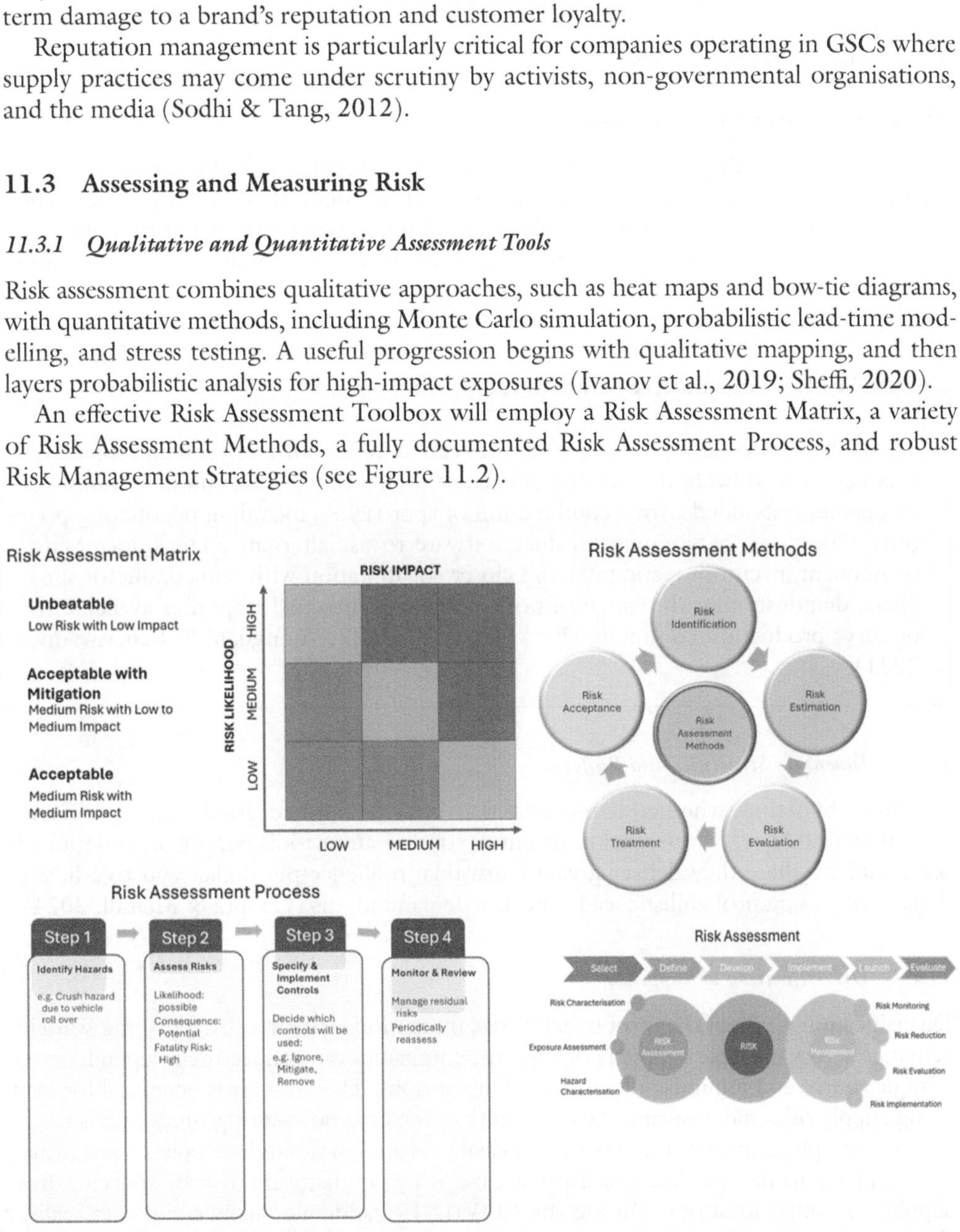

Figure 11.2 Risk Assessment Toolbox.

11.3.2 Multi-tier Visibility and Exposure Quantification

Many organisations lack visibility beyond tier-1 suppliers, yet disruptions often originate in lower tiers. Multi-tier mapping tools, augmented by supplier self-reporting and third-party data providers, enable exposure quantification by supplier location, criticality, and substitutability. For critical components, probabilistic exposure estimates should feed inventory policies, contractual terms, and contingency plans (Ivanov & Das, 2020; Monczka et al., 2016).

11.4 Mitigation Strategies

11.4.1 Portfolio and Sourcing Design

Mitigation starts with portfolio design, for example, diversification of supplier geography, dual sourcing for critical parts, and the use of strategic stock at risk-critical nodes. These changes can reduce the probability and impact of single-point failure, but they also affect cost and complexity, requiring a trade-off analysis anchored in business strategy (Chopra & Meindl, 2024).

Case Study – Automotive Semiconductor Shortages

The global semiconductor shortage that began in 2020–2021 disrupted automotive production worldwide due to chip concentration and long lead times. Automotive companies responded with a combination of approaches, including negotiating priority allocations, redesigning product software to use alternative chips, increasing component inventories, and pursuing closer collaboration with semiconductor suppliers, demonstrating the range of portfolio and contractual responses available to preserve production continuity (Burkacky et al., 2022; Youngdahl & Ramaswamy, 2021).

11.4.2 Inventory Strategies and Buffers

Inventory buffering, whether at raw material, WIP, or finished goods stages, remains a central tactical lever. Multi-echelon inventory optimisation tools permit organisations to place buffers where they deliver greatest marginal resilience per dollar, and to adjust SS dynamically using probabilistic lead time and demand inputs (Chopra & Meindl, 2024).

11.4.3 Diversification of Suppliers

Diversification is one of the most effective risk mitigation strategies. By spreading sourcing activities across multiple suppliers or regions, companies can reduce their dependency on a single source and minimise the impact of disruptions. This strategy is beneficial for managing supply risks and ensuring the continuity of material flow during times of crisis.

For example, suppose a company is heavily reliant on a single supplier located in a region prone to natural disasters. In that case, it can mitigate the risk by sourcing from suppliers in other locations. During the COVID-19 pandemic, many companies realised the importance of diversifying their supplier base to avoid the risk of total supply chain paralysis (Khajasteh et al., 2022).

11.4.4 Monitoring and Early Warning Systems

To proactively manage supply chain risks, companies can implement monitoring and early warning systems. These systems use real-time data to detect potential disruptions, allowing companies to take corrective action before risks escalate. By integrating advanced analytics, ML, and AI, organisations can identify risks related to supplier performance, inventory levels, shipping delays, and other factors that may indicate potential issues (Sodhi & Tang, 2012).

For example, AI-powered tools can track supplier performance in real time, alerting managers to quality issues, shipment delays, or financial instability, allowing the company to take prompt action.

11.4.5 Collaboration and Communication with Partners

Risk management in supply chains is not a solitary endeavour; it requires collaboration and communication between all stakeholders. By fostering strong relationships with suppliers, logistics providers, and customers, companies can work together to manage risks more effectively. Sharing information about potential disruptions, joint planning efforts, and collaborative risk management initiatives is critical to ensuring supply chain resilience (Taschner & Charifzadeh, 2023).

For instance, companies may work with suppliers to develop joint contingency plans in case of disruptions, or they may share resources and best practices to strengthen their collective ability to respond to unexpected events.

11.4.6 Contingency Planning and Scenario Analysis

Contingency planning and scenario analysis are essential techniques for preparing for uncertain events. Contingency planning involves developing backup plans and alternative strategies to address potential disruptions. Scenario analysis, on the other hand, simulates different risk scenarios to assess their impact on the supply chain. By examining various potential disruptions, companies can develop response strategies and ensure that they are prepared to act quickly when issues arise (Khajasteh et al., 2022).

For example, during the early stages of the COVID-19 pandemic, companies that had already developed contingency plans for disruptions were able to pivot to alternative supply sources quickly, whereas others faced significant delays and shortages.

11.4.7 Contractual and Financial Levers

Contracts can shift risk through capacity reservations, minimum off-take commitments, price adjustment clauses, and penalty/incentive mechanisms. Supply chain finance instruments, such as supplier credit lines and dynamic discounting, support supplier liquidity and reduce the probability of supplier failure, particularly for SMEs in emerging markets (Monczka et al., 2016).

Case Study – Vaccine Manufacturing and Contractual Complexity

During the COVID-19 pandemic, pharmaceutical companies, such as Pfizer, designed complex contractual and operational models to scale vaccine production and global distribution rapidly, investing in manufacturing capacity, cold-chain infrastructure, and contractual commitments with logistics providers to ensure speed and reach, which underscores how contractual and financial mobilisation is integral to timely mitigation (Garland, 2021; Pfizer, 2020).

11.4.8 Technology-Enabled Mitigation: Control Towers and Digital Twins

Digital control towers provide end-to-end visibility and real-time alerts across carriers, suppliers, and inventory, enabling faster root cause analysis and more effective rerouting. Digital twins and simulation enable scenario testing of mitigation plans before committing capital, and predictive analytics can surface leading indicators ahead of full-blown disruption (Ivanov, 2021; Ivanov et al., 2019).

Case Study – Port Digital Twin

Port operators and major carriers have piloted digital twins to simulate vessel arrivals, berth allocations, and hinterland constraints, improving resource allocation and resilience under surge conditions (DHL, 2023).

11.5 Enhancing Supply Chain Resilience

Supply chain resilience is the ability to recover from disruptions and maintain operational continuity. Companies can enhance resilience by building flexibility and redundancy into their operations. This includes maintaining SS, diversifying transportation routes, investing in flexible manufacturing capabilities, and designing systems that can quickly adapt to changes in demand or supply (Sodhi & Tang, 2012).

Investing in resilient infrastructure and flexible logistics systems also plays a key role in ensuring that a company can absorb shocks without severe consequences to its operations.

11.5.1 Resilience and Sustainability in Supply Chains

Building a resilient and sustainable supply chain is not just about managing risks but also about ensuring the long-term viability of supply chain operations. Sustainability encompasses not only environmental stewardship but also social and economic factors. The integration of sustainability into SCM requires companies to adopt practices that reduce their environmental impact, promote social responsibility, and ensure long-term profitability.

11.5.2 Sustainability in Practice

Sustainability involves integrating environmental, social, and economic considerations into SCM. Companies can reduce their carbon footprint by optimising transportation routes, using eco-friendly packaging, and sourcing materials from suppliers that adhere to sustainable practices. Furthermore, promoting fair labour practices, ensuring safe working conditions, and supporting local communities are essential for achieving social sustainability (Sheffi, 2007).

11.5.3 A Culture of Resilience and Sustainability

Ultimately, risk management and sustainability require a cultural shift within organisations. Businesses must foster a culture of resilience and sustainability by training employees on risk management practices, encouraging innovation, and promoting a proactive approach to managing risks. By embedding these values into the organisational mindset, companies can enhance their ability to weather disruptions and continue contributing to long-term success.

11.6 Response, Recovery, and Continuity Planning

11.6.1 Incident Response and Business Continuity Plans

Organisations should maintain playbooks that define decision rights, communication protocols, substitute suppliers, and critical stock release rules. Tabletop exercises, supplier continuity testing, and cross-functional rehearsals are essential to convert plans into practised capabilities (Sheffi, 2020).

Case Study – NotPetya Recovery Practices at Maersk

After NotPetya, Maersk reconfigured its IT and security posture, introduced network segmentation, strengthened backups, and improved cross-functional crisis coordination, offering a powerful example of learning from a major cyber incident and investing in resilience that has both operational and reputational value (Steinberg et al., 2021; Swinhoe, 2019).

11.6.2 Recovery Metrics and Post-incident Learning

Recovery should be measured by time-to-recovery, cost-to-restore, and residual business impact. Post-incident after-action reviews capture root causes and feed back into risk registers and supplier selection criteria, enabling continuous strengthening of resilience investments (Sheffi, 2020).

11.7 Governance, Culture, and Incentives

11.7.1 Board and Executive Oversight

Risk management requires visible executive sponsorship and board-level dashboards that connect supply chain exposures to financial and strategic KPIs. Integrating risk into S&OP or IBP cycles ensures that resilience is not siloed but aligned with commercial decision-making (Christopher, 2016; Simchi-Levi & Timmermans, 2021).

11.7.2 Incentives and Supplier Collaboration

Organisational incentives should reward both efficiency and resilience, for example, linking part of procurement bonuses to supplier continuity metrics and SRM performance. Collaboration with suppliers on joint contingency investments creates shared skin in the game and enhances collective recovery capacity (Monczka et al., 2016).

Case Study – Collaborative Inventory and VMI in Retail Networks

Retailers that partner with key suppliers through VMI, joint demand planning, and shared SS arrangements typically achieve better service with lower overall inventory across the network, illustrating how governance and shared incentives materially affect resilience outcomes (Christopher, 2016).

11.8 Global and Regional Perspectives

11.8.1 Geopolitics, Trade Policy, and Near-Shoring

Recent geopolitical tensions and trade policy shifts have encouraged some organisations to consider near-shoring or regionalisation to reduce exposure to distant chokepoints and trade frictions. In contrast, others maintain a global scale for cost reasons. A pragmatic regional strategy balances cost, speed, and political risk, and it must be revisited as political conditions change (He & Zhang, 2020; Sheffi, 2020).

Case Study – Rebalancing Post-pandemic Supply Chains

Post-2020, many companies reassessed their China dependence for critical components, diversifying factories to Southeast Asia, India, or Mexico for North American markets, illustrating trade-offs between labour cost advantages and geopolitical resilience (Burkacky et al., 2022).

11.8.2 Climate Risk and Adaptation

Climate change increases the frequency and severity of weather events, and organisations must incorporate climate-scenario modelling into network design, insurance planning, and supplier audits. Higher frequency flooding, droughts, and wildfires require both tactical contingency plans and strategic relocation or fortification of critical assets (Grant et al., 2017; Ivanov et al., 2019).

11.9 Conclusion

Risk management in supply chains is a continual process of anticipating, quantifying, and reducing exposures, and of embedding resilience into commercial strategy. The integrated case studies in this chapter illustrate that effective resilience combines portfolio design, contractual architecture, inventory tactics, digital visibility, and rehearsed response capabilities, and that global perspectives matter because exposures and mitigation costs vary by geography. Real-world events such as the NotPetya cyberattack, the Suez Canal blockage, semiconductor shortages, and vaccine cold-chain scaling illustrate theoretical concepts to the messy realities of contemporary supply networks and highlight the importance of designing robust, cost-effective mitigation strategies in practice (Ivanov & Das, 2020; Sheffi, 2020).

Q&A Section

Here is a short quiz to test your knowledge. The answers are provided in Appendix C.

1. Why is risk management essential in modern supply chains?
2. What are some key types of risks in supply chains?
3. What is demand risk, and why is it challenging?
4. How does supply risk impact GSCs?
5. What are operational risks, and how do they affect supply chains?
6. Why is financial risk a concern for supply chains?
7. How can environmental risk disrupt supply chain operations?
8. What is reputational risk in supply chains?
9. How does diversifying suppliers mitigate supply chain risks?
10. What role does resilience play in SCRM?

12 Case Studies

Learning Outcomes

By the end of this chapter, learners will be able to:

- Summarise key lessons from cross-industry SCM case studies and link them to theory.
- Analyse a case to identify the main trade-offs and managerial decisions that determined outcomes.
- Apply theoretical frameworks to explain why some companies succeeded and others failed.
- Create a short case brief (problem, analysis, recommendation) suitable for classroom discussion.
- Reflect on generalisable insights and propose one actionable policy or operational change.

Case studies are an essential tool for learning in the field of SCM. They provide real-world examples of both success and failure, illustrating the practical application of theoretical concepts and offering valuable insights into the intricacies and challenges businesses face. Examining case studies can reveal common trends, highlight best practices, and offer lessons on how companies can improve their supply chains to enhance efficiency, mitigate risks, and build resilience. This chapter explores some of the most prominent cases in SCM, focusing on both the successes and failures that have shaped the industry.

12.1 Toyota: The Benchmark for Supply Chain Success

Toyota is widely regarded as a model for effective SCM, with its JIT production system being one of the most revolutionary innovations in the automotive industry. The JIT system, pioneered by Toyota in the 1970s, focuses on minimising inventory and reducing waste by delivering components to the production line exactly when they are needed, in the right quantity. This system relies on precise coordination with suppliers, efficient transportation networks, and accurate forecasting. By reducing the need for large inventories, Toyota was able to lower costs, enhance product quality, and improve operational efficiency (Liker, 2020).

DOI: 10.4324/9781003740568-12

The JIT model is not without its challenges, especially when it comes to potential disruptions. However, Toyota's approach to supplier relationships and inventory management allows it to react quickly to changes in demand and supply, reducing the impact of any disruptions. For instance, Toyota's ability to recover quickly from the 2011 earthquake and tsunami in Japan demonstrated the resilience of its supply chain. While many manufacturers faced significant disruptions, Toyota was able to resume production faster than its competitors due to its strong supplier network and contingency planning.

Toyota's JIT system has helped the company maintain a competitive edge, not only by reducing costs but also by enhancing customer satisfaction through high product quality and OTD. The company's approach to lean manufacturing, which is grounded in eliminating waste at every level of the supply chain, remains a benchmark for companies across various industries looking to streamline their operations and increase efficiency (Liker, 2020).

12.2 Nokia: The Failure to Adapt

In contrast to Toyota's success, Nokia's failure to adapt its supply chain strategy provides a cautionary tale about the consequences of neglecting flexibility and contingency planning. Nokia was once a leader in the mobile phone market, with a well-established supply chain that relied on strong relationships with suppliers and efficient production systems. However, the company's downfall began with a fire at one of its key suppliers' factories, which disrupted the supply of critical components.

Nokia's failure to secure alternative sources of these components led to significant production delays, which in turn caused a loss of market share. The company had not diversified its supplier base sufficiently, leaving it vulnerable to disruptions that it could not quickly overcome. The incident highlighted the importance of having robust risk management strategies, including contingency planning, supplier diversification, and real-time monitoring of supply chain activities. Nokia's inability to recover from this disruption, coupled with its failure to innovate and adapt to the rapidly changing smartphone market, ultimately led to its decline (Doz & Kosonen, 2008).

Nokia's experience underscores the necessity of preparing for unexpected events in SCM. While a well-structured supply chain can help companies operate efficiently, it is equally important to be agile and capable of responding to unforeseen challenges. Diversifying suppliers and building redundancy into the supply chain are critical strategies for mitigating risk, especially in industries where rapid technological changes and external disruptions are commonplace.

12.3 Amazon: Leveraging Technology for Efficiency and Resilience

Amazon provides a prime example of a company that has successfully harnessed technology to build an efficient and resilient supply chain. Amazon's use of robotics, AI, and big data analytics has transformed its logistics operations, allowing the company to meet the ever-growing demands of its customers. One of the key factors in Amazon's success is its ability to optimise warehouse operations through automation. Robots in Amazon's fulfilment centres help with sorting, picking, and packing items, improving speed and accuracy while reducing labour costs (Stone, 2013).

In addition to automation, Amazon has also built a highly resilient supply chain by establishing a vast network of fulfilment centres around the world. This strategic expansion enables Amazon to offer fast and reliable delivery to customers, regardless of their location. By locating fulfilment centres near major population hubs, Amazon reduces transportation costs and improves delivery times. Furthermore, the company has developed strong partnerships with logistics providers, which help to ensure the smooth flow of goods from suppliers to customers.

Amazon's supply chain is characterised by a high degree of flexibility and responsiveness. The company uses sophisticated algorithms to forecast demand, which allows it to adjust its inventory levels in real time. This approach has enabled Amazon to continue growing despite the challenges posed by seasonal demand fluctuations, supply chain disruptions, and global trade uncertainties. The company's commitment to innovation and CI ensures that it remains at the forefront of supply chain excellence (Stone, 2013).

12.4 Rana Plaza: Ethical Considerations in SCM

While successful supply chains are often the focus of case studies, failures can also provide critical lessons, particularly in the area of ethics and social responsibility. The collapse of the Rana Plaza factory in Bangladesh in 2013 serves as a tragic example of how poor supply chain practices can lead to catastrophic consequences. The factory, which produced garments for several well-known global brands, collapsed due to substandard construction and inadequate safety measures, resulting in the deaths of over 1,100 workers.

The tragedy highlighted the ethical and social responsibilities that companies must consider when managing their supply chains. Many of the brands sourcing products from Rana Plaza had failed to ensure that their suppliers adhered to basic safety standards, which ultimately led to the disaster. This failure to prioritise worker safety not only resulted in human suffering but also caused significant reputational damage to the companies involved.

In the wake of the disaster, many companies took steps to improve the safety standards of their supply chains, including conducting regular audits, ensuring compliance with local labour laws, and engaging in more transparent communication with suppliers. The Rana Plaza collapse emphasised the need for companies to take a more holistic approach to SCM, incorporating ethical considerations and ensuring that their supply chains are socially responsible. It also underscored the importance of monitoring suppliers and holding them accountable for their actions (Taplin, 2014).

12.5 Apple: Mastering Complex Supply Chains

Apple Inc. is another example of a company that has built a highly successful supply chain, characterised by its close relationships with suppliers, rigorous quality control, and ability to manage complex logistics. Apple's supply chain strategy is designed to ensure the company maintains its competitive advantage in the technology industry. One of the key factors in Apple's success is its ability to manage a global network of suppliers while maintaining high standards of quality and reliability (Dormehl, 2012).

Apple works closely with its suppliers to ensure that components meet the company's exacting standards for quality, performance, and sustainability. The company also invests heavily in R&D to stay at the cutting edge of technology and ensure that its products remain innovative. Apple's ability to manage inventory effectively has been another critical factor in its success. By using sophisticated forecasting techniques and leveraging its GSC network, Apple can ensure that products are delivered to market on time, without the need for excess inventory.

Apple's supply chain success is also attributable to its ability to manage risks. The company has established contingency plans to mitigate potential disruptions, including the diversification of suppliers and the establishment of strategic partnerships with logistics providers. Apple's strong relationships with its suppliers and its focus on quality control have helped it maintain a dominant position in the technology sector (Dormehl, L. (2012)).

12.6 Conclusion

This chapter demonstrates how carefully selected case studies make theoretical concepts concrete, create a laboratory for reasoning about trade-offs, and support the combination of lecture content with applied problem-solving. The cases selected here, drawn from manufacturing, retail, logistics, and food sectors, span geographies and strategic priorities, and they show that supply chain choices are simultaneously technical, organisational, and political. The suggested exercises, case packs, and infographics can be adapted to fit course level and time constraints, and the integrated references below provide starting points for deeper student research.

Appendix A

Inventory Management KPIs

Inventory Turnover Ratio (ITR): Measures how often inventory is sold and replaced over a period. A higher ratio indicates efficient inventory management.

$$\text{ITR Formula} = \text{Cost of Goods Sold}\left(\text{COGS}\right) / \text{Average Inventory}$$

Days Sales of Inventory (DSI): Indicates the average number of days it takes to sell the entire inventory.

$$\text{DSI Formula} = \left(\text{Average Inventory} / \text{COGS}\right) * \left(\text{days in period}\right)$$

Return on Investment (ROI): Assesses the profitability of inventory by evaluating the gross profit earned for every dollar of inventory investment.

$$\text{ROI Formula} = \text{Gross Profit} / \text{Average Inventory Cost}$$

Stockout Rate: Measures the frequency of stockouts, indicating how often inventory levels are insufficient to meet demand.

$$\text{SR Formula} = \left(\text{Number of Stockouts} / \text{Total Orders}\right) * 100$$

Order Cycle Time (OCT): The average time taken to fulfil an order from the moment it is placed until it is delivered to the customer.

$$\text{OCT Formula} = \text{Total Order Fulfilment Time} / \text{Number of Orders}$$

Supplier Delivery Performance (DIFOTIS)

- **Delivered In Full (DIF)**

$$\text{Formula}: \left(\text{qty supplied}\right) / \left(\text{qty ordered}\right)$$

- **On Time (DOT)**

$$\text{Formula}: \left(\text{qty delivered on time}\right) / \left(\text{qty supplied}\right)$$

- **In Specification (DIS)**

  Formula : (qty supplied) – (quality issues) / qty supplied

DIFOTIS

  Formula : (DIF + DOT + DIS) / 3

  Formula : (beginning inventory) + (ending inventory) / *2 can be expressed in \$ or quantities*

Inventory Carrying Cost (a)

- **Annual Interest Cost**

  Formula : (inventory value) × (interest rate)

- **Cost for Days in Inventory**

  Formula : ((annual interest cost) / 365) × (days in inventory)

Inventory Carrying Cost (b)

- **Annual Interest Cost**

  Formula : (inventory value) × (interest rate)

- **Cost/Unit/Year**

  Formula : (annual interest cost) / (stock on hand)

Service Level: Measures the ability to meet customer demand without a stockout. It is often expressed as a percentage and may be set by contractual arrangements.

SL Formula = (Number of Orders Fulfilled Without Stockout / Total Orders) * 100

Reorder Point (ROP): The inventory level at which a new order should be placed to replenish stock before it runs out.

ROP Formula = Lead Time Demand + Safety Stock

Return on Assets (ROA): Indicates how profitable a company is relative to its total assets, including inventory.

ROA Formula = Net Income / Total Assets

Costs Per Order (CPO):

$$\text{CPO Formula} = \text{Total Selling and Fulfilment Costs} / \text{Total Orders}$$

Backorder Rate (BOR): Measures the percentage of orders that cannot be filled at the time of purchase and are placed on backorder.

$$\text{BOR Formula} = (\text{Number of Backorders} / \text{Total Orders}) * 100$$

Average Inventory: The average amount of inventory held over a certain period.

$$\text{Average Inventory Formula} = (\text{Beginning Inventory} + \text{Ending Inventory}) / 2$$

Obsolete Inventory: The amount or percentage of inventory that is no longer sellable due to being outdated or expired.

$$\text{Obsolete Inventory Formula} = (\text{Value of Obsolete Inventory} / \text{Total Inventory Value}) * 100$$

Ordering Cost:

$$\text{Formula}: (\text{SQRT}((2 * \text{annual demand} * \text{cost per order}) / \text{carrying cost})$$

see above for carrying cost

Safety Stock Fixed (SSF):

$$\text{SSF Formula} = \text{No.of Days} \times \text{Daily Sales}$$

Safety Stock – Time-Based (SST):

$$\text{SST Formula} = (\text{max Daily Use} \times \text{max Lead Time}) - (\text{Avg Daily Use} \times \text{Avg Lead Time})$$

Economic Order Quantity (EOQ):

$$\text{EOQ Formula} = \text{SQRT } 2 \times \text{Annual Demand} \times \text{Holding Cost}$$

Appendix B
Warehouse and Supply Chain Performance Formulae

Inventory Accuracy

Formula : (No.of items counted) / (Items on record) × 100

Storage Utilisation Rate

Formula : (inventory size cubed) / (total warehouse size cubed)

Total Order Cycle Time

Formula : (time order received by customer – time order placed) / (total number of orders shipped)

Internal Order Cycle Time

Formula : (time order shipped – time order received) / (number of orders shipped)

Perfect Order Percentage

Formula : (% orders on time) × (% orders shipped complete) × (% orders shipped no damage) × (% orders with correct documentation)

On-Time Shipping Percentage

Formula : (number of orders shipped on time) / (number of orders shipped)

Order Fill Rate

Formula : (total orders filled to customer request) / (total orders filled)

Line-Item Fill Rate

Formula : (total order lines filled complete) / (total order lines filled)

Orders Picked Per Hour

Formula : (total orders picked and successfully shipped) / (total hours worked in picking and shipping)

Lines Picked and Shipped Per Hour

Formula : (total order lines picked and successfully shipped) / (total hours worked in picking and shipping)

Distribution Costs (As a Percentage of Sales)

Formula : (total of distribution costs) / (total sales)

Appendix C
Quiz Answers

Chapter 1

1 **What is the core purpose of SCM?**
The core purpose of SCM is to efficiently manage the flow of goods and services from suppliers to consumers, ensuring cost minimisation, enhanced efficiency, and customer satisfaction.

2 **How does SCM contribute to reducing operational costs for businesses?**
SCM reduces operational costs by optimising production schedules, improving inventory management, reducing waste, and enhancing logistics efficiency.

3 **Why is flexibility important in SCM, particularly during global disruptions like the COVID-19 pandemic?**
Flexibility allows businesses to quickly adapt to unforeseen disruptions, ensuring continuity by adjusting supply sources, production schedules, and logistics processes.

4 **What is the JIT system, and how does it benefit companies like Toyota?**
The JIT system reduces inventory costs by ensuring that components arrive precisely when needed for production, reducing waste and improving efficiency, as seen in Toyota's operations.

5 **How does lean manufacturing support production efficiency in SCM?**
Lean manufacturing minimises waste and maximises efficiency by streamlining production processes, improving quality, and aligning output closely with demand.

6 **What role does logistics play in SCM, and how does it affect customer satisfaction?**
Logistics ensures the timely and cost-effective movement of goods, directly impacting customer satisfaction by delivering products on time and in the correct condition.

7 **How has Amazon's logistics network contributed to its success?**
Amazon's logistics network allows for rapid order fulfilment, leveraging technology and strategically placed fulfilment centres to provide fast, reliable delivery.

8 **In what ways can SCM help businesses align with sustainability goals?**
SCM supports sustainability by integrating environmentally responsible sourcing, reducing waste, and optimising transportation to lower carbon emissions.

9 **What technologies are driving the evolution of modern supply chains?**
Technologies such as data analytics, AI, blockchain, robotics, and the IoT are enhancing supply chain efficiency and visibility.

10 **How can businesses build resilient supply chains that are capable of adapting to unforeseen disruptions?**
Businesses can build resilient supply chains by diversifying suppliers, adopting flexible strategies, investing in technology, and preparing proactive risk management plans.

Chapter 2

1 **What is the SCOR Model used for?**
The SCOR Model provides a standard approach to supply chain operations, helping businesses optimise their processes and improve performance.

2 **How does Lean SCM benefit businesses?**
Lean SCM reduces waste and enhances efficiency by focusing on value-added activities and minimising non-value-added processes.

3 **What is the main focus of Agile SCM?**
Agile SCM prioritises flexibility and responsiveness to changing market demands and unpredictable conditions.

4 **What is TOC?**
The TOC focuses on identifying and optimising bottlenecks within a system to improve overall performance.

5 **How does the Bullwhip Effect impact supply chains?**
The Bullwhip Effect causes larger fluctuations in orders as demand moves up the supply chain, leading to inefficiencies like excess inventory and stockouts.

6 **What is Systems Thinking in SCM?**
Systems Thinking views supply chains as interconnected systems, emphasising collaboration and the impact of changes on the entire network.

7 **What role does JIT play in Lean SCM?**
JIT reduces inventory by producing only what is needed when it is needed, improving cash flow and reducing storage costs.

8 **How does Zara use Agile SCM?**
Zara uses Agile SCM by quickly designing and producing new styles in response to changing fashion trends, maintaining low inventory levels.

9 **What is the importance of VSM in Lean SCM?**
VSM helps identify inefficiencies in supply chain processes, enabling businesses to eliminate waste and optimise performance.

10 **Why is flexibility important in SCM?**
Flexibility allows businesses to respond to unforeseen disruptions, changes in demand, and other unpredictable events that affect supply chains.

Chapter 3

1 **What are the two primary strategies for achieving competitive advantage that the document centres on?**
The two primary strategies are Cost Leadership and Differentiation.

2 **Name three key practices that a company would use in its supply chain to achieve Cost Leadership.**
Three key practices to achieve Cost Leadership in SCM are:

a Implementing Lean Supply Chain Practices (like JIT and CI) to eliminate waste and reduce operational costs.
b Employing Efficient Procurement (e.g., strategic sourcing, bulk purchasing, strong supplier relationships) to reduce input costs.
c Utilising Optimised Logistics (e.g., advanced route planning, automation, data analytics) to minimise distribution and inventory holding costs.

3 **What are three ways a company can use its supply chain to achieve Differentiation?**
The two strategic enablers are Technology (e.g., Big Data, AI, IoT) and Sustainability (e.g., resource efficiency, ethical sourcing).

4 **According to the document, what are the two strategic enablers that amplify competitive advantage in SCM?**
Lean Supply Chain Practices are designed to eliminate waste and reduce operational costs, and an example technique is JIT inventory management or CI (Kaizen).

5 **What are Lean Supply Chain Practices designed to eliminate, and what is one example technique mentioned?**
The company that uses an agile replenishment model with real-time POS data to enable bi-weekly restocking and trend-driven design launches is Zara.

6 **The document mentions that an agile supply chain, drawing real-time POS data to enable bi-weekly restocking and trend-driven design launches, is characteristic of which company?**
The three factors of the "Triple Bottom Line" (also known as ESG) are Environmental, Social, and Governance.

7 **What three factors make up the "Triple Bottom Line" that is increasingly driving business strategy?**
Blockchain technology strengthens SCM by providing a secure, transparent, and immutable record of transactions, which improves traceability, enables compliance monitoring, and enhances trust among supply chain partners.

8 **How does Blockchain technology strengthen SCM?**
Two examples of how Process Optimisation is achieved in SCM are through:

a Lean Manufacturing principles to eliminate non-value-adding activities, such as implementing JIT to reduce holding costs.
b Implementing Six Sigma to reduce process variability, improve quality, and address defects.

9 **Give two examples of how Process Optimisation can be achieved in SCM to support cost leadership.**
The central aim of Strategic Alignment in SCM is the synchronisation of supply chain activities with a company's overarching business strategy to ensure every component contributes to achieving the organisation's competitive goals (whether cost leadership, differentiation, or sustainability).

10 **What is the central aim of Strategic Alignment in SCM?**
The central aim of Strategic Alignment in SCM is the synchronisation of supply chain activities with a company's overarching business strategy to ensure every component contributes to achieving the organisation's competitive goals (whether cost leadership, differentiation, or sustainability).

Chapter 4

1 **What is a GSC?**
A GSC involves sourcing, manufacturing, and distributing goods across international borders.

2 **What are the primary sources of disruption in GSCs?**
Natural disasters, political instability, and economic fluctuations are key sources of disruptions.

3 **How did the COVID-19 pandemic impact GSCs?**
It caused widespread disruptions through lockdowns, travel restrictions, and production delays.

4 **Why is regulatory compliance challenging in GSCs?**
Each country has different trade policies, tariffs, and safety standards that companies must adhere to.

5 **What cultural differences can impact GSCs?**
Variations in communication styles, business practices, and decision-making processes can create misunderstandings.

6 **How does big data analytics support GSCs?**
It helps companies analyse data to forecast demand and optimise inventory and production.

7 **What is the role of blockchain in supply chains?**
Blockchain provides secure, transparent records that enhance traceability and reduce fraud risks.

8 **Why is supplier diversification important for resilience?**
It reduces dependency on a single source, helping companies manage risks from regional disruptions.

9 **What is the advantage of localisation or near-shoring?**
It brings production closer to markets, reducing lead times and exposure to geopolitical risks.

10 **How do collaborative partnerships benefit SCM?**
They improve communication and coordination, allowing companies to address challenges jointly.

Chapter 5

1 **What is the main purpose of demand forecasting in SCM?**
Demand forecasting helps businesses predict customer demand, enabling them to plan operations, manage inventory effectively, and optimise production schedules.

2 **What is the difference between qualitative and quantitative forecasting?**
Qualitative forecasting relies on expert judgement and opinion, while quantitative forecasting uses historical data and statistical models to predict future demand.

3 **Why is the Delphi method used in qualitative forecasting?**
The Delphi method gathers insights from a panel of experts through multiple rounds of surveys to reach a consensus on future demand, especially in uncertain or complex situations.

4 **What are some common techniques in quantitative forecasting?**
Common techniques include time series analysis, regression analysis, and econometric modelling, which use historical data to identify trends, seasonality, and influencing factors.

5 **How can companies improve the accuracy of their forecasts?**
Companies can combine both qualitative and quantitative methods, using a hybrid approach to leverage the strengths of each and create more robust demand forecasts.

6 **What role does demand planning play in SCM?**
Demand planning ensures that supply chain activities align with anticipated demand, helping businesses optimise inventory, reduce stockouts or overstock situations, and improve customer satisfaction.

7 **Why is collaboration important in demand planning?**
Collaboration across departments like sales, marketing, and operations ensures that the demand plan reflects business goals, customer trends, and market dynamics, fostering alignment and accuracy.

8 **What advanced technologies are transforming demand planning?**
Advanced technologies such as demand planning software, big data analytics, and ML enable more accurate forecasting by processing vast amounts of data and adjusting to changing variables.

9 **What challenges do businesses face in demand planning?**
Challenges include managing demand uncertainty, dealing with seasonal variations, and ensuring alignment with broader business objectives, all of which require flexible and responsive planning processes.

10 **How can companies address demand uncertainty in their forecasts?**
Companies can use flexible forecasting models that are regularly updated with new data and external factors, allowing them to adjust forecasts in response to unexpected events and market changes.

Chapter 6

1 **What is the main purpose of inventory management in supply chain operations?**
To maintain optimal stock levels to meet customer demand while minimising costs.

2 **What are the primary objectives of inventory management?**
To minimise costs, ensure sufficient stock levels, and maximise service levels.

3 **What does the EOQ model calculate?**
It calculates the optimal order size that minimises total inventory costs.

4 **What is the formula for EOQ based on?**
It balances ordering and holding costs to determine the ideal order quantity.

5 **What is JIT inventory management?**
A method that aligns production schedules with demand, minimising inventory levels.

6 **What are the key requirements for JIT to work effectively?**
Accurate demand forecasting, strong supplier relationships, and efficient production processes.

7 **What is SS and why is it held?**
Additional inventory held to prevent stockouts due to demand or supply uncertainties.

8 **How is SS typically calculated?**
Using either fixed SS levels or time-based calculations considering demand and lead-time variability.

9 **What role does technology play in modern inventory management?**
It enables real-time tracking, predictive analytics, and automated reordering to optimise inventory levels.

10 **Name one best practice for effective inventory management.**
Regularly review inventory levels to identify excess stock or potential stockouts.

Chapter 7

1 **What is the main goal of procurement in SCM?**
To efficiently and cost-effectively acquire goods and services that meet organisational needs.

2 **Why is need identification important in the procurement process?**
It ensures that purchased items align with organisational goals without overburdening inventory.

3 **What is the purpose of conducting a market analysis in procurement?**
To evaluate and shortlist potential suppliers who can meet organisational needs at competitive prices.

4 **What is a RFP used for?**
To outline requirements and invite suppliers to submit competitive offers.

5 **How are bids evaluated during supplier selection?**
Based on criteria like price, quality, delivery time, and terms of service.

6 **Why is contract finalisation crucial in procurement?**
It establishes legally binding terms to protect both parties' interests and resolve potential disputes.

7 **What is SRM?**
A strategic approach to developing long-term, value-generating partnerships with key suppliers.

8 **Why is a supplier's reputation important in the selection process?**
It provides insight into their reliability and trustworthiness, helping reduce risks.

9 **How does SRM contribute to risk management?**
Fostering collaboration allows organisations to anticipate and mitigate potential supply chain issues.

10 **What is a key benefit of aligning suppliers with ethical and sustainability standards?**
It supports responsible procurement practices and strengthens the organisation's brand.

Chapter 8

1 **What is the main goal of production and operations management?**
To use resources efficiently to produce goods and services that meet customer demand.

2 **What is production planning?**
Production planning is the scheduling and control of production activities to maximise efficiency.

3 **What does a MPS outline?**
The MPS details the quantities and timing for each product to align with demand and resource availability.

4 **What is the purpose of capacity planning in production?**
To ensure sufficient resources, like labour and equipment, are available to meet production demands.

5 **What is lean manufacturing focused on?**
Lean manufacturing focuses on minimising waste and maximising customer value.

6 **Name two types of waste that lean manufacturing seeks to eliminate.**
Overproduction and unnecessary transportation are two types of waste lean manufacturing targets.

7 **What is TQM?**
TQM is a comprehensive quality management approach involving all employees in CI.

8 **What is the goal of Six Sigma?**
To minimise defects and process variability, aiming for fewer than 3.4 defects per million opportunities.

9 **How does SPC support quality management?**
SPC uses statistical techniques to monitor process performance and control quality.

10 **What is Kaizen, and why is it important?**
Kaizen is the practice of CI, helping organisations make incremental changes for better efficiency and quality.

Chapter 9

1 **What is the role of logistics and distribution in SCM?**
Logistics and distribution ensure efficient, reliable product delivery, enhancing supply chain effectiveness.

2 **Why is transportation management important?**
Transportation management optimises movement of goods, impacting costs and supply chain reliability.

3 **What are the main modes of transportation in logistics?**
The primary modes are road, rail, air, and maritime, each suited to different needs and constraints.

4 **What advantages does road transport offer?**
Road transport provides flexibility for direct-to-door delivery and is ideal for short to medium distances.

5 **Why is rail transport cost-effective for long distances?**
Rail transport handles bulk goods efficiently, with lower fuel consumption per tonne-kilometre.

6 **How does air transport benefit high-value, time-sensitive goods?**
Air transport offers the fastest delivery, ideal for urgent shipments, despite being costly.

7 **What makes maritime transport indispensable for global trade?**
Maritime transport supports high-volume, long-distance shipping at cost-effective rates.

8 **What is warehouse management's primary focus?**
Warehouse management ensures goods are stored and dispatched efficiently to support the supply chain.

9 **How does inventory control improve logistics operations?**
Inventory control prevents overstock and stockouts, maintaining optimal stock levels to meet demand.

10 **Why is adaptability crucial in distribution networks?**
Adaptability allows distribution networks to meet changing customer demands and market conditions.

Chapter 10

1 **How does IT enhance SCM?**
IT improves supply chain efficiency, reduces costs, and enables better collaboration and competitive advantage.

2 **What role do ERP systems play in SCM?**
ERP systems integrate business processes, enabling real-time visibility and control over the supply chain.

3 **How do ERP systems benefit data accuracy in SCM?**
ERP systems centralise information, providing a "single source of truth" that minimises errors and enhances decision-making.

4 **Why is supply chain visibility important, and how do ERP systems support it?**
ERP systems provide real-time visibility, helping organisations detect and address potential disruptions early.

5 **What is SCA, and why is it valuable?**
SCA uses data to improve demand forecasting, inventory management, and logistics, supporting data-driven decisions.

6 **How does demand forecasting benefit from SCA?**
SCA enables accurate forecasts, aligning production and inventory with customer demand to prevent stockouts or overstock.

7 **How does the IoT enhance supply chain visibility?**
IoT enables real-time tracking of goods and equipment, improving inventory management and reducing losses.

8 **What advantages does AI bring to SCM?**
AI optimises forecasting, inventory management, and automation, making SCM more efficient and responsive.

9 **How does blockchain technology improve transparency in SCM?**
Blockchain provides a secure, transparent record of transactions, enhancing trust and accountability among partners.

10 **In what ways do emerging technologies support sustainability in SCM?**
IoT, AI, and blockchain reduce waste, emissions, and verify sustainable practices, aligning with environmental goals.

Chapter 11

1 **Why is risk management essential in modern supply chains?**
Risk management helps supply chains remain resilient and sustainable amidst global uncertainties.

2 **What are some key types of risks in supply chains?**
Key risks include demand fluctuations, supply disruptions, operational failures, financial uncertainties, environmental factors, and reputational concerns.

3 **What is demand risk, and why is it challenging?**
Demand risk involves unpredictable changes in customer demand, which can lead to excess inventory or stockouts.

4 **How does supply risk impact GSCs?**
Supply risk can lead to material shortages or delays due to factors like geopolitical instability or natural disasters.

5 **What are operational risks, and how do they affect supply chains?**
Operational risks, like equipment failure or cyberattacks, can disrupt production and increase costs.

6 **Why is financial risk a concern for supply chains?**
Financial risk arises from currency fluctuations and commodity price changes that impact supply chain costs.

7 **How can environmental risk disrupt supply chain operations?**
Extreme weather events and climate change can damage infrastructure, delay shipments, and require regulatory compliance.

8 **What is reputational risk in supply chains?**
Reputational risk involves potential harm to a company's image from unethical practices within its supply chain.

9 **How does diversifying suppliers mitigate supply chain risks?**
Diversifying suppliers reduces dependency on a single source, minimising disruption risks.

10 **What role does resilience play in SCRM?**
Resilience enables supply chains to adapt and recover quickly from disruptions, ensuring continuity and stability.

Appendix D

Classroom Worksheet – Supplier Scorecard and Smallholder Yield Simulation

Classroom Worksheet – Supplier Scorecard and Smallholder Yield Simulation

Context Summary (for Students)

You are a procurement analyst in an organisation that sources cocoa/palm oil from aggregated smallholder cooperatives across several regions. The organisation runs a supplier development programme that aims to increase smallholder yields by 20% and reduce yield variability. The dataset supplier_scorecard_simulation.csv contains baseline and improved scenarios for eight supplier aggregations, with scorecard metrics and simulated monthly volatility.

Data file: (Supplier_Scorecard_Simulation)

Learning Objectives

1 Interpret a supplier scorecard and justify supplier selection using combined commercial and social metrics.
2 Quantify the supply impact of a smallholder yield-improvement programme.
3 Measure changes in supply volatility and compute the SS implications for a chosen service level and lead time.
4 Re-weight a composite supplier scorecard to prioritise traceability and social outcomes and observe ranking effects.
5 Practise sensitivity thinking and critique the limits of single-run simulation.

Part A – Data Familiarisation (10 Minutes)

Open the CSV and briefly inspect these columns:

1 SupplierID, Name, Country, Region
2 Baseline_yield_t_ha, Improved_yield_t_ha
3 Baseline_Annual_tonnes, Improved_Annual_tonnes
4 Baseline_Mean_Monthly_t, Baseline_SD_Monthly_t
5 Baseline_Volatility_pct, Improved_Volatility_pct
6 Price_USD_t, Price_Score, Quality_Score, OnTime_Score, Traceability_Score, Social_Score
7 Weighted_Score (original weights: Price 30%, Quality 25%, OnTime 15%, Traceability 15%, Social 15%)

Task A1. State which supplier has the highest weighted score under the original weighting scheme and give the value.

Part B – Supply Aggregate Impact (15 Minutes)

Task B1. Calculate the total baseline annual supply across all suppliers, the total improved annual supply after the 20% yield uplift, and the overall percentage increase in total supply. Show formulae.

Part C – Volatility and SS (30 Minutes)

Background

Volatility here is the coefficient of variation of the monthly supply (SD / mean * 100). SS (months) at a chosen service level is computed from:

$$Safety\ stock = z \times \sigma\ monthly \times Lead\ time(months)$$

$$\text{Safety stock} = z \times \sigma_{\text{monthly}} \times \sqrt{\text{Lead time}(\text{months})}$$

$$Safety\ stock = z \times \sigma\ monthly \times Lead\ time(months)$$

where zzz is the standard normal z-value for the target service level.

Assumptions for Exercise

1 Target service level: 95% → z ≈ 1.65z \approx. 1.65z ≈ 1.65.
2 Lead time: two months.

Task C1. For each supplier, compute the absolute and relative reduction in volatility (Baseline Volatility % – Improved Volatility %), and identify which suppliers show the largest and smallest reductions.

Task C2. Compute SS (tonnes) under baseline and improved scenarios for each supplier using the formula above and identify how SS needs change after the programme for each supplier.

Part D – Re-weight the Scorecard (20 Minutes)

Task D1. Re-weight the scorecard to reflect a strategic decision to prioritise traceability and social outcomes. Use these alternative weights:

- Price 20%, Quality 20%, On-time 15%, Traceability 25%, Social 20%.

Recompute the weighted scores and rank suppliers. Which three suppliers are top-ranked under the new weighting? Comment on any rank changes and what that implies for procurement strategy.

Part E – Sensitivity and Interpretation (15 Minutes)

Task E1. Re-run the "improved yield" scenario in your head with two other uplift assumptions: 10% and 30%, holding the improved variability profile proportional to the original assumptions. For one supplier of your choice, compute the marginal increase in annual supply when moving from 10% → 20% and 20% → 30% lift. Comment on diminishing returns, if any.

Task E2. Discuss the limitations of using a single random simulation run to estimate volatility improvements and propose how the organisation should present evidence to senior management.

Submission Format

Submit an Excel workbook or CSV with worksheet answers and supporting calculations, and a one-page memo to procurement leadership summarising the recommended supplier prioritisation and the expected changes in supply stability.

Instructor Guide – Supplier Scorecard and Smallholder Yield Simulation

Purpose and Learning Outcomes

- Teach students to interpret combined commercial/social supplier scorecards, quantify supply impacts from yield-improvement programmes, compute volatility and SS implications, and apply scorecard re-weighting and sensitivity thinking.
- By the end students should: (1) justify supplier prioritisation using combined metrics; (2) calculate aggregate supply change from a 20% uplift; (3) compute volatility reductions and SS changes; (4) re-rank suppliers under new strategic weights; (5) critique single-run simulation limits.

Materials and Set-up

- Files to give each student or team: Supplier_Scorecard_Simulation.csv (dataset from Supplier_Scorecard_Solutions.xlsx) and the worksheet brief (this Appendix).
- Recommended classroom tools: Excel (preferred) or Google Sheets; projector to show model-answer worksheet.
- Suggested class format: 90 minutes (can be split into two 45-minute sessions).

Suggested Timings (Classroom/Workshop)

- Introduction and context: 10 minutes
- Part A (data familiarisation): 10 minutes
- Part B (aggregate supply): 15 minutes
- Part C (volatility and SS): 30 minutes
- Part D (re-weight scorecard): 20 minutes
- Part E (sensitivity and interpretation): 15 minutes
- Presentation/debrief: 20 minutes Total flexible time: 90–120 minutes.

Marking Rubric (Total 100)

- Data familiarity and interpretation (Part A): 5
- Supply aggregate calculations and formulae (Part B): 15
- Volatility reductions and identification (Part C1): 15
- SS calculations and interpretation (Part C2): 15
- Scorecard re-weighting, recomputed ranks, commentary (Part D): 20
- Sensitivity calculations + critical thinking on simulation limits (Part E): 20 Score guidance: award partial credit for correct method even if arithmetic slips.

Model Answers and Instructor Notes (Task-by-task)

Use these to verify student work. Show formulae first, then numeric results.

Part A – Data Familiarisation

- Task A1 (original weighted score formula)
  - Formula: $\text{Weighted\_Score} = 0.30 Price\_Score + 0.25 \text{Quality\_Score} + 0.15 OnTime\_Score + 0.15 \text{Traceability\_Score} + 0.15 * \text{Social\_Score}$
  - Model answer: Highest weighted score = Sumatra Smallholders (S3) with Weighted_Score = 81.7.
  - Marking note: accept correct identification and value within ±0.1 if rounding differences.

Part B – Supply Aggregate Impact

- Task B1 formulae
  - $\text{Baseline total} = \text{SUM}(\text{Baseline\_Annual\_tonnes\_}i)$ for i = 1.8
  - $\text{Improved total} = \text{SUM}(\text{Improved\_Annual\_tonnes\_}i)$ for i = 1.8
  - $\%\text{increase} = (\text{Improved total} - \text{Baseline total}) / \text{Baseline total} \times 100\%$
- Model numeric answers (from provided data)
  - Baseline total = 1,985.40 t
  - Improved total = 2,382.48 t
  - Percentage increase = 20.00%
- Instructor note: students must show the cell-range sums and the per cent formula; 20% uplift applied consistently explains the exact 20% aggregate.

Part C – Volatility and SS

Background and formulae

- $\text{Volatility}(\%) = (\text{SD\_monthly} / \text{Mean\_monthly}) \times 100$
  (already provided as Baseline_Volatility_pct and Improved_Volatility_pct in dataset)
- $\text{Volatility absolute reduction (pp)} = \text{Baseline\_Volatility\_pct} - \text{Improved\_Volatility\_pct}$

- Volatility relative reduction(%) = (Volatility_abs_reduction / Baseline_Volatility_pct) × 100%
- SS (tonnes) formula used in dataset (corrected form): Safety Stock = $z \times \sigma$_monthly × √(Lead time in months)
  - Use z = 1.65 (95% service level), Lead time = 2 months → √2 ≈ 1.4142
  - So Safety Stock ≈ 1.65 × σ_monthly × 1.4142 ≈ 2.3334 × σ_monthly
- Students should compute baseline and improved SS per supplier from Baseline_SD_Monthly_*t* and Improved_SD_Monthly_*t*.
- Marking note: accept intermediate rounding; check formula implementation (multiplying *z* by σ then by √LT).

Model numeric results (volatility reductions and SS guidance):

- Volatility reductions (abs, rel) – model table (abs reduction in percentage points; rel reduction in %):
  - S1 Kumasi Co-op: Baseline 12.72 → Improved 12.91 → Abs = –0.19 pp → Rel = –1.49% (note: negative means simulated volatility increased slightly)
  - S2 Abidjan Growers: 16.73 → 11.35 → Abs = 5.38 pp → Rel ≈ 32.16%
  - S3 Sumatra Smallholders: 10.22 → 7.24 → Abs = 2.98 pp → Rel ≈ 29.16%
  - S4 Sarawak Growers: 14.90 → 5.95 → Abs = 8.95 pp → Rel ≈ 60.07%
  - S5 Amazon Agro: 11.15 → 10.73 → Abs = 0.42 pp → Rel ≈ 3.77%
  - S6 PNG Village Co-op: 23.23 → 14.68 → Abs = 8.55 pp → Rel ≈ 36.81%
  - S7 Mekong Planters: 8.59 → 7.85 → Abs = 0.74 pp → Rel ≈ 8.61%
  - S8 Lagos Cocoa Co-op: 18.09 → 9.72 → Abs = 8.37 pp → Rel ≈ 46.27%
- Largest absolute reductions: S4 (8.95 pp), S6 (8.55 pp), S8 (8.37 pp).
- Smallest absolute reductions: S1 (–0.19 pp, increase) and S5 (0.42 pp).

SS calculations (model guidance)

- Multiplicative factor ≈ 2.3334 × SD_monthly
- Example checks (rounded):
  - S1 Baseline safety stock ≈ 2.3334 × 1.29 ≈ 3.01 t (dataset shows 3.01) – Improved ≈ 2.3334 × 1.38 ≈ 3.22 t.
  - S2 Baseline ≈ 2.3334 × 2.02 ≈ 4.71 t – Improved ≈ 2.3334 × 1.63 ≈ 3.80 t.
  - S3 Baseline ≈ 2.3334 × 3.70 ≈ 8.63 t – Improved ≈ 2.3334 × 3.16 ≈ 7.37 t.
  - Continue similarly for S4–S8 using SD values in spreadsheet; provided sheet contains SS baseline and improved values for instructor verification.
- Interpretation: SS needs fall for suppliers with reduced SD; for S1, SS increases because improved SD rose slightly in the simulated run.

Marking guidance: full credit for correct formula, correct multiplier derivation, and matching these example numbers within rounding tolerance; partial credit for correct approach but arithmetic errors.

Part D – Re-weight the Scorecard

- New weights: Price 20%, Quality 20%, On-time 15%, Traceability 25%, Social 20%
- New Weighted_Score formula: $0.20 Price\_Score + 0.20 \text{Quality\_Score} + 0.15 OnTime\_Score + 0.25 \text{Traceability\_Score} + 0.20 * \text{Social\_Score}$
- Model top 3 under new weighting (with values from provided sheet):

  1 S3 Sumatra Smallholders – New_Weighted_Score = 76.40
  2 S4 Sarawak Growers – New_Weighted_Score = 74.60
  3 S7 Mekong Planters – New_Weighted_Score = 74.21

- Instructor commentary to prompt student discussion:
  - Compare original and new rankings. S3 remains top; S4 and S7 rise due to higher traceability/related scores; suppliers with strong commercial/pricing but weaker traceability/social scores may drop.
  - Procurement implication: shifting strategic weight towards traceability/social outcomes changes supplier prioritisation; discuss trade-offs (cost vs ESG objectives, supply security).

Marking note: award points for recalculation, for correctly identifying rank changes, and for reasoned procurement strategy commentary.

Part E – Sensitivity and Interpretation

- Task E1 (marginal supply increases)
  - Method: For a chosen supplier, marginal increase from $x\% \rightarrow y\% \text{uplift} = \text{Baseline\_Annual\_tonnes} \times (y\% - x\%)$.
  - Example (use S3 Sumatra Smallholders baseline = 432 t):
    - $10\% \rightarrow 20\% \text{marginal increase} = 432 \times (0.20 - 0.10) = 432 \times 0.10 = 43.2\,\text{t}$
    - $20\% \rightarrow 30\% \text{marginal increase} = 432 \times (0.30 - 0.20) = 43.2\,\text{t}$
    - For linear uplift assumption, marginal increases are equal; discuss whether diminishing returns may appear in real systems (land constraints, input limits, adoption rates) even if simple proportional model shows constant marginal gains.
- Task E2 (limitations of single-run simulation)
  - Key points to require students to state:
    - Single-run results are subject to sampling noise; may show counterintuitive increases in SD for some suppliers (e.g., S1) because of random seed.
    - A single random draw does not provide confidence intervals or probabilistic guarantees.
    - Recommend robust approach for senior management: run Monte Carlo with many replications (e.g., 1,000+ runs), report mean, median, percentile bands (P10–P90), and confidence intervals for volatility and SS changes; provide

scenario analysis (different adoption rates, uplift magnitudes, correlated risks across regions); present sensitivity tables and clear visualisations (boxplots, fan charts).

- Marking note: full credit for recognising sampling variability, recommending multiple runs, and proposing clear summary statistics and visualisations.

Expected Student Deliverables (for Marking)

- Excel/CSV with:
  - All calculations shown (explicit formula cells for sums, % changes, volatility reductions, SS formulae, re-weighted scores).
  - A short results sheet/tabs labelled A–E matching the worksheet parts.
- One-page memo to procurement leadership summarising:
  - Top recommended suppliers under the chosen strategic weighting (explicitly name top 3).
  - Expected change in aggregate supply and high-level SS impacts.
  - Key caveats from sensitivity analysis and recommended next steps (e.g., run Monte Carlo, monitor early adoption KPIs).

Common Student Errors to Watch For

- Misapplying SS formula (forgetting √LeadTime or using LeadTime instead of √LeadTime).
- Using wrong z-value (must use 1.65 for 95% per exercise).
- Forgetting to show formulae or to reference the cell ranges used for sums.
- Rounding inconsistently leading to small mismatches – acceptable within ±1–2% unless method is wrong.
- Treating improved volatility as automatically lower for every supplier; discuss observed increases (e.g., S1) as opportunity to teach randomness and the importance of multiple simulation runs.

Extensions and Exam-Style Questions

- Ask students to implement a Monte Carlo exercise (e.g., 1,000 runs) and report mean and 90% confidence intervals for improved volatility and SS per supplier.
- Ask for a constrained optimisation: given a fixed budget premium for supplier development, which supplier set maximises expected additional tonnes while meeting minimum traceability thresholds.
- Ask students to model correlated shocks (climate event affecting multiple suppliers) and re-evaluate SS and diversification strategy.

Final Instructor Tips

- Encourage students to produce clear tables and charts: (1) baseline vs improved annual supply, (2) volatility reduction bar chart, (3) SS before/after comparison, (4) rank-change table.
- Use S1 and S5 examples to prompt discussion on why simulated improvements may not uniformly reduce volatility and what business monitoring (field trials, farmer training metrics) would look like in practice.
- Use the memo task to assess students' ability to translate technical outputs into actionable procurement recommendations for leadership.

Bibliography

AI Expert Network. (2024). *Case study: FedEx's AI-powered supply chain revolution.* [Online]. Available at: https://aiexpert.network/ai-at-fedex [Accessed 06 August 2025].

Analytics Insights. (2025). *Analytics insights: IoT meets AI.* [Online]. Available at: https://www.analyticsinsight.net/internet-of-things/iot-meets-ai-how-sensor-data-optimizes-lead-tracking-in-industrial-sales? [Accessed 06 August 2025].

Anamika. (2025). *Techpacker.* [Online]. Available at: https://techpacker.com/blog/design/indefinite-guide-to-3d-printing-in-fashion [Accessed 06 August 2025].

APICS. (2017). *Supply chain operations reference (SCOR) model.* [Online]. Available at: https://www.apics.org/apics-for-business/frameworks/scor [Accessed 12 November 2024].

Armstrong, J. S. (2001). *Principles of forecasting: A handbook for researchers and practitioners.* New York: Springer Science & Business Media.

ASCM: Association of Supply Chain Management. (2024). *What is supply chain management?.* [Online]. Available at: https://www.ascm.org/topics/supply-chain-management/ [Accessed 27 September 2024].

ASEAN Secretariat. (2024). *ASEAN digital integration and trade facilitation Progress report 2024.* Jakarta: Association of Southeast Asian Nations.

Ashcroft, S. (2022). *SupplyChain Digital.* [Online]. Available at: https://supplychaindigital.com/digital-supply-chain/keith-oliver-the-man-who-gave-us-supply-chain-management [Accessed 10 April 2025].

Ashton, K.. (2009). *That "Internet of Things" thing.* [Online]. Available at: https://www.rfidjournal.com/that-internet-of-things-thing [Accessed 13 December 2024].

Australian Competition and Consumer Commission. (2020). *Digital platforms inquiry – Final report, Australian Government.* [Online]. Available at: https://www.accc.gov.au/publications/digital-platforms-inquiry-final-report [Accessed 12 November 2024].

Australian Government. (2022). *Sustainable procurement guide, Australian Government Department of the Environment and Energy.* [Online]. Available at: https://www.environment.gov.au/protection/national-waste-policy/sustainable-procurement-guide [Accessed 12 November 2024].

Australian Industry Group. (2020). *The impact of COVID-19 on Australia's Manufacturing Industry, Australian Industry Group.* [Online]. Available at: https://www.aigroup.com.au [Accessed 12 November 2024].

Bailey, P., et al. (2015). *Procurement, principles & management* (11th ed.). Pearson Education.

Basu, R. (2023). *Global supply chain strategies: Managing risk and complexity.* London: Routledge.

Battacharya, S., & Battacharyya, R. (2024a). *Sustainable supply chains: Strategies and best practices.* Singapore: Palgrave Macmillan.

Battacharya, S., & Battacharyya, S. (2024b). IT for sustainable supply chains. *Journal of Sustainable Logistics, 12*(2), 45–63.

Blanchard, D. (2022). *Supply chain management best practices* (4th ed.). New York: McGraw Hill.

Bolstorff, P., & Rosenbaum, R. (2017). *Supply chain operations reference (SCOR) model version 12.0* (3rd ed.). New York: AMACOM.

Bowersox, D. J., Closs, D. J., Cooper, M. B., & Bowersox, J. C. (2013). *Supply chain logistics management* (4th ed.). New York: McGraw-Hill.

Burkacky, O., Deichmann, J., Pfingstag, P., & Werra, J. (2022). *McKinsey & Company*. [Online]. Available at: https://www.mckinsey.com/industries/semiconductors/our-insights/semiconductor-shortage-how-the-automotive-industry-can-succeed [Accessed 11 August 2025].

Caserio, C., & Trucco, S. (2018). *ERP systems for SMEs: Implementation and management*. London: Routledge.

Castañeda-Navarrete, J., Hauge, J., & López-Gómez, C. (2021). COVID-19's impacts on global value chains, as seen in the apparel industry. *Development Policy Review*, *39*(6), 953–970.

Chawla, P., Kumar, A., Nayyar, A., & Naved, M. (2023). *Blockchain, IoT, and AI technologies for supply chain management*. CRC Press.

Chopra, S., & Meindl, P. (2020). *Supply chain management: Strategy, planning, and operation* (7th ed.). Boston: Pearson.

Chopra, S., & Meindl, P. (2024). *Supply chain management: Strategy, planning, and operation* (8th ed.). Boston: Pearson.

Christopher, M. (2016). *Logistics & supply chain management* (5th ed.). Harlow: Pearson Education.

Christopher, M. (2022). *Logistics and supply chain management: Creating value-adding networks* (6th ed.). London: Pearson.

Christopher, M., & Peck, H. (2004). Building the resilient supply chain. *The International Journal of Logistics Management*, *15*(2), 1–14.

Cohen, S., & Roussel, J. (2013). *Strategic supply chain management: The five core disciplines for top performance* (2nd ed.). McGraw Hill Professional.

Colehower, K. (2023). *Innovations in transportation and logistics*. London: Kogan Page.

Coyle, J. J., Langley, C. J., Novack, R. A., & Gibson, B. J. (2017). *Supply chain management: A logistics perspective* (10th ed.). Boston, MA: Cengage Learning.

Destino, M., Fischer, J., Müllerklein, D., & Trautwein, V. (2022). *McKinsey & Company*. [Online]. Available at: https://www.mckinsey.com/capabilities/operations/our-insights/to-improve-your-supply-chain-modernize-your-supply-chain-it [Accessed 7 August 2025].

DHL. (2023). *DHL Group*. [Online]. Available at: https://group.dhl.com/content/dam/deutschepostdhl/en/media-center/investors/documents/business-profiles/DHL-Group-Business-Profile-2023.pdf [Accessed 7 May 2025].

Dormehl, L. (2012). *The Apple revolution: Steve Jobs, the counterculture and how the crazy ones took over the world*. Virgin Books.

dotData. (2022). *How a manufacturer saved $10M in inventory costs with AI*. [Online]. Available at: https://dotdata.com/blog/how-an-automobile-manufacturer-saved-10m-per-year-with-ai/#:~:text=With%20dotData%2C%20the%20client%20automatically,used%20in%20ML%20model%20development [Accessed 07 August 2025].

Doz, Y., & Kosonen, M. (2008). *The Nokia revolution: The story of an extraordinary company that transformed an industry*. Oxford: Oxford University Press.

DP World. (2024). *DP World*. [Online]. Available at: https://www.dpworld.com/-/media/project/dpwg/dpwg-tenant/corporate/global/media-files/annual-report-2024/final-web---dp-world-ar-2024-eng.pdf?hash=8F3E2EC65C43188D99D97E12BCAE2397&rev=21babacf07c842dd811f211f1e39e46d [Accessed 4 August 2025].

Drake, M. (2012). *Global supply chain management*. New York: Business Expert Press.

Durak, N. (2023). *Logistics Viewpoints: How technology makes continuous innovation possible: A case study with Unilever*. [Online]. Available at: https://logisticsviewpoints.com/2023/10/05/how-technology-makes-continuous-innovation-possible-a-case-study-with-unilever/#:~:text=Centralized%20Demand%20Planning%20became%20the,turn%20in%20the%20market%20landscape [Accessed August 07 2025].

Ellahi, R. M., Wood, L. C., & Bekhit, A. E.-D. A. (2023). *PubMed Central: Blockchain-based frameworks for food traceability: A systematic review*. [Online]. Available at: https://pmc.ncbi.nlm.nih.gov/articles/PMC10453023/ [Accessed 06 August 2025].

Engineering with Management. (2025). *Engineering with management*. [Online]. Available at: https://engineeringwithmanagement.com/8-types-of-waste-lean-manufacturing/ [Accessed 6 June 2025].

Eriquez, M., Fenies, P., Grimaud, T., & Lounnas, M. (2023). *Strategic procurement: Managing complexity and risk in global supply chains*. Berlin: Springer.

Evans, J. R., & Linday, W. M. (2014). *Managing for quality and performance excellence* (9th ed.). Cengage Learning.

FAO. (2019). *E-agriculture in action: Blockchain for agriculture*. Food and Agriculture Organization of the United Nations (FAO).

Fisher, M. (1997). What is the right supply chain for your product? *Harvard Business Review*, *75*(2), 105–116.

FreightAmigo. (2025). *The Suez Canal crisis: How the ever given blockage impacts global trade*. [Online]. Available at: https://www.freightamigo.com/blog/the-suez-canal-crisis-how-the-ever-given-blockage-impacts-global-trade [Accessed 06 August 2025].

Garland, M. (2021). *How Pfizer transformed its supply chain to deliver vaccines at lightspeed*. [Online]. Available at: https://www.supplychaindive.com/news/pfizer-jim-cafone-covid-vaccine-manufacturing-distribution-cscmp/606867 [Accessed 11 August 2025].

Gaur, V. (2021). *Supply chain analytics*. New York: McGraw Hill.

Ghosh, S. K. (2022). Artificial intelligence in supply chain management: Enhancing efficiency and resilience. *Journal of Supply Chain Management Science*, *8*(3), 245–265.

Goldratt, E. M. (2004). *The goal: A process of ongoing improvement* (3rd rev ed.). Great Barrington, MA: North River Press.

Govindan, K., Loleimani, H., & Kannan, D. (2015). Reverse logistics and closed-loop supply chain: A comprehensive review to explore the future. *European Journal of Operational Research*, *240*(3), 603–626.

Grant, D. B., Trautrims, A., & Wong, C. Y. (2017). *Sustainable logistics and supply chain management* (2nd ed.). London: Kogan Page.

Greenberg, A. (2018). *Wired*. [Online]. Available at: https://www.wired.com/story/notpetya-cyberattack-ukraine-russia-code-crashed-the-world [Accessed 12 August 2025].

Gujarati, D. N., & Proter, D. C. (2009). *Basic econometrics*. McGraw-Hill Education.

Gurtu, A., & Johny, J. (2021). Supply chain risk management: Literature review. *Risks*. https://doi.org/10.3390/risks9010016

Handfield, R. B., & Nichols, E. L. (2002). *Supply chain redesign: Transforming supply chains into integrated value systems*. Ft Press.

Harland, C. (2024). *Supply chain strategy and management* (3rd ed.). Oxford: Oxford University Press.

Hart, R. (2021). *Forbes*. [Online]. Available at: https://www.forbes.com/sites/roberthart/2021/07/07/giant-ever-given-ship-that-blocked-suez-canal-is-freed-after-months-long-fight-over-compensation [Accessed 12 August 2025].

He, X., & Zhang, W. (2020). The impact of the US-China trade war on global supply chains. *Journal of International Business Studies*, *51*(5), 1003–1015.

Heizer, J., Render, B., & Munson, C. (2020). *Operations management: Sustainability and supply chain management* (13th ed.). Pearson.

Hofmann, E., & Knébel, S. (2016). Supply chain differentiation: Background, concept and examples. *Journal of Service Science and Management*, *9*(2), 160–174. https://doi.org/10.4236/jssm.2016.92020

Hubner, A., Kuhn, H., & Sternbeck, M. (2013). Demand and supply chain planning in grocery retail: An operations planning framework. *International Journal of Retail & Distribution Management*, *41*(8), 512–530.

Hugos, M. H. (2018). *Essentials of Supply chain management* (4th ed.). Hoboken: Wiley.

IKEA. (2023). *IKEA sustainability report FY23*. [Online]. Available at: https://www.ikea.com/global/en/images/IKEA_SUSTAINABILITY_Report_FY_23_20240125_1b190c008f.pdf [Accessed 4 August 2025].

Imai, M. (1986). *Kaizen: The key to Japan's competitive success*. McGraw-Hill.

Ivanov, D. (2021). Supply chain viability and the COVID-19 pandemic: A conceptual and formal generalisation of four major adaptations. *International Journal of Production Research*, *59*(12), 3535–3552.

Ivanov, D., & Das, A. (2020). Coronavirus (COVID-19/SARS-CoV-2) and supply chain resilience: A research note. *International Journal of Integrated Supply Management*, *13*(1), 90–102.

Ivanov, D., & Dolgui, A. (2020). A digital supply chain twin for managing the disruption risks and resilience in the era of Industry 4.0. *Production Planning & Control*, *32*(9), 775–788.

Ivanov, D., Dolgui, A., & Sokolov, B. (2019). The impact of digital technology and industry 4.0 on the ripple effect and supply chain risk analytics. *International Journal of Production Research*, *57*(3), 829–846.

Kamath, R. (2018). Food traceability on Blockchain: Walmart's pork and mango pilots with IBM. *The Journal of the British Blockchain Association*, *1*(1), 47–53.

Khajasteh, H., Kelle, P., & Mansouri, S. A. (2022). Supplier diversification strategies to mitigate risk in global supply chains. *International Journal of Production Economics*, *244*, 108346. https://doi.org/10.1016/j.ijpe.2021.108346

Kleindorfer, P. R., & Saad, G. H. (2022). Managing risk in supply chains: A comprehensive framework. *International Journal of Production Research*, *60*(24), 7318–7336.

Kojaster, Y., Xu, H., & Zofaghari, S. (2022). *Supply chain risk mitigation: Strategies, methods and applications.* Springer.

Kotler, P., Keller, K. L., Manceau, D., & Hemonnet-Gougot, A. (2015). *Marketing management.* Pearson.

Lee, H. L. (2004). The triple-a supply chain. *Harvard Business Review*, *82*(10), 102–113.

Lee, H. L., Padmanabhan, V., & Whang, S. (1997). The bullwhip effect in supply chains. *Sloan Management Review*, *38*(3), 93–102.

Leonard, M., & Kapadia, S. (2021). *Informa: Supply chain dive.* [Online]. Available at: https://www.supplychaindive.com/news/timeline-ever-given-evergreen-blocked-suez-canal-supply-chain/597660 [Accessed 11 August 2025].

Liao, Y., Deschamps, F., Loures, E. F. R., & Ramos, L. F. P. (2017). Past, present and future of industry 4.0 – A systematic literature review and research agenda proposal. *International Journal of Production Research*, *55*(12), 3609–3629.

Liker, J. K. (2020). *The Toyota way: 14 management principles from the world's greatest manufacturer* (2nd ed.). New York: McGraw-Hill Education.

Liker, J. K., & Choi, T. Y. (2020). Building deep supplier relationships: Toyota's unique approach. *MIT Sloan Management Review*, *61*(3), 18–25.

Linstone, H. A., & Turoff, M. (Eds.). (1975). *The Delphi method: Techniques and applications.* Addison-Wesley.

Lowe, A. (2021). *Supply chain challenges in Australia: Logistics solutions for regional markets.* [Online]. Available at: https://www.austlogistics.com.au [Accessed 12 November 2024].

Maarmoun, M. (2015). Financial risk management in international supply chains: Hedging strategies and practices. *Journal of International Business and Economics*, *3*(2), 56–65.

Makridakis, S., Wheelwright, S. C., & Hyndman, R. J. (1998). *Forecasting: Methods and applications.* John Wiley & Sons.

Manokhin, V. (2025). *Benefits of improving forecast accuracy in supply chains.* [Online]. Available at: https://valeman.medium.com/benefits-of-improving-forecast-accuracy-in-supply-chains-29f6d8b37c80 [Accessed 07 August 2025].

Mathews, L. (2017). *Forbes.* [Online]. Available at: https://www.forbes.com/sites/leemathews/2017/08/16/notpetya-ransomware-attack-cost-shipping-giant-maersk-over-200-million [Accessed 12 August 2025].

Mentzer, J. T., Moon, M. A., Smith, C. D., & Garver, M. S. (2023). *Sales forecasting management: A demand management approach.* SAGE Publications.

Min, H. (2010). Artificial intelligence in supply chain management: Theory and applications. *International Journal of Logistics: Research and Applications*, *13*(1), 13–39.

Min, H. (2019). Blockchain technology for enhancing supply chain resilience. *Business Horizons*, *62*(1), 35–45.

Moncza, R. M., Handfield, R. B., Giunipero, L. C., & Patterson, J. L. (2015). *Purchasing and supply chain management* (6th ed.). Cengage Learning.

Monczka, R. M., Handfield, R. B., Giunipero, L. C., & Patterson, J. (2016). *Purchasing and supply chain management.* Boston: Cengage Learning.

Monk, E., & Wagner, B. (2013). *Concepts in enterprise resource planning* (4th ed.). Boston: Cengage Learning.

Montgomery, D. C. (2013). *Introduction to statistical quality control* (7th ed.). John Wiley & Sons.

Muller, M. (2019). *Essentials of inventory management.* HarperCollins Leadership.

Nestlé. (2024). *Nestlé.com.* [Online]. Available at: https://www.nestle.com/media/pressreleases/allpressreleases/full-year-results-2023 [Accessed 13 July 2025].

O'Brien, J. (2018). *Supplier relationship management: Unlocking the hidden value in your Supply Base* (2nd ed.). Kogan Page Publishers.

Oakland, J. S. (2014). *Total quality management and operational excellence: Text with cases* (4th ed.). Routledge.

Olson, D. L. (2011). *Advanced planning and scheduling in ERP systems.* New York: Wiley.
Ørsted. (2024). *Ørsted corporate responsibility report.* [Online]. Available at: https://orsted.co.uk/about-us/corporate-responsibility/environment [Accessed 5 August 2025].
pdfs.semanticscholar. (2022). *Redesigning global supply chains during compounding.* [Online]. Available at: https://chatgpt.com/c/68803be0-a840-8004-8b29-622509a0a894 [Accessed 05 August 2025].
Pfizer. (2020). *Pfizer 2020 annual report.* [Online]. Available at: https://annualreview2020.pfizer.com/pgs-ingenuity-solves-covid-19-cold-chain-storage-challenge [Accessed 11 August 2025].
Porter, M. E. (1985). *Competitive advantage: Creating and sustaining superior performance.* New York: Free Press.
Porter, M. E. (2008). *Competitive advantage: Creating and sustaining superior performance.* Simon and Schuster.
Prescienceds. (2024). *Prescience: Case studies.* [Online]. Available at: https://prescienceds.com/case-studies/achieved-95-accuracy-in-demand-forecasting-for-an-africa-based-company-manpower-and-logistics-challenges-also-resolved/#:~:text=With%20the%20new%20demand%20forecasting,drop%20metric%20for%20the%20company [Accessed 11 August 2025].
PWC. (2020). *Nearshoring: A solution to global supply chain disruptions.* PricewaterhouseCoopers (PwC) Report.
Pyzdek, T., & Keller, P. (2014). *The six sigma handbook* (4th ed.). McGraw-Hill Education.
Quadratyx AI Solutions. (2024). *LinkedIn.* [Online]. Available at: https://www.linkedin.com/pulse/improving-demand-forecasting-accuracy-ai-nestl%C3%A9-k7irf/ [Accessed 8 May 2025].
Richards, G. (2021). *Warehouse management: The definitive guide to improving efficiency and minimizing costs in the modern warehouse* (4th ed.). London: Kogan Page Publishers.
Rossi, R. (2021). *Advanced inventory management techniques.* Melbourne: Inventory Publishing.
Rushton, A., Croucher, P., & Baker, P. (2017). *The handbook of logistics and distribution management: Understanding the supply chain* (6th ed.). London: Kogan Page.
Rushton, A., Croucher, P., & Baker, P. (2022). *The handbook of logistics and distribution management* (7th ed.). London: Kogan Page.
Sabet, E., Yazdani, N., & De Leeuw, S. (2017). Supply chain integration and its impact on business performance. *International Journal of Logistics Research and Applications, 20*(4), 316–329.
Samsung. (2024). *Samsung SDS: Digital SCM.* [Online]. Available at: https://www.samsungsds.com/en/scm/scm.html [Accessed 24 July 2025].
Schneider-Petsinger, M. (2021). The impact of trade and regulatory policies on global supply chains. *International Journal of Supply Chain Management, 18*(4), 234–249.
Senge, P. (2006). *The fifth discipline: The art and practice of the learning organization* (Revised ed.). New York: Crown Business.
Senge, P. M., & Prokesch, S. E. (2020). *The necessary revolution: How individuals and organizations are working together to create a sustainable world* (Updated ed.). New York: Crown Business.
Sheffi, Y. (2007). Building a resilient supply chain. *Harvard Business Review, 85*(1), 29–31.
Sheffi, Y. (2020). *The new (ab)normal: Reshaping business and supply chain strategy beyond Covid-19.* MIT Press.
Shih, W. C. (2020). Global supply chains in a post-pandemic world. *Harvard Business Review, 98*(5), 39–45.
Siemens, A. G. (2024). *Smart manufacturing at Amberg electronics plant: Industry 4.0 in action.* Munich: Siemens Press Office.
Simchi-Levi, D., Kaminsky, P., & Simchi-Levi, E. (2024). *Designing and managing the supply chain: Concepts, strategies, and case studies.* New York: McGraw-Hill Education.
Simchi-Levi, D., & Timmermans, J. (2021). *Operations rules: Delivering customer value through flexible operations.* Boston: MIT Press.
Slack, N., Chambers, S., & Johnston, R. (2019). *Operations management* (9th ed.). Pearson.
Sodhi, M. S., & Tang, C. S. (2012). *Managing supply chain risk.* Berlin: Springer.
Sollish, F., & Semanik, J. (2012). *The procurement and supply manager's desk reference* (2nd ed.). Wiley.
Sony. (2024). *Sony new releases: Development of blockchain "Soneium™".* [Online]. Available at: https://www.sony.com/en/SonyInfo/News/Press/202408/24-029E [Accessed 24 July 2025].
Steinberg, S., Stepan, A., & Neary, K. (2021). *NotPetya.* New York: Columbia University.

Sterman, J. D. (2000). *Business dynamics: Systems thinking and modelling for a complex world.* Boston: McGraw-Hill.

Stevenson, W. J. (2021). *Operations management* (14th ed.). McGraw-Hill Education.

Stone, B. (2013). *The everything store: Jeff Bezos and the age of Amazon.* New York: Little, Brown and Company.

Swinhoe, D. (2019). *CSO.* [Online]. Available at: https://www.csoonline.com/article/567845/rebuilding-after-notpetya-how-maersk-moved-forward.html [Accessed 11 August 2025].

Taplin, I. M. (2014). The Rana plaza disaster: The role of global supply chains in shaping labour practices. *Business Ethics Quarterly, 24*(2), 167–194.

Taschner, H., & Charifzadeh, M. (2023). Collaborative risk management in supply chains: A case study. *Supply Chain Management: An International Journal, 28*(1), 112–126.

Three Group Solutions. (2025). *Three Group Solutions.* [Online]. Available at: https://groupsolutions.three.com/insights/logistics-iot [Accessed 06 August 2025].

Tran, N. K., Haralambides, H., & Notteboom, T. (2025). The costs of maritime supply chain disruptions: The case of the Suez Canal blockage by the 'Ever Given' megaship. *International Journal of Production Economics, 279,* 109477. https://doi.org/10.1016/j.ijpe.2024.109477

Tseng, M. L., Wu, K. J., Chien, C. F., & Ali, M. H. (2024). Circular supply chain practices: challenges, innovation and development. *International Journal of Logistics Research and Applications, 27*(1), 1–5. https://doi.org/10.1080/13675567.2024.2305519

Unilever. (2023). *Sustainable living plan.* [Online]. Available at: https://www.unilever.com [Accessed 3 December 2024].

Waller, M. A., & Fawcett, S. E. (2013). Data science, predictive analytics, and big data: A revolution that will transform supply chain design and management. *Journal of Business Logistics, 34*(2), 77–94.

Wang, G., Gunasekaran, A., & Papadopoulos, T. (2016). Big data analytics in logistics and supply chain management: Certain investigations for research and applications. *International Journal of Production Economics, 176,* 98–110.

Waters, D. (2023). *Supply chain risk management: Vulnerability and resilience in logistics* (2nd ed.). London: Kogan Page.

Westerlund, M., Nene, S., Leminen, S., & Rajahonka, M. (2021). Distributed ledger technologies for smart digital economies. *Technology Innovation Management Review, 11*(6).

Wisner, J. D. (2022). *Principles of supply chain management: A balanced approach.* South-Western Cengage Learning.

Womack, J. P., & Jones, D. T. (1996). *Lean thinking: Banish waste and create wealth in your corporation.* Simon & Schuster.

Womack, J. P., Jones, D. T., & Roos, D. (1990). *The machine that changed the world: The story of lean production.* New York: Harper Perennial.

Woolworths Group. (2023). *Woolworths group: 2023 sustainability report.* [Online]. Available at: https://www.woolworthsgroup.com.au/content/dam/wwg/investors/reports/2023/f23-full-year/Woolworths%20Group%202023%20Sustainability%20Report.pdf [Accessed 23 July 2025].

Youngdahl, B., & Ramaswamy, K. (2021). *Toyota's disrupted global supply chain: COVID-19 and the global chip shortage.* Arizona State University.

Index

Pages in *italics* refer to figures, pages in ***bold-italics*** refer to boxes and pages in **bold** refer to tables.